NO ONE TO FIGHT

Everywhere Kuter looked, the skies over the English Channel, and as far away as he could see with his high-powered binoculars, was full of airplanes. Yet everywhere that he looked, the airplanes were marked with stars or roundels. Nowhere did Kuter see the black cross and swastika of the *Luftwaffe*.

"We kept watching and gradually it became clear to us that if an air battle *was* taking place, it must be an extremely compressed affair, because few aircraft ever burst through the top of the cloud and those few were friendly," Kuter later recalled. "Not only that, the radio produced none of the usual German air controller's battle directions. We knew then that we were right. The air was full of American and British fighters. Columns of Flying Fortresses stretched back to England as far as the eye could follow. We had over eighteen hundred 'heavies' over France that morning. The Hun never showed up. He couldn't because he had nothing left. His bluff had been called."

This book is the story of how events were molded to create the week in which that bluff was called.

"Recounted in stunning detail, rich in history and with the pace and verve we have come to expect from Bill Yenne, *Big Week* soars like the hero pilots and crews he describes in the air war over the Third Reich."

—Brian Sobel, author of *The Fighting Pattons*

BIG WEEK

SIX DAYS THAT CHANGED THE COURSE OF WORLD WAR II

BILL YENNE

BERKLEY CALIBER, NEW YORK

THE BERKLEY PUBLISHING GROUP
Published by the Penguin Group
Penguin Group (USA) LLC
375 Hudson Street, New York, New York 10014

USA • Canada • UK • Ireland • Australia • New Zealand • India • South Africa • China

penguin.com

A Penguin Random House Company

Berkley Caliber trade paperback ISBN: 978-0-425-27224-4

The Library of Congress has catalogued the Berkley Caliber hardcover edition as follows:

Yenne, Bill, date.
Big Week : six days that changed the course of World War II / Bill Yenne.—1st ed.
p. cm.
Includes bibliographical references.
ISBN 978-0-425-25575-9
1. World War, 1939–1945—Aerial operations.   2. World War, 1939–1945—
Campaigns—Western Front.   3. United States. Army Air Forces—History—World War,
1939–1945.   4. Great Britain. Royal Air Force—History–World War, 1939–1945.
5. Germany. Luftwaffe—History—World War, 1939–1945.   I. Title.
D785.Y45 2013
940.54'4973—dc23
2012038542

PUBLISHING HISTORY
Berkley Caliber hardcover edition / January 2013
Berkley Caliber trade paperback edition / February 2014

PRINTED IN THE UNITED STATES OF AMERICA

10   9   8   7   6   5   4   3   2   1

Cover photo by Keystone (Getty Images)
Cover design by Sharanya Durvasula

The week of 20–26 February, 1944, may well be classed by future historians as marking a decisive battle of history, one as decisive and of greater importance than Gettysburg.

—General Henry H. "Hap" Arnold,
Commanding General of the USAAF,
in his report to the Secretary of War, February 27, 1945

CONTENTS

viii   CONTENTS

ACKNOWLEDGMENTS

The author would like to thank Colonel J. A. (Bill) Saavedra, USAF (Ret.) of the Office of Air Force History in Washington, DC, and Thomas P. Lauria of the Air Force Historical Research Agency at Maxwell AFB, both of whom provided an immense volume of research material. It is through them that I had access to information about the life of Archie Mathies, an inspiration to us all, and access to the memoirs of Richard D'Oyly Hughes, the most influential unsung hero in the story of Big Week and the events that led to it. Finally, the author wishes to thank Tom Colgan of Berkley Caliber, who made this book possible.

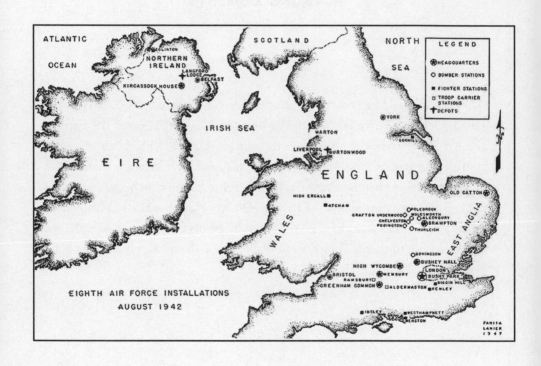

EIGHTH AIR FORCE INSTALLATIONS
AUGUST 1942

ATLANTIC OCEAN

SCOTLAND

NORTH SEA

LEGEND
⊛ HEADQUARTERS
○ BOMBER STATIONS
■ FIGHTER STATIONS
□ TROOP CARRIER STATIONS
✝ DEPOTS

NORTHERN IRELAND
EGLINTON
LANGFORD LODGE
KIRCASSOCK HOUSE
BELFAST

IRISH SEA

EIRE

YORK

WARTON
LIVERPOOL
BURTONWOOD

GOXHILL

ENGLAND

HIGH ERCALL
ATCHAM

OLD CATTON

EAST ANGLIA

WALES

POLEBROOK
GRAFTON UNDERWOOD
CHELVESTON
PODINGTON
MOLESWORTH
ALCONBURY
BRAMPTON
THURLEIGH

BOVINGDON
BUSHEY HALL

HIGH WYCOMBE
BRISTOL
RAMSBURY
GREENHAM COMMON
NEWBURY
ALDERMASTON

LONDON
BUSHY PARK
BIGGIN HILL
KENLEY

IDSLEY
WESTHAMPNETT
MERSTON

FANITA LANIER 1947

NORTH
SEA

BALTIC SEA

IRELAND

GREAT
BRITAIN

DENMARK

SWEDEN

LATVIA

LITHUANIA

EAST
PRUSSIA

POLAND

ROSTOCK • TUTOW

• DIEPHOLZ

NETHER
LANDS

• BRUNSWICK
• HALBERSTADT
• BERNBERG
• ASCHERSLEBEN
• LEIPZIG

BELGIUM

• GOTHA

G E R M A N Y

• SCHWEINFURT

• FURTH

• REGENSBURG

SLOVAKIA

F R A N C E

STUTTGART •

• AUGSBURG

• STEYR

HUNGARY

BAY of
BISCAY

SWITZERLAND

YUGOSLAVIA

SPAIN

C O R S I C A

I T A L Y

ADRIATIC
SEA

SARDINIA

M E D I T E R R A N E A N   S E A

SICILY

F. J. KANE

MAIN OBJECTIVES
of
"BIG WEEK" OPERATIONS

INTRODUCTION

On a blustery June day in 1944, Larry Kuter took an airplane ride. Far beneath him, one of the greatest military enterprises in world history, certainly one of the biggest in World War II, was unfolding. Down below, across a fifty-mile swath of the shores of France's ancient province of Normandy, 156,000 Allied soldiers were going ashore to begin the great campaign to drive the German armies out of the nations of Western Europe they had occupied for the previous four years.

The Allied soldiers, including 57,500 Americans, came ashore in places with code names alien to those who actually lived in Normandy—especially Normandy's newest residents, the Germans manning the artillery and the reinforced concrete fortresses. They came ashore on beaches named Sword, Gold, Juno, and Utah. At a fifth beach called Omaha, the Americans took it especially hard, chopped to pieces by heavy machine gun fire and shelling.

Allied planners aboard some of the five thousand ships that stood offshore in the English Channel, or in the various headquarters in Britain, were fixated on this great battle unfolding in surf and sand and rocky cliff.

However, Larry Kuter's eyes were on the *sky*. As the Flying Fortress in which he was a passenger flew almost listlessly through the freezing air, his binoculars were trained not on the vast drama unfolding two thousand feet below, but on the eastern fringes of the great blue dome of sky.

He saw a cluster of airplanes at his own altitude, marked with the same white star as the B-17 in which he flew. He saw another cluster of airplanes beneath him, and their wings were marked with the roundels of Britain's Royal Air Force.

The bomber diverted from overflying the channel and drifted inland over France, then back over the channel, crisscrossing the invasion beaches—Sword, Gold, Juno, Utah, and Omaha. Down there, Allied soldiers were being hammered relentlessly by a well-armed enemy, but up where Kuter scanned the skies, things were downright peaceful.

The sky was full of airplanes that day, but they were all friendly. It was not supposed to have been that way. Once, a very short time before, Germany's Luftwaffe had been the most powerful and effective air force in the world. Indeed, only a few months ago, Flying Fortress crews who ventured into the skies over Europe did so at considerable peril, knowing that the Luftwaffe maintained total air superiority in the skies across the continent.

Six months earlier, any Allied aircraft that ventured into continental airspace was liable to be pounced upon by a gaggle of angry Messerschmitts hurling 20mm explosive shells at the rate of seven hundred rounds per minute. Indeed, many Flying Fortresses like the one in which Kuter now rode had been turned into crumpled, falling piles of wreckage by those shells—and in these skies. Dozens of times, the floors of these Flying Fortresses, like the floor beneath Kuter's feet, had been covered with pools of American blood because of the Luftwaffe.

Four years earlier, when Adolf Hitler's legions had swept across Europe, defeating nations as powerful as France in a matter of weeks, they had done so beneath an umbrella of airpower that attacked and pounded Germany's enemies into submission. Nothing moved on the ground but that it was seen from above and strafed by a Messerschmitt or bombed by a Stuka.

This was the fear that had haunted Allied planners when they imagined the great battle now taking place in Normandy. It had kept them awake at night, and it had caused chills to run up their spines and nest in the bases of their skulls like icy rodents.

"If I were the German operations officer and Providence had promised to allow me to select the weather in which to make my defense, these were the conditions I would have chosen," Kuter thought as he looked beneath him. "A solid bank of overcast covered the Normandy coast and extended to mid-Channel. The top was at twelve thousand feet and the bottom down to thirteen hundred. Here was perfect concealment for German airmen. They could dive out of the dense cloud on the packed Channel below, bomb or strafe any ship and climb back into the protecting clouds in a matter of seconds. They could come and go before a gun was brought to bear or any of our thousands of fighters were able to intercept. I was apprehensive more than I would care to admit."

With his Clark Gable mustache and his energetic demeanor, Major General Laurence Sherman Kuter was one of a group of young men who had helped form and define the US Army Air Forces. One week from his thirty-ninth birthday, Kuter was the youngest general in the US Army when he was promoted in 1942, and the first man since William Tecumseh Sherman to receive a "jump" promotion to general without having served as a colonel.

In 1929, the young officer from Rockford, Illinois, was two years out of the US Military Academy at West Point and serving as a coast artillery officer in Monterey, California. Soon, however, he had transferred to the Army's Air Corps and earned his wings in the skies over Texas. By the time that Hitler's armies were subjugating Europe, he was in Washington, DC, as part of that cadre of brilliant young officers who clustered around their revered chief, Henry Harley "Hap" Arnold, to form this service that would become the largest air force in the world, *and* to formulate the strategy that would use this weapon to win World War II.

"The cloud bank could be swarming with Germans," Kuter observed. Left unsaid was the phrase "the cloud bank *should* be swarming with Germans."

Everywhere he looked, the skies over the English Channel, and as far away as he could see with his high-powered binoculars, were full of airplanes. Yet everywhere that he looked, the airplanes were marked with stars or roundels. Nowhere did Kuter see the black cross and swastika of the Luftwaffe.

"We kept watching and gradually it became clear to us that if an air battle *was* taking place, it must be an extremely compressed affair, because few aircraft ever burst through the top of the cloud and those few were friendly," Kuter later recalled. "Not only that, the radio produced none of the usual German air controller's battle directions. We knew then that we were right. The air was full of American and British fighters. Columns of Flying Fortresses stretched back to England as far as the eye could follow. We had over 1,800 'heavies' over France that morning. The Hun never showed up. He couldn't because he had nothing left. His bluff had been called."

This book is the story of how events were molded to create the week in which that bluff was called.

Big Week was a watershed moment in World War II, and in the military history of the twentieth century. It was the point after which nothing would be as it had been before. After a long and difficult gestation, it marked the birth of strategic airpower as a means of effecting the outcome of military action.

A year and a half earlier, when British armies achieved their first important ground victory against the Germans in three years of war—at El Alamein—Britain's wartime prime minister, Winston Churchill, delivered one of his most memorable wartime speeches.

"We have a new experience. We have victory—a remarkable and definite victory," Churchill said. "The Germans have received back again that measure of fire and steel which they have so often meted out to others. Now this is not the end. It is not even the beginning of the end. But it is, perhaps, the end of the beginning."

Big Week *was* the beginning of the end.

It was not so much a turning point as it was a *tipping* point.

As defined by the physicists, a tipping point is a threshold, the point at which an entity is displaced from a position of established balance into a new equilibrium significantly unlike what has existed previously. A tipping point is a moment of critical mass.

The threshold was the last week of February 1944. The entity that was about to be displaced from its established balance was the economy and war-making capacity of the Third Reich. The critical mass that was achieved that week was in the number of heavy bombers that comprised the strategic airpower of the USAAF Eighth Air Force.

Between February 20 and 25, 1944, the US Army Air Forces began running massive raids against the economic heart of Hitler's Germany. It was a battle of epic proportions on a three-dimensional battlefield.

In six days, the Eighth Air Force bombers based in England would fly more than 3,300 missions and the Fifteenth Air Force based in Italy more than 500. Together they dropped roughly 10,000 tons of bombs on targets that accounted for 90 percent of German aircraft production. The British Royal Air Force Bomber Command flew more than 2,350 nighttime missions against the same targets during Big Week.

Big Week had been a long time in the making.

Indeed, it had its origins in World War I, when forward-thinking strategists looked at airpower and saw its *big* picture. From this evolved the theory that in wartime, airpower could be used, not just as a *tactical* weapon near the battlefront, but as a *strategic* weapon that could profoundly and decisively affect the outcome of the war.

Strategic airpower had many fathers, but none more outspoken and influential in United States military circles than William Lendrum "Billy" Mitchell, the man who had commanded the aviation component of the American Expeditionary Force during the First World War.

"The world stands on the threshold of the 'aeronautical era,'" Mitchell wrote in his 1925 book, *Winged Victory*. "During this epoch the destinies of all people will be controlled through the air. Airpower has come to stay. But what, it may be asked, is airpower? Airpower is the ability to do something in or through the air, and, as the air covers the whole world, aircraft are able to go anywhere on the planet. They are not dependent on the water as a means of sustentation, nor on the land, to keep them up. Mountains, deserts, oceans, rivers, and forests, offer no obstacles. In a trice, aircraft have set aside all ideas of frontiers. The whole country now becomes the frontier and, in case of war, one place is just as exposed to attack as another place."

Mitchell died exactly eight years, to the day, before the eve of Big Week, but his words and his ideas had a profound and consequential effect on the men who planned it.

Mitchell died three years before the start of World War II, the first war in which airpower would be decisive, but he had a profound effect on the American air officers who were the founding fathers of the concept that the USAAF could make airpower decisive. These men were led by General Hap Arnold, the commanding general of the USAAF throughout World War II, who gathered around him the men who won the war in the air.

Most significantly, these men included General Carl "Tooey" Spaatz, a veteran pilot and staff officer who headed Arnold's Air Staff when the war began, and went on to be the field officer at the top of the USAAF chain of command in Europe when Big Week came. Among the coterie of young officers—not yet generals when the war began—were those who drafted the master plan that would turn Billy Mitchell's vision into a war-winning reality. They included Larry Kuter, as well as Harold L. "Hal" George, Orvil Anderson, Hoyt Vandenberg, and Haywood S. "Possum" Hansell.

Among the officers in the field who would, under the watchful eye of Tooey Spaatz, execute the master plan that culminated with Big Week, were men whose names became, and in some cases still remain, as house-hold words. They included Ira Clarence Eaker, Frederick Lewis Anderson, James Harold "Jimmy" Doolittle, and Curtis Emerson LeMay.

Burning the midnight oil to provide the specific details of the targets that made up the incomprehensibly vast mosaic of strategic aerial victory in World War II were men, and a few women, whose names *never* became household words. Significant among them was Richard D'Oyly Hughes.

Flying in the airplanes that executed the plans were the thousands of young men—of 2.4 million in USAAF uniform in June 1944—who sweated the missions, dropped the bombs, and shed the blood. These men included young airmen, barely into their twenties, like Archie Mathies, as well as Bill Lawley and Wally Truemper. Their names are not household words, but they are iconic within today's US Air Force because of their heroism during Big Week.

Everything that came together during Big Week was about one thing—the use of American airpower to defeat German airpower in order to ensure the success of an epic campaign on the ground.

"On that first and crucial day, with our troops clinging to at least one beachhead 'by an eyelash,' the soldiers who were bombed and strafed were not Americans but Germans," Kuter observed. "German airpower, far from being a factor in the final struggle for Europe, was practically non-existent."

As Larry Kuter pondered the scene above, around and beneath him on June 6, 1944, it was clear that the beginning of the end had come at last. The war was not over, not by a long shot, but its outcome had been assured.

It was a terrible thing, this enormous battle that spread across fifty miles of Norman coastline. By the time the sun set on June 6, the Allied casualty count had reached ten thousand young, human lives, a quarter of whom would never see the sun rise on June 7. However, the important thing was that they were still *in* Normandy. Terrible, difficult battles lay ahead, but the Allied soldiers would not step back into the English Channel, and on the first anniversary of Operation Overlord, the loudest thunder on the Normandy beaches would not be gunfire and exploding shells, but the surf—and Adolf Hitler would be gone forever.

As Billy Mitchell had written two decades earlier, "Even if hostile armies and navies come into contact with each other, they are helpless now unless they can obtain and hold military supremacy in the air."

PROLOGUE

One day, two boys were headed home from school. It was a day like many others, a day like those that live in our memories more as a day than a date, a day whose date might have fallen in the spring, or the early summer before school let out, or even the early autumn. It might have been in the waning months of their fifth-grade year, but it was certainly *around about* that time. It was a day when the willows were leafed out, but a day on which the green leaves of the willows were unimportant, a backdrop, not a fixture. One of the boys idly grabbed a fistful of leaves, and just as idly tossed them away, as a country boy might idly pull up a long stalk of grass to chew on for a moment or two before casually discarding it.

It was one of those years that is inclined to be recalled, by those who were there as well as by those who can experience them only in their imagination, as from a "simpler" time. The year was 1929, though it could just as easily have been 1928, or even 1920. For boys who are ten or eleven, years are years, not dates in a history book. In retrospect, for those of us who were not there, and who experience them only in our imagination, these were the formative years of the Americans whom we have called, since Tom Brokaw coined the term, the Greatest Generation.

As is often the case, people destined for greatness do not know it.

Usually, it is for us who were not there, and who know them only in retrospect, to bestow the mantle of greatness.

The latterly named Greatest Generation grew up believing that they were merely the "younger generation." Like all generations, they grew up in the us-and-them world that placed them in the shadow of that enigmatic cast of characters known as the "older generation."

Archie Mathies and Johnny Ferelli had been friends since the second grade, sharing laughs, sharing tall tales, sharing secrets, and sharing adventures. Sharing adventures was then, as always, something that boys did. Sharing secrets was part of the age-old divide between the generations, and the punch line to the phrase "if our mothers knew half of the trouble we got into . . ."

For Archie Mathies and Johnny Ferelli, one of the stories that would be most often shared—though not willingly with their respective mothers—was the one that began on that day as the two boys were headed home from school in the waning months of their fifth-grade year.

Somewhere along the way, they met up with some other boys and continued on their way. Their destinations were their homes in a row of duplexes on the west side of Library, Pennsylvania. In some recountings of Archie's early days, the town is called "Liberty," which would fit the narrative more smoothly, but the town bore a more eccentric name. It was called "Library," because someone along about the turn of the twentieth century remembered that a man named John Moore had set up a library in these environs way back in 1833. Before it was so named, the place had been known for years as "Loafer's Hollow," a name that would be even more idiosyncratic when set to the kind of serious narrative that you might want to take home to your mother.

In fact, Library was not then, and *still* is not, a town at all, but merely an unincorporated corner of South Park Township in Allegheny County, about a dozen or so highway miles south of downtown Pittsburgh. It was, in the lexicon of the Greatest Generation, "just a wide spot in the road."

Pittsburgh was then, and for some years before and after, a steel town. Indeed, for America, it was *the* steel town. The steel industry runs on iron ore and coal, and it came to Pittsburgh because the ground under your feet there is filled with coal. They call them "coal patches" and they are everywhere in western Pennsylvania. You cannot usually see them, but you can see the mine entrances and the former mine entrances everywhere.

Dirty, dusty, black, and choking, coal became the lifeblood of western Pennsylvania. When Archie Mathies and Johnny Ferelli were growing up, nearly everybody's dad worked in the coal industry, mostly at the Montour Number 10 Mine, and nearly everybody lived in the duplexes that were bully and owned by the Pittsburgh Coal Company.

The terrain around southern Allegheny County, like the terrain in most of coal country, is comprised of steep hills and deep valleys. The valley around which Library had been built was cut long ago by the stream folks knew as Piney Fork. To get from one side to the other, you had to go down, then climb up—*or* take a shortcut.

Boys being boys, and boys being disinclined to exert more effort than necessary in the accomplishment of a walk home, they elected to take a shortcut. That which presented itself most conveniently, and which had been used so often as to make it a routine part of the route, was the trestle used by the Montour Railroad, which crossed the canyon one hundred feet above Piney Fork. Walking the trestle thus saved considerable trouble in climbing down and climbing up.

As this writer can attest, having used railroad trestles as a boy of ten or eleven himself, trestles are unnerving in the first crossing but grow less daunting with the frequency of their use.

Another truism about being ten or eleven that is obvious only in retrospect is that boys this age have not yet seen everything. This was about to be illustrated most dramatically.

Archie and Johnny, and their friends, were about halfway across the trestle, when the ties and the rails upon which they walked shivered and shook with the portent of an oncoming coal train. They had never previously encountered one while in mid-span. By the time they looked up, the train was coming around the bend, and there was nowhere to run, nowhere to hide.

With fifty tons of coal in every car he was pulling, there was no way the engineer could stop, and nothing he could do but frantically blow his whistle.

Being one hundred feet above the safety of the ground, there was nothing the boys could do but to crawl beneath the ties, hang on and pray.

"I can still see Archie high above us, hanging by his toes from the railroad ties as the train crossed the trestle," Johnny later told Archie's brother, David. "We were clinging to the girders for dear life."

As Archie later explained to his brother, he had slipped down between the ties and immediately cantilevered his feet up into another set of ties.

"He wasn't really holding by his toes," David recalled in a recording in the collection of the Air Force Historical Research Agency at Maxwell AFB. "He was hanging by his arches. . . . You can imagine the vibration that was set up in that trestle. . . . I have had occasion to stop by that trestle on several occasions just to look at it. It's still there. I judge that from the point where they were trapped, it is at least seventy-five to one hundred feet off the ground. That might not seem like much, but when you're hanging like a bat, and you fall, you're going to break your neck."

Archie Mathies had embraced danger and looked death in the eye. On that day in 1929, death blinked.

Archie was meant for greater things.

Archie Mathies was born Archibald Hamilton on June 3, 1918, in Stonehouse, South Lanarkshire, twenty miles southeast of Glasgow, Scotland. He never knew his father, nor did he ever know Scotland. His earliest memories formed on Jacobs Creek in Westmoreland County, Pennsylvania. When his mother remarried in 1921, to William James Mathies, the family, including Archie's older sister, Jessie, immigrated to the United States. William Mathies went to work for the Pittsburgh Coal Company at Van Meter, in Rostraver Township, north of Pittsburgh.

It was a few years after David Mathies was born, in 1922, that the family moved to another coal patch. Mary Mathies was relieved to get out of Van Meter, where they were still mourning one of the worst mining disasters in American history, which had claimed 239 lives in 1907. The Mathies family was now living in Library, on the south side of America's great steel town, where William went to work at the Montour Number 10 Mine, also owned by Pittsburgh Coal.

As David would recall, soon after they arrived in Library, Archie was challenged by the "patch bully" in his age bracket, but promptly "turned him everywhere but loose."

Archie Mathies faced adversity and the bully more than blinked.

Those were the days when dairies still made home deliveries, and the milkman serving Library had a particular dilemma. It seems that the same bully who had challenged Archie had also been stealing from the milkman, slipping into the milk truck as the driver made his rounds to the backs of the houses.

When the milkman learned of Archie's having thrashed the bully, he hired Archie to ride shotgun. His pay at the end of the day was 50 cents and a quart of chocolate milk.

Around the time of the Piney Fork trestle incident, Archie's mother informed William that, in brother David's words, "she'd had enough of that coal patch living," meaning that she was tired of raising her family in a company-owned duplex. The family, which included Jessie, now at the threshold of becoming a teenager, along with seven-year-old David, and Nettie May, just turned two, lived in four rooms, with an outhouse in the backyard. Mary was ready for a place of their own, so she sent William down to the small town of Finleyville, four miles away—where he was able to rent another house—with *five* rooms.

Archie adapted quickly to life in Finleyville, and discovered Patton's Garage, where the proprietor ran a car repair shop by day and a boxing club by night. Pugilism suited Archie's competitive nature, and he boxed continuously until he hurt his arm one night in 1933.

"That's enough," William Mathies told his knight errant son. "There's no money for hospitals, and furthermore, it's time to start high school."

The older generation had spoken.

When he graduated from Monogahela High School, Archie went to work. This being coal country, he went to work in the mines, specifically up in Library, at the Champion 3 Preparation Plant, adjacent to the Montour Number 10 Mine where his father had worked since Archie was a little boy. He got on working at the tipple, where they loaded the coal cars, for five dollars a day.

"He could have made a lot more money if he had worked *inside* the mine," David explained. "But my dad was not about to hear tell of that. There's too much danger involved in coal mining."

In 1939, when Archie turned twenty-one, he joined the volunteer fire department. "He loved that, flying around on the back of the truck going to all the field fires—there were very few house fires." David laughed in the recollection. "He liked the speed, but there was an extra bonus involved. We had the volunteer fireman's marching band. It was a bonus because he got to see all the girls. They played music by America's greatest band master, John Philip Souza. His favorite tune then, and my favorite tune now, is 'Stars and Stripes Forever.'"

David went on to recall that even though Archie was making only five dollars a day working for Pittsburgh Coal, he wasn't selfish. "I remember coming home from school one day and there was two pairs of Chicago roller skates. There was a pair for him and a pair for me. In 1941, the first year that Archie was in the service, he bought my mother a four-hundred-dollar fur coat. I wondered how he managed this. Did he rob a bank or something? Then I remembered that Archie was good with cards and he was also good with the galloping dominoes."

On December 30, 1940, Archie decided that, in David's words, "it was time for a new adventure," and he joined the US Army Air Corps.

Archie Mathies would never meet Richard D'Oyly Hughes, but their lives were intertwined. Both were born in the United Kingdom, both became citizens of the United States, both served in the uniform of the USAAF, and both men went on to become iconic figures in the story of Big Week. Their stories become intertwined in the narrative of this book.

Aside from that, the two men were as different as night and day. A generation older than Mathies, Hughes was born into one of those upper class British families where military service is a sacred duty. He attended Wellington College in Berkshire, founded as a national monument to the Duke of Wellington, and where the faculty still includes commissioned officers from the Duke of Wellington's regiment. He went on to the Royal Military Academy at Sandhurst, the British equivalent of West Point, where the British Army trains its officers, and he served in World War I. An item in the *London Gazette* of December 1916 finds him assigned to

King George's Own 1st Gurkha Rifles, also known as the Malaun Regiment, who had fought the Germans at Ypres and who were then battling the Ottoman Turks in what later became Iraq.

A dozen years later, Dick Hughes would be found in the Northwest Frontier Province in India. It was here that he met and fell in love with an American woman. He pursued Frances back to St. Louis, Missouri, married her, settled down, and started a family. Their daughter, also named Frances, was born in 1929, and the twins, Richard and Guy, were born in 1934. Dick went into business and developed an excellent reputation for understanding the nuances of the interrelationship of businesses and economic forces, which would make him uniquely qualified to serve as one of the key men in the later planning and execution of the Big Week mission.

Guy D'Oyly Hughes, the namesake of one of Dick and Franny's twins, had taken the route in life that led him to His Majesty's Royal Navy. As Dick was with the British Army, fighting Turks in Iraq, Guy was fighting the Turks beneath the waves of the Mediterranean, as first officer aboard the submarine HMS *E11*. Mainly during the Dardanelles Campaign, the sub was credited with sinking more than eighty vessels of various sizes. In 1915, Guy earned a Distinguished Service Order by swimming ashore to blow up a portion of the Constantinople-to-Baghdad railroad.

World War II would find Guy above the waves as captain of the aircraft carrier HMS *Glorious*. On June 8, 1940, the carrier and two escorting destroyers were intercepted near Norway by the infamous German battlecruisers *Scharnhorst* and *Gneisenau*. In one of the war's major surface actions involving the German Kreigsmarine and the Royal Navy, all three British vessels were sunk. Guy was killed by a shell from the *Scharnhorst* before *Glorious* slipped beneath the icy waves.

By the late 1930s, Dick Hughes managed St. Albans Farms, a former dairy operation that was evolving into a comfortable suburban residential community. Overlooking the Missouri River in northeastern Franklin County, about thirty-five miles west of St. Louis, St. Albans Farms once provided around 2 percent of the milk that was sold in that city. Over time, it would supply a similar proportion of commuters to St. Louis.

When the war began in Europe, and especially after his own brother was killed by the Germans, Dick Hughes yearned to get into the war somehow. It was partly an eagerness for revenge, or so he stated in his unpublished memoir, and partly a yearning to be a part of the twentieth century's biggest adventure.

ONE

THE BIRTH OF AN IDEA

"I can see it falling through the sky for a couple of seconds and then it disappears," a thirty-year-old Italian pilot named Giulio Gavotti recalled breathlessly of his first bomb run over a target in Libya. "After a little while, I can see a small dark cloud in the middle of the encampment. I have hit the target!"

In 2011, the world watched as NATO airpower provided the critical edge in the defeat of Muammar Gaddafi's forty-two-year rule in Libya. In the history of airpower, compared to the great battles of World War II, the Libyan campaign of 2011 was a footnote.

In the history of airpower, 2011 was neither a turning point nor a tipping point. It was the *centennial*.

Exactly one hundred years earlier, in 1911, in the skies over exactly the same place, Lieutenant Gavotti's first bomb run had been the first bomb run in the history of aerial warfare.

With the advent of heavier-than-air flight early in the twentieth century, the armies of the world had been buying airplanes, but as with the balloons used by the armies of the nineteenth century, they were only intended as passive observation platforms.

Among the wars being fought by European countries in the early twentieth century was a land grab by Italy that involved the seizure of Ottoman Turkish colonial possessions in North Africa, specifically in the area that later became Libya. November found a squadron of Italian aircraft involved. One of the pilots was Giulio Gavotti.

"Today two boxes full of bombs arrived," Gavotti wrote in a letter to his father in Naples. "We are expected to throw them from our planes. It is very strange that none of us have been told about this, and that we haven't received any instruction from our superiors. So we are taking the bombs on board with the greatest precaution. It will be very interesting to try them on the Turks."

The rest is history.

Three years later, the armies of Europe's great powers, each of them now equipped with small aviation sections, were in the opening throes of World War I.

Meanwhile, the mainstream technical establishment had been slow to grasp the tactical importance of such operations. In October 1910, *Scientific American* dismissed the idea of airplanes as war machines, noting that "outside of scouting duties, we are inclined to think that the field of usefulness of the aeroplane will be rather limited. Because of its small carrying capacity, and the necessity for its operating at great altitude, if it is to escape hostile fire, the amount of damage it will do by dropping explosives upon cities, forts, hostile camps, or bodies of troops in the field to say nothing of battleships at sea, will be so limited as to have no material effects on the issues of a campaign."

Between 1914 and 1918 in the skies over World War I battlefields, the young men of Gavotti's generation would prove the fallacy of the venerable journal's assumptions.

In that conflict, aircraft were, indeed, first used as observation platforms, but air-to-air combat was a natural step in the evolution of aerial warfare. Both sides had airplanes and aviators, and soon they encountered one another over the trenches. The first confrontations were gentlemanly, indeed, probably chivalrous, for the knights of the air had something in common with other airmen that their respective countrymen on the ground could only dream of.

It didn't take long, however, for the realization to sink in that the enemy in the trenches, with his Mauser trained on your skull, saluted the same flag as the silk-scarved enemy gliding by in his lacquered Albatros. Somebody took his sidearm aloft, the first airplane went down, and air combat was born.

Soon, like Gavotti, aerial observers flying over the enemy's lines realized that they could as easily drop something that exploded. Tactical bombing, as a doctrine, was born. To use *Scientific American*'s phrasing, aerial bombing had actually started to have "material effects on the issues of a campaign."

Meanwhile, there were some farsighted airpower theorists who began imagining that aviation might potentially be deployed in such a way as to have "material effects" *beyond* the battlefield, thereby shaping the course and outcome of the war itself. This is what came to be known as *strategic* airpower.

Tactical bombing, simply stated, is aerial bombardment of enemy targets, such as troop concentrations, airfields, entrenchments, and the like, as part of an integrated air-land battlefield action at or near the front. Tactical airpower generally is used toward the same goals as, and in direct support of, naval forces or ground troops in the field.

Strategic airpower, by contrast, seeks targets without a specific connection with what is happening at the front. Strategic airpower is used to strike far behind the lines, at the enemy's *means* of waging war—such as factories, power plants, cities—and ultimately, the enemy's very *will* to wage war.

Strategic aircraft naturally differ from tactical aircraft in that they have a much longer range and payload capacity—certainly more than the average 1914 airplane.

It was not until around the time of World War I that aviation technology had developed to the point where such large aircraft were practical. One of the original pioneers of strategic airpower was a Russian engineer and aviation enthusiast. The year was 1913, and the man was Igor Sikorsky, the same man who would amaze the world thirty years later with the first practical helicopters. The airplane was named the Ilya Mourometz (or Muromets) after the tenth-century Russian hero, and it was the world's first strategic bomber. The big plane was designed as an airliner but was adapted as a bomber when the war began. It was powered by four engines, as no other plane before it had been, with the single exception of its own prototype, the unarmed Russky Vityaz (Russian Knight).

By the winter of 1914–1915, a sizable number of these big bombers were in action against German targets. The bomb load of each plane exceeded half a ton, and with a range of nearly four hundred miles, they were able to hit targets well behind German lines. The Russians conducted more than four hundred raids without the Germans mounting a similar campaign in retaliation, but in the end, other factors intervened. After initial victories, the Russian Army was defeated on the ground by 1917, the tsar had abdicated, and the events leading to the Russian Revolution were rapidly under way. The Ilya Mourometz had been successful in what it did, but it played only a minor part in one of mankind's biggest dramas. Igor Sikorsky emigrated from Russia to the United States, and the theory of strategic airpower would remain largely dormant in Russia until after the next world war.

Strategic air operations on the western front were soon to follow those in the east, with British aircraft launching strikes against German positions in occupied Belgian coastal cities in February 1915. The Germans countered with zeppelin attacks on Paris and on British cities as far north as Newcastle. On the night of May 31, after ten months of war, London looked upon its own dead for the first time. About a week later, Austrian aviators launched the first long-range strategic mission on the southern front, causing several fires in and around the Piazza San Marco in Venice. By 1917, the Germans were using long-range, fixed-wing Gotha bombers against London.

In April 1918, shortly after being established as an independent service, Britain's Royal Air Force (RAF) conducted a series of raids on German cities in the Ruhr and even ranged as far south as Frankfurt, though the raids were more a strategic bombing *experiment* than a strategic bombing *offensive*. A full-scale strategic air offensive against Germany *was* scheduled for the spring of 1919, with Berlin on the target list, but the war ended in November 1918 with the plan untried.

Though the intervention of United States manpower in World War I may have been of pivotal importance to the Allies, the involvement of

American *air*power was not extensive and consisted almost entirely of tactical operations. Nevertheless, the *idea* of strategic airpower made a great impression on the commander of the American Expeditionary Force (AEF) air units in the war, Colonel Billy Mitchell.

Mitchell's boss, General John J. "Blackjack" Pershing, the overall commander of the AEF, saw airpower strictly as tactical ground support, the conventional view of the time. Mitchell, however, saw the potential for a broader application. He wanted to see the AEF airmen striking the enemy at his source of supply, rather than being simply another weapon for ground commanders to use as they would use artillery.

Mitchell became the first major American exponent of strategic airpower, but his ideas were never implemented during the war. Part of the reason was that strategic bombing, though experimental in British and French doctrine, was not yet accepted by the American military establishment at all.

"Aircraft move hundreds of miles in an incredibly short space of time, so that even if they are reported as coming into a country, across its frontiers, there is no telling where they are going to go to strike," the prescient Mitchell wrote, describing a method of warfare that was still many years in the future. "Wherever an object can be seen from the air, aircraft are able to hit it with their guns, bombs, and other weapons. Cities and towns, railway lines and canals cannot be hidden. Not only is this the case on land, it is even more the case on the water, because on the water no object can be concealed unless it dives beneath the surface."

After the war, Mitchell, now a brigadier general, became the central figure in the crusade for strategic airpower. Mitchell argued that strategic bombers were cheaper to build and operate than battleships, and they could be used faster and more easily to project American power wherever it might be needed around the world.

"Neither armies nor navies can exist unless the air is controlled over them," Mitchell wrote in 1925. "Air forces, on the other hand, are the only independent fighting units of the day, because neither armies nor navies can ascend and fight twenty thousand feet above the earth's surface."

He raised hackles in 1921 when he told Congress that his bombers could sink any ship afloat. To prove him wrong, the US Navy agreed to let him try out his theories on some captured German warships they had inherited at the end of the war and that needed to be disposed of.

The rules of engagement were written by the Navy's Atlantic Fleet commander. The Navy would regulate the weight of the bombs and the number of planes, and reserved the right to call off the engagement at any time. In a series of demonstrations held in July 1921, Mitchell and the Army Air Service attacked the German ships anchored in Chesapeake Bay. A destroyer went down, followed by the light cruiser *Frankfurt*, and ultimately the heavily armored battleship *Ostfriesland*. Mitchell had dramatically proven his point, but both the US Army and the US Navy remained officially unconvinced.

"Aircraft possess the most powerful weapons ever devised by man," Mitchell cautioned. "They carry not only guns and cannon but heavy missiles that utilize the force of gravity for their propulsion and which can cause more destruction than any other weapon. One of these great bombs hitting a battleship will completely destroy it. Consider what this means to the future systems of national defense. As battleships are relatively difficult to destroy, imagine how much easier it is to sink all other vessels and merchant craft."

As Mitchell became more and more outspoken, the US Army transferred him from Langley Field in Virginia (too close to Washington for their comfort) to Kelly Field near San Antonio, Texas. In 1925, after the loss of life from the crash of the Navy dirigible *Shenandoah*, Mitchell called the management of national defense by the War and Navy Departments "incompetent" and "treasonable." The army had had enough. Mitchell was court-martialed, convicted, reduced to colonel, and drummed out of the service on half pension. He died in 1936, just a few years short of seeing strategic airpower play a key role in the Allied victory in World War II.

Nevertheless, even before the death of Billy Mitchell, the proponents of the still-unproven concept of strategic airpower had risen to places of influence within the major air forces of the world. In both Britain and the United States, large, four-engine heavy bombers were in development, while in Germany, airpower in general would become fully integrated into battlefield doctrine.

TWO

THE WAR WILL BE AN AIR WAR

Even as Billy Mitchell was uncannily predicting the use of airpower in future conflicts, events were in motion on the other side of the Atlantic that would propel the nations of Europe and the world into the Second World War.

In the Treaty of Versailles, which concluded the First World War, the wartime Allies had imposed steep reparations demands and economic restrictions that shoved Germany's already tottering economy to the brink. In so doing, they were creating the environment which would breed the next great war.

While the rest of the world was enjoying a decade of prosperity in the 1920s, Germany imploded. Having been the industrial powerhouse of continental Europe before the war, that nation collapsed economically because of its defeat and the Versailles restrictions. Unemployment and hyperinflation reached staggering levels that have few, if any, comparisons in the history of modern industrialized nations. Also part of the Versailles restrictions was the policy forbidding Germany to have an air force, or even an aircraft industry.

The treaty handed Germany insult on top of injury, demanding that it accept sole responsibility for the war. While Germany had been the principal combatant among the Central Powers, there were plenty of nations on both sides who had a share in the blame for the war having started. Because Germany had been so obviously singled out, it provided German extremists of all stripes a gift on which they could agree. The treaty became a lightning rod for the harangues of rabble-rousers from all political persuasions.

Out of the swirling sea of leaderless chaos, there at last emerged a powerful and charismatic leader who promised much and was embraced by masses yearning for prewar glories.

Germany's downward economic spiral reversed its course when Adolf Hitler's National Socialists came to power in 1934. When Hitler became *Führer und Reichskanzler* (leader and Reich chancellor), he began rearming Germany in violation of the terms of the Treaty of Versailles. In 1936, his armies occupied the German Rhineland, again in direct violation of the Treaty of Versailles.

Tensions between Germany and its wartime enemies, Britain and France, quickly increased, but neither of them was keen to challenge Hitler and risk another war. Neither did the Soviet Union relish the idea, despite the ferocious ideological divide between the Nazis and the Communists. Hitler had written at length in his 1926 manifesto, *Mein Kampf* (*My Struggle*), about his desire to incorporate large slices of the Soviet Union into his Third Reich, but as with so much about his tome, the world did not take it seriously.

The ticking of the time bomb of World War II began with Hitler's grab for the territory of Germany's closest neighbors. In March 1938, Hitler annexed Austria in a move that was called *Anschluss*, or "Connection." This fulfilled the dreams of Germanic ethnocentrists in both countries who wished to see all German-speaking people united in a single Reich. There were also large numbers of ethnic Germans in Czechoslovakia, and Hitler next demanded that Czechoslovakia's German-speaking Sudetenland region also be folded into his Third Reich. There were also a large number of Germans in the nominally independent port city of Danzig, which had alternated between Poland and Prussia for centuries before the League of Nations took it away from Germany in 1920, when Poland was reconstituted, and made it a "free city." Known as Gdansk in

Polish, it was coveted by Poles, whose territory surrounded it, and it was coveted by Germans, who had owned it for more than a century and wanted it back.

In September 1938, at the now infamous summit conference, Britain's Prime Minister Neville Chamberlain and France's President Édouard Daladier flew to Munich, the mother city of the Nazi Party, to meet with Adolf Hitler. The Führer told these gentlemen that the Sudetenland should properly be part of Germany, and he promised that this was the end of his territorial ambitions. Czechoslovakia naturally complained, but Chamberlain and Daladier ignored the Czechs and acceded to the Führer's demands. When Chamberlain flew home, he happily announced that he had helped to negotiate "peace for our time."

In March 1939, Hitler decided that he wanted the rest of Czechoslovakia. The price tag for "peace for our time" had gone up. Chamberlain and Daladier were willing to go to almost any lengths to appease Adolf Hitler and avoid war. Like a terminal patient in his hospital bed, Czechoslovakia had no choice. The poor country was chopped into bits. Slovakia was sliced off as a quasi-autonomous satellite of Germany, while the remainder of Czechoslovakia became the Reich Protectorate of Bohemia and Moravia.

Two months later, Hitler inked a deal with Italy's Fascist "Duce," Benito Mussolini. Known as the Pact of Steel, the agreement called for cooperation in time of war, a war that seemed all that much closer because of the pact. With a name like "Pact of Steel," it didn't even sound like an alliance with friendly intentions.

On August 24, Hitler sent his foreign minister to Moscow. There, Joachim von Ribbentrop signed a nonaggression pact with the Soviet Union's own brutal strongman, Josef Stalin. Much to the surprise of the global media that demonized and caricaturized them both, the right-wing demon, Hitler, had tumbled into bed with the left-wing demon, Stalin.

A week later, on the morning of September 1, 1939, as German troops raced across the border, German bombs began falling on Poland. In London, Neville Chamberlain proposed more negotiations, but Hitler held the best hand—and he had just decreed that the time for negotiating was over.

Chamberlain consulted with Daladier, and together they came to realize that the time for negotiating was indeed over. On September 3, Britain and France declared that a state of war between them and the Third Reich had existed for two days. There would be no "peace in our time."

Not only did the German invasion stun the world politically, the precision of the integrated German war machine stunned the world militarily. It was the most well-trained, best-equipped, and overall superior military force in the world. Their coordinated air and ground offensive, known as blitzkrieg (lightning war), was the most rapid and efficient mode of military attack the world had ever seen. The use of fast-moving tanks, mobile forces, dive bombers, and paratroop units—all working together as one tight, well-disciplined force—stunned the world, especially the Polish defenders. Germany was able to subjugate Poland in just three weeks. The Luftwaffe played such a crucial role in this action that it surprised airpower advocates and airpower skeptics alike.

After Germany had conquered Poland—naturally annexing the great port at Danzig—Britain and France dispatched a few bombers over Germany but, for the most part, took no offensive action. A lull in the action of World War II descended over Europe. Throughout the winter of 1939–1940, Allied and German troops sat and stared at one another across the heavily fortified Franco-German border. So little was happening that newspaper writers dubbed the situation the "sitzkrieg" or the "phoney war."

On April 9, 1940, Germany attacked to the west.

Sitzkrieg became blitzkrieg once again. German troops quickly occupied Denmark and Norway. On May 10, the Germans began a great offensive to the west that duplicated their advance on Belgium and France in 1914 at the beginning of World War I. By May 28, Luxembourg, Belgium, and the Netherlands had surrendered and German forces were pouring into France. By June 14, Germany had seized control of Paris, having accomplished in five weeks what it had been unable to do in four years of protracted fighting in World War I.

France finally surrendered on June 22, leaving Britain to face the onslaught of Germany's blitzkrieg alone. Only twenty-one miles of English Channel separated Germany's crack troops from an army that had abandoned all of its equipment in France when it barely managed to escape from the Germans at Dunkirk on the French coast on June 4.

While Hitler's forces prepared for a cross-channel invasion of Britain, the English people rallied around Prime Minister Winston Churchill, who had taken office on May 10 telling them he had "nothing to offer but blood, toil, tears and sweat." He defied Hitler by informing him that his troops would meet relentless opposition on the beaches, on the streets, and in every village. However, Luftwaffe commander Field Marshal Hermann Göring insisted that his bombers could easily subdue Britain, making the planned sea invasion a simple walk-over.

In August, the Luftwaffe began a brutal, unremitting bombing assault on Britain's ports, factories, and cities. Soon the assault turned to the British capital, with the ruthless London Blitz.

The only thing that stood in the way of an easy victory was the courageous, but vastly outnumbered, pilots of the Royal Air Force, who met the Germans like gnats attacking crows. Despite the fact that the British had fewer than one thousand fighters to face a Luftwaffe onslaught four times as large, the RAF was able to destroy twelve bombers for each one of their own losses. Churchill called it the RAF's "finest hour."

The Luftwaffe had eradicated the will of the Netherlands to resist German armies by leveling downtown Rotterdam in June, but failed to do the same to the British a few months later. Nevertheless, the London Blitz stunned and nearly demoralized Britain.

In their use of integrated tactical air operations in support of the blitzkrieg, the Luftwaffe had revolutionized tactical air warfare. They had developed the right aircraft and had mastered the right tactics to achieve frighteningly successful results.

The Germans had shown the world that this war would be an *air* war.

THREE

AMERICA PREPARES FOR THE AIR WAR

Billy Mitchell had resigned in February 1926, and died a decade later, in February 1936, having spent the last ten years of his life predicting that the next world war would be an air war, *and* insisting that the United States should get ready for it. While there were young officers throughout the US Army and US Navy who had heard Mitchell, the upper levels of command were scarcely more willing to believe the premise of his argument than they had been in 1921.

Though his own countrymen had remained deaf to Mitchell's message, the idea had obviously taken root in Europe, especially in Germany. While the air forces of Europe were expanding during the 1930s, there was no corresponding urgency among the upper echelon leadership of the United States armed forces to do the same. For nearly two centuries, vast oceans had been both physical and psychological barriers which insulated America from foreign wars. Even eighteen years after Billy Mitchell had proven that bombers could sink battleships, the US Navy defense planners still insisted that oceans and battleships were the only line of defense that the United States needed to avoid war. The US Army, meanwhile, still believed that its subsidiary Air Corps existed only to support troops in the field, not to undertake offensive actions behind enemy lines independent of the ground troops.

However, within the Air Corps, Billy Mitchell's vision for an independent air force capable of decisive action had resonated with many junior officers since the 1920s. By the 1930s, these men were no longer *junior* officers. One of the leading voices of airpower advocacy within the Air Corps was the officer who became its chief in 1938—General Henry Harley "Hap" Arnold, West Point class of 1907.

Until the early 1930s, the types of aircraft that were being acquired by the Air Corps were principally single-engine trainers and combat aircraft. By the late 1930s, more and more longer range "multi-engine" warplanes were being added to the mix by forward-thinking officers who were rising in the ranks, graduating from bars to oak leaves.

The development of the technology for such aircraft began in 1933, with two secret Air Corps programs that were called Project A and Project D. With this, the seeds of the strategic airpower doctrine, sewn by Billy Mitchell, were germinated. The two secret projects were the first whisper of a breeze in the winds of change blowing into airpower doctrine. The idea in both projects was to examine the feasibility of very large, very long-range bombers.

These projects were significant in that they were conceived as harbingers of aircraft that would be part of a strategic doctrine. Though the United States was being outproduced elsewhere in the world, especially in Germany and the United Kingdom, when it came to combat aircraft, at least the Air Corps was *looking* ahead in conceptualizing strategic airpower.

Project A and Project D spawned a series of very large aircraft designs, of which the Boeing XB-15 and Douglas XB-19 became one-of-a-kind prototypes. However, the real value of the projects came in the manufacturers, especially Boeing, having developed the technology base for large bombers. This led to the Boeing Model 299.

Designed by a team of brilliant young engineers, notably Edward Curtis Wells, and built at company expense, the Boeing Model 299 first flew on July 28, 1935. At the rollout, *Seattle Times* reporter Richard

Williams described the huge, four-engine bomber as a "flying fortress." The name was adopted as the official name. In January 1936, after several months of testing, the Air Corps ordered the first Flying Fortresses under the designation Y1B-17, and by 1938, they were ordering small numbers of operational B-17Bs.

During 1939, as Europe went to war, the Luftwaffe took delivery of 8,295 new aircraft, and Britain's Royal Air Force acquired 7,940. The US Army Air Corps bought 2,141, mainly trainers. In August, they had ordered 38 B-17C Flying Fortresses for delivery in 1940.

In July 1940, with the German armies in control of most of Western Europe, and England seeming to be ripe for the picking, the United States government and military services were faced with the problem of expanding the army and the Navy, and the air services of both. Nevertheless, the acquisition of four-engine bombers still moved at a timid pace. In 1940, the Air Corps would order just 80 B-17C and B-17D aircraft. Among these, 20 were acquired for Britain's Royal Air Force in the autumn of 1940 under the designation Fortress Mk.I.

The latter is illustrative of how the world viewed four-engine bomber development, and how planners in England had failed to embrace the doctrine of strategic airpower. Even one year into World War II, the Flying Fortress was the only operational four-engine bomber of which significant numbers were in the pipeline.

By this time, the RAF had awakened and the British Air Ministry had ordered the development of aircraft such as the Short Stirling and the Handley Page Halifax, but their operational careers would not be under way until 1941. The Avro Lancaster, considered Britain's best strategic bomber of the war, would not be in service until 1942.

Meanwhile, a second American four-engine bomber type was coming on line in 1941. Developed by Consolidated Aircraft of San Diego as its Model 32, the aircraft was designated as the B-24 by the Air Corps, and named Liberator. As with the Flying Fortress, some early Liberators were delivered to the RAF in 1941. The first mass-production variant, the B-24D, would make its squadron service debut in the United States the following year.

For all their meticulous planning in terms of aircraft and tactics—not to mention their superior numbers of first-rate aircraft—the Luftwaffe had yet to seriously consider four-engine strategic bombers. Those four-engine aircraft the Germans had developed, such as the Fw 200, were long on range but short on combat durability and payload.

The Luftwaffe had proven itself as an undisputed master of tactical air warfare, but they had failed to develop either the long-range aircraft, or a long-rang plan, for *strategic* air warfare. Meanwhile, the US Army Air Corps had taken a significant step toward developing the aircraft. Soon it would take a step toward developing a plan.

In June 1941, big changes came to the US Army's conception of air-power. In a move that would have been unthinkable just a few years ear-lier, Chief of Staff General George Marshall ordered the creation of an autonomous US Army Air Forces as the operational successor to the Air Corps.

General Arnold, as the commander of the new USAAF, formed an Air Staff and named General Carl Spaatz as its chief. He charged Spaatz, who had already spent time working with the British Air Staff in London, with creating an Air War Plans Division (AWPD). This organization would coordinate with the US Army's existing War Plans Division (WPD) but would remain independent from it. Headed by Lieutenant Colonel Harold L. "Hal" George, the AWPD came into being in July 1941 and began developing the plan that would be implemented if, or *when*, the United States became involved in World War II. This plan, known as AWPD-1, would be integrated into the larger joint US Army–US Navy contingency plan known as Rainbow 5.

The cast of young officers who came together around AWPD-1, as part of Hal George's staff, not only helped draft the plan, but many would go on to play key roles in its implementation. They included Lieutenant Colonel Orvil Anderson, Major Hoyt Vandenberg, and a World War I flight instructor turned businessman, Lieutenant Colonel Malcolm Moss, as well as a pair of West Pointers, Major Laurence Kuter and Major Haywood Hansell. Hansell would go on to command the first B-17 combat wing in Europe, while Vandenberg would command the wartime Ninth Air Force, and go on to serve as chief of staff of the postwar US Air Force.

Ground had yet to be broken for the Pentagon, so these men, among the best and the brightest in the USAAF, rolled up their sleeves and went to work in the Munitions Building on the Washington Mall.

Officially entitled *Munitions Requirements of the Army Air Forces to Defeat Our Potential Enemies*, AWPD-1 went beyond determining aircraft production goals and developed the comprehensive outlines for a strategy of deploying them to win the war. As Robert Futrell writes in his book, *Ideas, Concepts, Doctrine*, President Roosevelt himself heartily agreed that the mission of the AWPD was to draft the "requirements required to defeat our potential enemies."

Completed early in August, AWPD-1 included a strategy for fighting a war not just in Europe, but around the world, from the Western Hemisphere to the Western Pacific. Subsequent AWPD planning, such as AWPD-2 in September 1941, which considered aircraft production, would be based on the general outlines of AWPD-1.

Though Hal George and his team were looking ahead, nobody realized how soon the anticipated American entry into World War II would come.

By the end of November 1941, as an Imperial Japanese Navy carrier group was closing in on the Hawaiian Islands, the USAAF had 3,305 combat aircraft in its inventory. Of these, 145 were Flying Fortresses, and only 11 were Liberators.

FOUR

GOING TO WAR

On a sober morning after, the United States went to war.

Before a joint session of Congress on December 8, 1941, as Franklin Roosevelt described the previous day as "a date which will live in infamy" and asked a joint session of Congress for a declaration of war, they were picking up the pieces at Pearl Harbor. Among those pieces were the fragments of a B-24 and eight B-17Ds that had once belonged to the 5th Bombardment Group at Hickam Field. On that same day, most of the nineteen Flying Fortresses based at Clark Field near Manila in the Philippines were also destroyed.

On December 21, Prime Minister Winston Churchill and high-ranking British military officers arrived in Washington, DC, for the Anglo-American summit conference designated as Arcadia. The purpose was to sit down with President Franklin Roosevelt and his top brass—including Hap Arnold and Carl Spaatz—to plan a strategy to defeat Germany and Japan, both of which, at that moment, appeared unbeatable.

The Arcadia Conference was not without precedent. Though the United States did not formally declare war on Germany until December 11, there had been overt as well as covert cooperation with Britain since the beginning of the year. The most overt example of an Anglo-American alliance had been the Lend-Lease Act of March 11, 1941.

When the war began in 1939, British arms buyers came to the United States to buy everything from Flying Fortresses to tommy guns. By the start of 1941, though, His Majesty's government was running out of money. President Roosevelt feared Hitler as much as the British did, and he knew that the United States was not, despite his buildup for national defense, ready to fight the German war machine. He wanted to keep the British fighting, and he desired very much to keep the fighting British *between* Hitler and the United States.

Perhaps the second to last thing that Roosevelt wanted to see was Britain running out of money to *pay* for all the materiel they had ordered during 1940—so he came up with a plan. The plan was called Lend-Lease. The idea was that the United States would "sell, transfer title to, exchange, lease, lend, or otherwise dispose of" weapons and materiel to any government whose defense the president deemed vital to the defense of the United States. The way it worked was the United States government purchased the weapons from the manufacturers and then delivered them to the Allies.

Payment for the Lend-Lease goods, or their return to the United States, was to be made after the war. In fact, few of the goods that survived the war were actually returned, and repayment was delayed. Britain finally settled up its bill, at a deeply discounted rate, at the end of 2006.

On the covert side, American officers had already met secretly with British and Canadian military leaders between January and March in the "ABC-1" (First American-British-Canadian) staff conferences to discuss strategy for "if" the United States entered the war against Germany. Indeed, elements of the ABC-1 plan had been incorporated into AWPD-1, specifically the part about the implementation of a joint Anglo-American strategic bombing campaign against Germany.

The seeds of a wartime working relationship had sprouted earlier, in August 1941, when Roosevelt and Churchill themselves met at sea off Newfoundland to announce an optomistic postwar cooperative agreement, which came to be known as the Atlantic Charter. The Arcadia Conference in Washington that winter was both a confirmation of previously understood cooperation, and a nuts-and-bolts planning session for specific collaboration toward what should be and *could be* done next—now that the two parties had become wartime allies.

In the dark days of December, what *could be* done next was summarized as not much. What *would be* done next was up to the British and American officers who knew they faced an uphill climb.

In the Pacific, in the previous two weeks, the Japanese had used airpower to decimate the United States Pacific Fleet and sink two of Britain's biggest warships. They had landed in the Philippines and were headed for Manila, washing over American and Filipino defenders with ease—and with air superiority. While the Arcadia conferees were in the midst of their talks, the Japanese captured the British Crown Colony of Hong Kong, even as the Germans were banging on Moscow's door.

With 20/20 hindsight, we know that the German failure to capture the Soviet capital in December 1941 was a watershed moment, but at the time, the only hindsight available told the planners that since their invasion of the Soviet Union six months earlier, the Germans had captured more territory faster than any army in history. In addition to dominating virtually all of continental Europe, they occupied an area of the Soviet Union more than twice as large as Germany itself.

At their historic December meeting, the American and British leaders created a "Combined Chiefs of Staff" (CCS) to direct the war effort, and they decided on a strategy. They decided to put their principal military efforts in the war against Germany, while attempting to contain the Japanese offensive.

They knew that one day, they would have to fight a major land battle against the German Army that had defeated France in a couple of weeks and *appeared* to have defeated the Soviet Union in a few months.

There was not an American in the room who did not get a nervous lump in his throat when he thought of having to fight the blitzkrieg. The British knew that their expeditionary force *had* fought the blitzkrieg in France in 1940—and they barely escaped with their lives. In the meantime, the Germans were turning the continent into their *Festung Europa* ("Fortress Europe"), fortifying the coastline opposite Britain into an impregnable citadel.

Though the failure of the Germans to capture Moscow in December was touted by the Soviets as a great victory, the Arcadia conferees interpreted it merely as a minor setback for an army that had thus far proven invincible. They based their planning on the correct assumption that the Germans would try again to crush the Soviets in the spring of 1942, and the very plausible fear that the Soviet Union could be knocked out of the war before the Anglo-American Allies could launch any kind of land assault on *Festung Europa*.

The Soviets, naturally, shared this fear. As a consequence, they demanded, and continued to demand at every opportunity, that the Americans and the British launch a "second front" against the Germans sooner rather than later. No one knew better than the Arcadia conferees that this would be impossible in 1942. Instead, they agreed to Operation Bolero, the buildup of forces necessary to launch a second front against *Festung Europa* in 1943. The date for this invasion of Europe by way of northern France, code-named Operation Roundup, was originally set for April 1943.

As the German army seemed all-powerful, in the air the Luftwaffe commanded an equivalent fear and respect. Even though the Royal Air Force had challenged them successfully in 1940 over Britain, they still controlled the skies over Europe.

That which concerned the men most about Germany—the elephant in the room, so to speak—was the might of German industry that had made all this possible. There was no way that the Anglo-American Allies could challenge Hitler's mighty war machine on the ground in Europe so long as the mighty German industrial machine continued to churn out the tanks and aircraft that had thus far proven unstoppable.

The men in the room also knew that the *only* way to do anything to impact the mighty German industrial machine was with strategic airpower.

The Combined Chiefs of Staff found themselves facing the situation that Billy Mitchell had predicted.

The RAF needed no convincing when it came to strategic airpower. Arnold and Spaatz, longtime advocates of Mitchell's strategic vision, found kindred spirits in the commander of RAF Bomber Command, Air Marshal Arthur Travers "Bomber" Harris, and his boss—and predecessor as head of Bomber Command—RAF commander Air Chief Marshal Sir Charles "Peter" Portal. It was only a matter of coordinating the effort.

The ABC-1 report from early in the year had already concluded that "US Army air bombardment units [would] operate offensively in collaboration with the Royal Air Force, primarily against German Military Power at its source." The emphasis on "German Military Power" was reiterated in AWPD-1. The foresight of AWPD-1, which had gone beyond its mandate of merely calculating production numbers, had given the USAAF the operational framework that was so badly needed.

As for the basing of the Anglo-American strategic force, Britain was the only viable option. As with the existing and planned British bombers, the range of the Flying Fortress and the Liberator dictated that targets in the German industrial heartland could be attacked only from bases in southeast England.

Of course, in early 1942, any kind of sustained air offensive was merely theoretical, because of the small number of heavy bombers available. British production of four-engine bombers was moving at so slow a pace that the Brits were still anxious to continue receiving Flying Fortresses and Liberators from America. Meanwhile, the USAAF now had fewer Flying Fortresses than they'd had on December 6.

The USAAF was also spread very thin. Even though the Allies had adopted the "Germany first, contain Japan" approach at the Arcadia Conference, the USAAF still had commitments in the Pacific. The British, though impatient to strike a major blow against Hitler from the air, understood. The rapid movement of Japanese forces threatened their interests as well—especially Australia and their great bastion at Singapore. When the latter was, in fact, captured by the Japanese in February, it underscored the fact that, while the Pacific Theater might be secondary to the European Theater, it could not be ignored.

Indeed, it was against Japan, not Germany, that the USAAF would strike first.

Early in 1942, as the Arcadia Conference was adjourned, two schools of thought were holding court within the American military establishment. One called for a methodical and comprehensive plan of action for substantial, if plodding, steps to defeat the Axis. The other, driven by the requirements of morale-building, called for something to be done quickly.

The former was embodied in the work being done by the Air War

Plans Division. The latter manifested itself in two important actions that were undertaken in the spring and summer of 1942, well before the USAAF was anywhere near being ready to undertake truly decisive strategic air operations.

The first of the two was the heroic and iconic April 18 attack on Japanese cities led by prewar aviation pioneer and daredevil air racer Lieutenant Colonel James Harold "Jimmy" Doolittle. The sixteen carrier-launched B-25 medium bombers on Doolittle's mission did slight damage to Japan but immensely buoyed American morale by demonstrating that the United States was *capable* of bombing the country.

The second action was the June 12 attack on the oil refineries at Ploeşti (now Ploieşti), Romania, the Achilles' heel of the Third Reich's oil production and the largest refinery complex in continental Europe. Having allied itself with the Axis in November 1940, Romania had contributed troops for the June 1941 German invasion of the Soviet Union and was providing the petrochemicals that oiled and fueled the German war machine.

The Ploeşti mission was flown by a contingent of B-24D Liberators, commanded by Colonel Harry "Hurry-Up" Halverson, which had reached Egypt en route to India, where they were intended to operate against the Japanese from bases in China. Given that the previously considered airfields were now under threat from Japanese forces, and that the Burma Road supply route had been cut, the Halverson Project (HALPRO) was diverted. They would, instead, attack Ploeşti from Egypt.

Like Doolittle's raid, this attack on the oil refineries at Ploeşti was much longer on symbolism and propaganda value than on concrete results. As Hap Arnold wrote of the Ploeşti mission in his memoirs, "The target was not much damaged. The improbability of this two-thousand-mile round trip was its best protection, and enemy opposition was not heavy."

It would be more than a year before Allied bombers returned to attack, Ploeşti and more than two for Tokyo, but Halverson and Doolittle had shown that "improbable" was not the same as "impossible."

Mainly, Doolittle and Halverson proved to the American public—and to the enemy—that the USAAF was doing *something*. Of course, the people in USAAF uniform understood that it would take time before anything substantial could be done.

For all the prior planning, the fact that the war came sooner than the Americans had anticipated required the Air Staff to play catch-up. James Lea Cate points out, in *Army Air Forces in World War II*, that "it had been presumed that at outbreak of war, or even before, a substantial air contingent should be sent to the British Isles. Now that war had come, there were more pressing needs. The British naturally were interested in the projected bomber force, but were anxious that it be provided without jeopardy to current allocation of heavy bombers [via Lend-Lease] to the RAF."

Harris and Portal were wondering how soon that "substantial air contingent" could get into action against Germany.

As recorded in the notes of the Arcadia Conference, Arnold and Spaatz told Portal on January 1 that it might be possible to send two heavy bombardment groups to England "before too long," but as Cate reminds us, an estimate of "about March or April [was only] a shot in the dark."

In a Combined Chiefs of Staff memorandum of February 22, entitled *Policy for Disposition of US and British Air Forces*, it was determined that for the present the RAF would assume responsibility for the air offensive against Germany, with the USAAF joining in "at the earliest dates practicable."

As an operational organization to join with RAF Bomber Command to execute the strategic air offensive, the USAAF created the VIII Bomber Command, which was, along with other units, an element of the larger Eighth Air Force, which was formed to control and manage USAAF assets in Britain.

The numbered air forces were the largest operational components of the USAAF during World War II. As the plural in "US Army Air Forces" implies, the USAAF was composed of multiple numbered air forces. The original four had been created in the four quadrants of the continental United States. The Fifth was the former Philippine Department Air Force in the Western Pacific, the Sixth Air Force originated as the Panama Canal Air Force, and the Seventh Air Force was born out of the Hawaiian Air Force. All had been prewar components of the Air Corps.

An additional eight air forces would be added during the war. The Ninth would operate first in North Africa and later from Britain as the tactical airpower parallel to the strategic Eighth. The Tenth and Fourteenth would operate in the China-India-Burma Theater, and the Thirteenth in the South Pacific. In the Mediterranean Theater, the Twelfth and Fifteenth would evolve into the tactical and strategic counterparts to the Ninth and the Eighth in the European Theater. Indeed, the Eighth and Fifteenth would ultimately coordinate their efforts in the strategic campaign against Germany. The Sixteenth through Nineteenth were not activated during World War II, and the Twentieth would become operational in 1944 as a strategic force that operated the Boeing B-29 Superfortress against Japan.

As the decisions of the Arcadia Conference were implemented early in 1942, the VIII Bomber Command was placed under the command of General Ira Eaker. Preceding the arrival of the heavy bombers that would put teeth into his command, Eaker went overseas to observe the activities and tactics of RAF Bomber Command. His conclusions were fairly simple—and predictably obvious: The strategic airpower doctrine was sound, but the RAF, like the USAAF, did not have a sufficient number of four-engine bombers to fully exploit the doctrine.

"After two months spent in understudying British Bomber Command it is still believed that the original all-out air plan for the destruction of the German war effort by air action alone was feasible and sound, and more economical than any other method available," Eaker observed on April 26. "General Arnold points out, however, that the required means is not now available, and time does not allow for the completion of this total air effort, hence it now seems wise to combine a limited air effort with ground forces to open up a Western European front."

In fact, there would be no such front opened for more than two years, and in the meantime, strategic airpower would have to fulfill its promise.

Having been named by Arnold to command the Eighth Air Force, Spaatz arrived in England on June 18 against the backdrop of the official announcement that "the object in view is the earliest maximum concentration of Allied war power upon the enemy."

As James Cate writes, all the American "air units initially based there [in the United Kingdom] were to be integrated into the Eighth Air Force. General Spaatz as commander was to have his own headquarters."

This headquarters, code-named Widewing, would be located at Bushy Park, a suburb southwest of London.

Within a week, General Dwight Eisenhower arrived in London to assume his role as the commander for the recently delineated European Theater of Operations, US Army (ETOUSA). As the highest ranking American officer in Europe, he assumed command of the growing buildup of American forces, of which the Eighth Air Force would be an important element.

In addition to the VIII Bomber Command, the Eighth Air Force expanded to also contain organizations such as the VIII Air Force Service Command, which provided the logistical and maintenance support to keep the aircraft flying, and the VIII Fighter Command, which was intended to supply the fighters that escorted the bombers through the curtain of interceptors the Luftwaffe threw across their paths. An VIII Ground Air Support Command (later Air Support Command), which was formed to operate medium bombers in a tactical role, was later inactivated and its assets transferred to the Ninth Air Force, which was located in England specifically for tactical operations.

Meanwhile, the Eighth Air Force began to break ground on dozens of new airfields, nominally RAF airfields, from which it would operate. Eventually, the Eighth Air Force would fly from more than a hundred air bases, which were concentrated mainly in East Anglia, northeast of London.

As Eisenhower told Spaatz in a July 21 memo, the broad objective of the Eighth Air Force, in coordination with the RAF Fighter Command and Bomber Command was to gain "air supremacy over Western Continental Europe in preparation for and in support of a combined land, sea, and air movement across the Channel into Continental Europe."

Strategic air operations would evolve as a key element of this very tall order.

By now, the total number of Flying Fortresses in the USAAF inventory had grown to 535, and the number of Liberators to 309. Though a majority were to be allocated to the Eighth Air Force, demands of the

Pacific Theater would also have to be met. Among these totals were an increasing number of B-17Es.

While the Flying Fortress had earned its nickname for a handful of machine guns protruding from its fuselage, the small number of B-17C and B-17D aircraft on hand when the war began were hardly equipped to defend against Luftwaffe interceptors. Having been designed with no provision for a turret in the extremely vulnerable tail, and built with no powered turrets, they were no more "fortresses" than the Luftwaffe's Fw 200. As British experience using the early model Flying Fortresses on strategic missions in 1941 had illustrated, the defensive armament was inadequate to an extreme.

The B-17E was an entirely different package. There was a powered turret on top behind the flight deck, a ball turret aft of the bomb bay, and the tail was redesigned for another gunner's position. Each was equipped with a pair of .50-caliber machine guns. Additional, side-firing guns were located in the nose and waist. The B-17E was the first Flying Fortress to be produced in large numbers—512 would be built, all at Boeing's Plant 2 in Seattle. The B-17E was also the first Flying Fortress to see combat on a regular basis.

The further improved B-17F was introduced in April 1942 with the same armament as the B-17E, but with more powerful engines and increased fuel capacity, which translated to increased range. The faceted Plexiglas nose of the earlier model had inhibited visibility, so the one-piece nose of the B-17E was a welcome improvement. Over the course of the fifteen months the B-17F was in production, 605 would be built by the Douglas factories and another 500 by Lockheed-Vega—all in Southern California. Meanwhile, Boeing's Plant 2 would roll out 2,300.

The first mass-produced Liberator, the B-24D, was introduced in January. Like the B-17E and B-17F, it had powered turrets top and bottom, as well as a tail turret. Over the coming months, Consolidated built 2,415 in San Diego and 303 at their new factory in Fort Worth, while Douglas began building them at their plant in Tulsa. Meanwhile, the USAAF brought the Ford Motor Company on line as a Liberator manufacturer, under the theory—subsequently proved correct—that the company could bring automobile assembly line efficiencies to aircraft production. Ford built a new state-of-the-art factory at Willow Run, Michigan, and beginning in September 1942, the company rolled out 490 B-24Es, which were similar to the B-24D. Through the end of the war, Ford would build a total of 6,792 Liberators, of several variants, at Willow Run.

As the aircraft flowed from American factories to the skies over *Festung Europa*, they flowed through the filter of operational doctrine.

Both the Eighth Air Force and RAF Bomber Command had committed themselves to the Combined Chiefs of Staff directive that they would coordinate their efforts in that upcoming strategic air campaign. However, their operational doctrines and principles turned out to be, in the understated words of Hap Arnold, "entirely different."

The RAF would choose to fly its missions at night, allowing the attackers to clothe themselves in darkness for protection. This meant that targets were harder to see, and therefore more difficult to hit without expending a great deal of ordnance. The USAAF doctrine called for precision raids in the daytime, when the targets were clearly visible.

James Cate explains that "to attack congested transportation centers surrounded by sprawling factory districts, [RAF Bomber Command] chose *area* rather than *pinpoint* bombing, and stray bombs—'overs' and 'shorts'—were absorbed by adjacent residential districts. Because targets thus defined were large, and more importantly because German defense was rugged, attacks were delivered at night from medium or high altitudes. Bomber Command was proving that its Stirlings and Manchesters (as later its Lancasters and Halifaxes) could deliver a heavy load of bombs in the general vicinity of a transportation-industrial complex without prohibitive losses. In view of lower costs of construction, the greater bomb load, and the smaller crew demanded, the night bomber seemed more economical than the day. The clinching argument was the factor of lower operational losses."

Despite the shortcomings of area bombardment—also called "carpet bombing"—the British genuinely believed that it would be effective in destroying specific industrial targets. A July 1939 contingency plan developed by the British Air Ministry cautioned that area attack strategy "is not intended to imply an indiscriminate scattering of projectiles over the whole or any part [of a specific industrial area]. . . . On the contrary, there will be definite objectives in the area itself normally consisting of industrial targets [which] . . . constitute the chief vital spots of the industrial body."

The report went on to discuss the dispersal of manufacturing facilities, noting that in "alternative manufacturing processes, the manufacture of an essential commodity . . . can readily be started in many different factories." Area bombing would theoretically catch dispersed factories.

The British also saw value in the nocturnal area raids as a weapon against the morale of the German people. When area bombardment was discussed, British officers often recalled that in World War I, Germany had ultimately agreed to an armistice after the collapse of the civilian will to continue the war. "Bomber" Harris insisted that the war could be won by attacking German cities and the morale of civilians.

During the London Blitz in 1940, as the Luftwaffe was bombing the British capital, Harris vowed to turn the same weapon back upon the Germans. Paraphrasing Hosea 8:7 from the Old Testament, he said to Portal, "The Nazis entered this war under the rather childish delusion that they were going to bomb everyone else, and nobody was going to bomb them. At Rotterdam, London, Warsaw, and half a hundred other places, they put their rather naive theory into operation. They sowed the wind, and now they are going to reap the whirlwind."

The British were as firmly convinced of the appropriateness of this approach as they were unconvinced of the practicality of the American doctrine. In July, when Harris wrote to General Eaker that "I, myself, and all the members of my command who have been in official or unofficial relations with you and yours, by now well appreciate that common doctrines prevail," he was speaking only of the final objectives.

RAF commander Peter Portal, like Harris, remained skeptical of the American approach and never missed an opportunity to politely suggest that Arnold and Spaatz reconsider. In August, however, the RAF and the Eighth Air Force agreed to disagree and to continue to operate by night and day respectively—and they issued a joint directive to that effect. It came down to an agreement as to ends, and dissent as to means.

The Americans went forward under the assumption that strategic targets could best be destroyed by precision bombing from high altitude, which was possible only in daylight. As Cate puts it, "Paralysis of selected key spots would be as effective as, and far cheaper than, total obliteration. . . . There was in the United States a traditional reverence for marksmanship which went back to the squirrel rifle of frontier days when scarcity of powder and shot put a premium on accuracy. Even if the facts sometimes belied the tradition, it was an element of American folklore which could be taken over by analogy to the new weapon. Emphasis on precision was also an antidote to widespread antipathy toward attacks on 'civilian' objectives."

When recalling the hardware that made American precision bombing practical, even possible, for the strategic bombers, one specific piece of equipment cannot be ignored. The "squirrel rifle" of American strategic airpower in World War II was the Norden bombsight.

The person who created the most sophisticated aiming device in history not to use electronics was a Dutch engineer named Carl Lukas Norden. Before World War I he had worked for the Sperry Gyroscope Company, where he had been recognized as a pioneer in the field of gyroscopically stabilized naval gun platforms. Having formed his own company, Norden began work on an aerial bombsight for the US Navy in 1921, and by 1935, his constantly improving design had evolved to the Norden Mk.IV, capable of hitting within 165 feet of a target from altitudes up to 15,000 feet. By World War II, the Norden M-Series was capable of hitting within a 50-foot radius from an altitude of more than 20,000 feet. This provided a level of precision up to eight times that of the contemporary British Mk.XIV bombsight.

The long-awaited first Eighth Air Force daylight bombing mission over *Festung Europa*, a strike against Luftwaffe fields in the Netherlands, finally took place on the Fourth of July in 1942. According to General John Huston, who edited Hap Arnold's wartime diaries for publication, the mission's timing originated in a June 10 memo to Churchill, in which Arnold optimistically claimed that the USAAF "will be fighting with you" by July 4. Given the American casualties that occurred during the mission, Secretary of War Stimson complained in his diary that Arnold's ebullient promise had been "half baked."

Half-baked or not, it was a beginning, but it was a very inauspicious beginning. The crews were Americans from the 15th Bombardment

Squadron, and the bombers had been made in Santa Monica, California, and this helped make it a milestone—albeit mainly a public relations milestone. However, the aircraft were not the heavy bombers that were the intended complement of the Eighth Air Force. They were Lend-Lease Bostons borrowed from the RAF, and there were just a half dozen of them.

Indeed, it was as of that date that there were only *two* Eighth Air Force Flying Fortresses on hand in England. This was, of course, *only* just the beginning.

FIVE

THE HOUSE OF MYSTERY ON BERKELEY SQUARE

In May 1942, Richard D'Oyly Hughes returned to England.

He came back from America, where he had gone after he departed from his service to His Majesty's army. Today, Hughes's is an unfamiliar name in the roll call of men who were involved in the American strategic air campaign, but among the obscure and forgotten, there are few names *more* important than that of Dick Hughes.

The names of the great airmen of that time—Hap Arnold, Tooey Spaatz, and Ira Eaker—were already household words. They were public figures, and they were quoted in the press. Men like Dick Hughes occupied such shadowy corners of the momentous work of the Eighth Air Force that even today few people know of them. The London headquarters of General Eisenhower, and the Bushy Park headquarters of the Eighth Air Force, would be featured in the datelines of newspaper articles. Nobody aside from a very select few ever knew what happened at 40 Berkeley Square.

The growing number of USAAF heavy bombers, spread out across a growing number of East Anglia airfields, took wing in execution of a doctrine of strategic airpower handed down by Billy Mitchell and nurtured by men like Arnold, Spaatz, and Eaker. They were flown into battle by tens of thousands of heroes from the "Greatest Generation" who comprised the largest strategic air force in history.

However, when the bomb bays opened and the five-hundred-pound bombs tumbled out, the *where*, *when*, and *why* were the work of Richard D'Oyly Hughes and the other mystery men of Berkeley Square.

Walt Whitman Rostow, who worked under Hughes at Berkeley Square, and who emerged from the shadows to serve as a national security advisor to John F. Kennedy and Lyndon Johnson in the 1960s, called Hughes "one of those selfless men of high intelligence, integrity, and dedication who play important roles in great enterprises but . . . leave little trace in the formal records."

In February 1941, Dick Hughes was managing St. Albans Farms near St. Louis, leading a comfortable life, reading the headlines and wishing that the great global events were not passing him by.

It was that month, as the Germans were remaking the map of Europe to conform to Hitler's vision of a Third Reich to last a thousand years, that two men had appeared on Dick Hughes's doorstep. He knew Malcolm Moss, though he was more used to seeing him in a business suit than in Air Corps khaki. Moss introduced Hughes to Haywood Hansell. The two men, destined to be star players on the Air War Plans Division dream team, explained that they needed Hughes's expertise. He had always enjoyed his informal discussions with Moss about world affairs and military matters, and he asked to hear more.

They got to the point and asked Hughes if he would consider joining the Air Corps as a staff officer. For "security reasons" they explained that they couldn't tell him exactly what his duties would entail, but if he would accompany them to Washington, they would provide more detail and fast-track him for an Air Corps officer's commission. The mysterious nature of the invitation was intriguing, and with World War II raging in Europe, Hughes could easily read between the lines.

"This was the kind of chance I had been waiting for," he recalls in an unpublished typescript memoir. "I at once agreed to their proposition."

Hughes arrived in Washington to find the Air Corps still crammed into a pigeonhole of an office. He described Hap Arnold's pre-USAAF staff as "a minute organization, completely dominated, suppressed, and hardly permitted to exist, by the Army. For instance, it was not supposed even to have an intelligence department of its own, and was under orders to request any intelligence information that it might require from the Army Intelligence Department G-2."

As he walked into the office, he discovered that the airmen were not taking this paternalism lying down.

"Certain far-sighted Air Corps officers were in active revolt against this stupid edict," he recalls. "Hansell and Moss had been instructed quietly to organize the nucleus of an independent Air Corps intelligence department, carefully concealed, to begin with, from the jealous eyes of the Army. I was one of the first three invited to work with this small group."

The newly minted Captain Hughes turned management of St. Albans Farms over to his bookkeeper, brought his wife Franny and their children east from Missouri, rented a house in Falls Church, Virginia, and went straight to work.

By now, the Air Corps was in the process of re-forming itself into the autonomous USAAF and shedding its afterthought status within the army bureaucracy. Tasked with creating an air intelligence branch out of whole cloth, Hughes and his colleagues were stepping into virgin territory. Intelligence gathering to date had been a hit-and-miss affair. The US Army, the US Navy, and the State Department maintained separate, poorly organized intelligence operations that almost never communicated with one another. The army depended on military attachés in foreign embassies, who were, as Hughes described them, "of very uneven quality and seldom appointed for their analytical brains."

Prior to World War II, espionage had yet to earn its James Bond caché and was even considered a tad bit sordid. The State Department had once maintained a small code-breaking section, but this had been dismantled a decade earlier by Henry L. Stimson, then the secretary of state in the Hoover Administration, who famously said, "Gentlemen don't read other gentlemen's mail."

In 1940, Stimson had been brought out of retirement to serve as secretary of war, the cabinet officer in charge of the US Army. Presumably, he now understood that those in Hitler's government and war machine were not gentlemen in the context of his earlier statement.

The situation with intelligence activities on a national level was appalling, and exasperating even to President Roosevelt. When he realized how completely inadequate the entire disjointed intelligence apparatus was, Roosevelt did not order it fixed, but called on New York lawyer and world traveler William J. "Wild Bill" Donovan to start from scratch and set up an entirely *separate* intelligence apparatus. No stranger to war, Donovan had served as an officer with the 69th Infantry Division in World War I and was awarded the Medal of Honor for gallantry under fire.

In July 1941, at the same time Dick Hughes was getting his feet wet in his new office in Washington, Roosevelt brought Donovan back into uniform as a general and named him as his coordinator of intelligence (COI), a position analogous to today's director of national intelligence. A year later, Donovan set up the Office of Strategic Services (OSS), the precursor to the Central Intelligence Agency. Many of the men with whom Hughes would work at Berkeley Square, including Rostow, came to him via the OSS.

In the meantime, the intelligence officers of the fledgling USAAF were in need of practical intelligence and getting almost nothing of value from US Army G-2—where the emphasis was almost exclusively focused on ground forces and ground operations.

However, across the pond an independent RAF intelligence apparatus was up and running, and developing useful and valuable information throughout the 1930s. Now, with the prospect of a wartime alliance with the Yanks on the horizon, they were in a mood to share. Indeed, Hansell traveled to Britain in the summer of 1941 and came back with a footlocker full of encyclopedic files on the entirety of German industry.

Hansell knew that, even within the USAAF, intelligence was not yet regarded as more than a second-tier priority. As described in earlier chapters, the foremost concerns of the Air Corps men prior to June 1941 had been divorcing themselves from the US Army, acquiring significant numbers of aircraft, and developing a strategic operational doctrine—pretty much in that order. Men such as Hansell and Moss understood that in order to implement the latter, they needed to develop a clear picture of where, when, and how to apply strategic airpower.

This is the place where Richard D'Oyly Hughes fit into the jigsaw puzzle of the USAAF. He came aboard just as the newly created Air Staff had tasked the new Air War Plans Division with writing the report that became AWPD-1, and his presence was why AWPD-1 focused on operations, rather than on procurement.

"Over the coming months we slowly built up the size of the target planning section," Hughes recalls. "[We] endeavored, from the best mass of British intelligence material which was at our disposal, not only to bring ourselves up to date with what was going on in the world . . . but also to hammer out in our brains a common sense, logical target selection process."

Hughes and Moss dug into the raw intelligence data provided by the RAF and went to work calculating the number and types of aircraft, the number of missions, and the tonnage of bombs that would be necessary for a sustained and effective campaign. Working backward, they came up with the number of bomber crews that would have to be trained, the number of training bases, the number of bomber bases in England, and so on. The plan even extrapolated the requirements for the Boeing B-29 Superfortress. Still nine months short of its first flight at the time of the Arcadia Conference, the Superfortress would go on to be the largest strategic bomber of World War II.

In their work, the men were guided by the doctrine laid down near two decades earlier by Billy Mitchell, who had written that "to gain a lasting victory in war, the hostile nation's power to make war must be destroyed—this means the manufactories, the means of communication, the food products, even the farms, the fuel and oil and the places where people live and carry on their daily lives. Not only must these things be rendered incapable of supplying armed forces but the people's desire to renew the combat at a later date must be discouraged."

Just as they were guided by Mitchell, they were also aware of the work of his contemporary, Italian General Giulio Douhet, who prescribed in his 1921 book, *The Command of the Air*, that "the selection of objectives, the grouping of zones and determining the order in which they are to be destroyed is the most difficult and delicate task in aerial warfare, constituting what may be defined as aerial strategy."

In April 1942, Colonel Henry Berliner from the Eighth Air Force planning staff walked into Hughes's office. He explained that General

Spaatz had sent him "to find out whether there was anybody who knew anything about the European Theater, and who had given any consideration whatsoever as to what the Eighth Air Force should do when it got over there. He had been shunted from office to office, until he finished up at my desk. From that moment began the operational planning for the Eighth and, subsequently, the Fifteenth Air Forces, which was to carry us through to VE-Day."

Berliner had come to the right place.

As Hughes recalls, the USAAF officers whom he had gotten to know were "superlatively capable" when it came to organizing, training, arming, and equipping their forces, and in the logistics required "to get them to where they were going." However, he notes that most of the USAAF staff officers had given woefully little consideration to the question of what to do when they arrived where they were going.

After a lengthy session with Berliner, Hughes was invited to bring his files and preliminary planning work to General Spaatz's office the following day. The Eighth Air Force commander gave Hughes his undivided attention for several hours, listening, nodding, and saying very little. A few days later, Hughes was summoned to give his briefing to the highest of top brass—Generals George Marshall and Hap Arnold. When he was done, they turned Hughes over to their staff officers.

"None of them ever made an operational war plan before in their lives," Hughes recalls. "None of them had had the opportunity to study the problems involved, and a more scared and nervous bunch of officers I have seldom seen. The unanimous appeal was 'Will you please make this plan for us?' Nothing of course could have pleased me more."

He promised them a plan in five days, and he delivered.

"For five days and nights, I worked like a dog and produced something which I considered rather a masterpiece. It was, of course, completely phony, as only actual battle in the skies over Europe would tell us what we were, or were not, capable of doing. However, with all my special knowledge and information, I had turned out a sufficiently slick and plausible job."

As Hughes recalls, he was asked "which industries in Germany and Japan, if destroyed by air power, would render these two countries incapable of continuing to fight a war?"

Working with Moss, Hughes came up with a list of three industrial cornerstones, without which "no country could wage modern war." These strategic objectives were the petroleum industry, the aluminum industry, and the aircraft industry. In retrospect, Hughes admitted that this was a very preliminary evaluation of the potential strategic campaign. However, in retrospect, it is worth noting that he had included the German aircraft industry, which was to be the cornerstone of the Big Week campaign two and a half years later.

The petroleum industry, meanwhile, was an obvious inclusion. In theory, its complete elimination could have the potential to bring an economy to a halt. President Roosevelt's Board of Economic Warfare had reached the same conclusion, and the HALPRO mission, the first American air attack into *Festung Europa*, would target the Third Reich's petroleum supply.

However, Hughes would later be critical of HALPRO, observing that Roosevelt's Board of Economic Warfare had convinced General Arnold of the importance of oil as a strategic target, but that neither Arnold nor the board "had analyzed and appreciated what size of air effort would be necessary to achieve, and maintain, any worthwhile damage. . . . The spring of 1942 was no time to launch an attack against the vast German oil industry."

Two weeks later, as Spaatz was getting ready to transfer the Eighth Air Force headquarters to England, he asked Arnold to transfer Hughes to his staff. His first order for Hughes was for him to precede to Eighth Air Force overseas.

Traveling in a B-24 by way of Presque Isle, Maine, and Prestwick, Scotland, through heavy turbulence over the Atlantic, Hughes returned to the land of his birth and reported for duty at the Eighth Air Force temporary headquarters on Davis Street in London on June 22. Here, he found himself in the turbulent world of wartime British bureaucracy.

He was, as he describes it, surrounded not only by the bureaucrats of the British Air Ministry, but by those of the Ministry of Economic Warfare, which had been the model for Roosevelt's Board of Economic Warfare. Even though Spaatz had pressed through the paperwork promoting Hughes to lieutenant colonel, he was still greatly outranked by the

RAF air commodores and air vice marshals with whom he dealt. Fortunately, his fourteen years as a British army officer—not to mention his accent—gave him a good working sense of the system.

"One of my most pressing, immediate needs was for competent, capable, people to examine, and evaluate for me, the mass of economic intelligence information being produced by the Ministry of Economic Warfare," Hughes writes. "Such individuals just did not exist in the Eighth Air Force, so I turned to the only other source of American personnel in England, the American Embassy in London. . . . They had a small civilian economic section and these people at once volunteered to do everything they could to help me."

The American ambassador, John Gilbert Winant, who had succeeded Joseph P. Kennedy in 1941, had been a US Army pilot in World War I and was sympathetic to Hughes's needs. Hughes was able to convince him that appropriately trained civilian economists should be sent to London to work under him.

When Winant cabled the State Department asking for such people to be sent over, it ignited a firestorm of turf warfare. The War Department was furious that the State Department was going behind their backs, interfering in the exercise of selecting potential targets for the Eighth Air Force. General Marshall contacted General Eisenhower, newly arrived in London himself, who contacted General Spaatz for an explanation. This, in turn, led to Hughes being called on the carpet in Eisenhower's office. The pragmatic Eisenhower listened as Spaatz and Hughes explained the situation, and he agreed that Hughes was on the right track. Naturally, Eisenhower had much larger issues on his plate at the time, not the least of these being Operation Torch, the impending Allied invasion of northwestern Africa, then occupied by Vichy French forces sympathetic to the Germans.

Given the blessing of both Eisenhower and Spaatz, Hughes worked with Henry Berliner, now also in London, to set up the organization that was to be called the Enemy Objectives Unit (EOU) of the Economic Warfare Division of the United States Embassy. Because it would be partially staffed by civilian analysts, the EOU was placed under the nominal administrative umbrella of the embassy, rather than under that of the Eighth Air Force headquarters.

When Spaatz moved his headquarters out to Bushy Park, Hughes and Berliner opted to remain in London, establishing the EOU headquarters in the nondescript building at 40 Berkeley Square in London's fashionable Mayfair area, not far from Hyde Park and a short walk from the embassy itself. Though the facility was *officially* associated with the embassy, it remained separate, and indeed secret, from the embassy. Winant was one of the few civilians, other than those who worked there, who knew that the unit existed, and he, along with a handful of Eighth Air Force people, were the only outsiders who had access to the place.

The EOU was as strange as it was mysterious. The arrangement defied precedent and thumbed its nose at correct and established procedure. Who could have guessed that behind the great bomber offensive there was to be a gaggle of mid-level USAAF and OSS officers and academics working together in an anonymous building maintained by the Department of State in an upper crust neighborhood in London?

"Except for the quality of the people on each side, such a military-civilian, bastard set-up could never have worked," Hughes admits. "Because of this quality, however, it worked better than any formally, logically constituted body."

Two of the "quality people" ranked most highly by Hughes among the EOU team were the whiz-kid economists Charles Poor "Charlie" Kindleberger and Walt Rostow. Both had already been recruited by Bill Donovan for the OSS when they were transferred to the EOU. Kindleberger had earned his PhD from Columbia University in 1937, and Rostow had earned his in 1940 from Yale—the school from which he had earlier graduated at age nineteen. Like Rostow, Kindleberger was a high achiever, having been named to the board of the Federal Reserve Bank of New York in his twenties and to the Board of Governors of the Federal Reserve System at age thirty.

Rostow joined Hughes in September, along with two other transferees from Donovan's OSS, economist Rosaline Honerkamp and Chandler Morse, also from the Federal Reserve. Having previously been assigned to the OSS Military Supplies Section, Kindleberger arrived on the last day of February 1943, replacing Morse.

In a paper entitled *Waging Economic Warfare from London*, presented at a 1991 OSS historical symposium, Rostow writes that "as a professional product of Wellington and Sandhurst, [Hughes] had long been trained in the principles of concentration of effort at the enemy's most vulnerable point and of prompt and maximum follow-through when a breakthrough was achieved. The members of EOU were, mainly, trained as economists, reflecting the assumption that the broad objective of the strategic bombing offensive was to weaken the German war economy. Our task was to develop and apply criteria for the selection of one target system versus another, one target within a system versus another, and, if the target was large enough and bombing precise enough, one aiming point versus another. . . . *EOU was the child of Air Corps Colonel Richard D'Oyly Hughes.*" [Author's italics.]

Rostow went on to describe the early days of the EOU, explaining that "Hughes took a little time to size up the small but overactive young crew he had evoked from Washington at long distance—a bit like a colonel in the field trying to figure out a batch of lieutenants sent from headquarters. He initially put EOU to work on a narrowly focused and painstaking task: aiming-point reports. These were analyses of particular German industrial plants or installations designed to establish the most vulnerable point of attack. The aiming-point reports were an invaluable education, requiring, among other things, visits to the nearest equivalent plants in Britain. They also required exploitation of virtually all the intelligence London could provide about the plant itself, the economic sector of which it was a part, and the role of that sector in the German war effort."

Inside the undisclosed location in Mayfair, such esoteric conclusions, calculated by scarcely more than a dozen people, would guide the actions of tens of thousands in the biggest air campaign in history.

Virtually no one knew they were there, or knew the source of the material that issued forth from 40 Berkeley Square over the course of thirty-two long months. Though the shroud of secrecy has long since been drawn back, the quiet anonymity of the mystery house on Berkeley Square still endures today.

SIX

A STEEP LEARNING CURVE

President Franklin Roosevelt often reviewed briefing papers as he ate his breakfast. They would arrive overnight and be brought to him by his closest advisor and troubleshooter, Harry Hopkins. On the morning of September 6, 1942, about a week before Walt Rostow and Chandler Morse joined Dick Hughes at 40 Berkeley Square, the document was entitled *Requirements for Air Ascendancy, 1942*, but it would be known simply as AWPD-42. The preparation of this report, essentially the sequel to AWPD-1 and AWPD-2 of 1941, had begun only eleven days earlier under the personal direction of the president. Through the spring and summer of 1942—with the exception of the unlikely but welcome American victory at Midway—the course of the war still favored Germany and Japan. Roosevelt asked Arnold what his airmen would have to do in order to have complete air ascendancy over the enemy.

The president reviewed the report while he sipped his coffee, then picked up the phone and called Secretary of War Henry Stimson to say that he approved it. Stimson was caught off guard. He hadn't *seen* the report. Nor had Chief of Staff General George Marshall, when Stimson phoned *him*. Nor had Marshall's fellow members of the Joint Chiefs of Staff—Admiral Ernest King (the chief of naval operations) and Admiral

William Leahy (the chief of staff to Roosevelt and, since July 1942, the Chairman of the Joint Chiefs of Staff)—although they all had their copies within hours.

Roosevelt had already approved it, so this was a moot point.

The fourth member of the Joint Chiefs, General Hap Arnold, had his copy before anyone. His was the name on the return address of the envelopes.

When the president had ordered him to assemble the report, Arnold had recalled Possum Hansell and Malcolm Moss from England and put them in a room with Hal George, Larry Kuter, and other veterans of the earlier air war plans.

AWPD-42 reiterated the agreements made earlier in the year, calling for the USAAF to undertake the "systematic destruction of selected vital elements of the German military and industrial machine through precision bombing in daylight." At the same time, in accordance with their own stated doctrine, the RAF would be making "mass air attacks of industrial areas at night, to break down morale [which was expected to have] a pronounced effect upon production."

A dramatic thousand-plane RAF raid on the night of May 30–31, 1942, was pointed to as an example. This single mission had destroyed an estimated 12 percent of the principal industrial and residential districts in the city of Cologne.

More importantly, AWPD-42 set out specific numbers, specific allocations of resources, to make it all happen. It called for the USAAF to have an operational bomber force of nearly three thousand four-engine bombers deployed in the European theater within sixteen months. The US Navy did not like the emphasis on allocation of resources to the USAAF at a time when they wanted an allocation of four-engine bombers to use as long-range patrol planes, but the president had spoken. In fact, he later insisted on American aircraft production being ramped up so that everyone would get the planes they wanted.

Like its predecessors, AWPD-42 was still just a road map, an educated guess, albeit a better educated guess than AWPD-1 and AWPD-2, even though the Eighth Air Force heavy bomber offensive had barely just begun.

Fewer than one hundred four-engine bombers were operational with the Eighth Air Force when AWPD-42 reached the president's bedside, but the report confidently promised that if the recommended force was in place by the first of January 1944, then the invasion of *Festung Europa* could be undertaken by the summer of that year. AWPD-42 may have been just a road map, but it was the road map that would lead the USAAF to Big Week, and ultimately to victory.

On August 17, 1942, six weeks after the Eighth Air Force made its Fourth of July raid with borrowed light bombers, the heavy bombers were finally ready to strike. A dozen Flying Fortresses of the 97th Bombardment Group took off from Polebrook in East Anglia on the first Eighth Air Force heavy bomber mission. Of the heavy bombardment groups allocated to the Eighth Air Force, only the 97th had become operational.

Led personally by General Eaker, commander of the VIII Bomber Command, they attacked a target selected by Hughes personally—the railroad marshaling yards at Rouen-Sotteville, near the city of Rouen in Normandy. Attacking a marshaling yard would theoretically impact the transportation network by damaging the interchange of freight trains on a number of intersecting lines.

It was a great boost to Eighth Air Force morale to know that the B-17s had finally bombed their first target, and that they had done so without losses *and* with greater accuracy than had been expected from fresh, inexperienced crews.

In Washington, the USAAF Air Staff seized upon this moment to insist that the previously theoretical doctrine of daylight precision bombing had been vindicated by this first mission. In a memo to General Marshall prepared for Arnold's signature, it was asserted that the result of the mission "again verifies the soundness of our policy of the precision bombing of strategic objectives rather than mass (blitz) bombing of large, city size areas [as the RAF was doing]. The Army Air Forces early recognized that the effective use of air power on a world wide basis equired the ability to hit small targets from high altitudes."

However, many USAAF officers, including Ira Eaker, later commented that the comparison to the British effort was unfair and "most unfortunate," given that those in the field wished to maintain a harmonious working relationship with the RAF.

Two days after Rouen, twenty-two B-17s attacked airfields near Abbeville, home of Jagdgeschwader 26, one of the Luftwaffe's most highly regarded fighter wings. The objective of this bombing was to divert German fighters at the same time the Allies made their commando raid on the French coastal city of Dieppe. According to Air Marshal Sir Trafford Leigh-Mallory, the air commander for the Dieppe operation, "The raid on Abbeville undoubtedly struck a heavy blow at the German fighter organization at a very critical moment during the operations [and thus] had a very material effect on the course of the operations."

Referring, no doubt, to Leigh-Mallory's comments, Ira Eaker effused contentedly in an August 27 memo to Hap Arnold that the British "acknowledge willingly and cheerfully the great accuracy of our bombing, the surprising hardihood of our bombardment aircraft and the skill and tenacity of our crews."

Five additional raids were flown by the Eighth Air Force through the end of August, striking targets ranging from shipyards to airfields across an arc from northern France to Rotterdam in the Netherlands.

As Dick Hughes observed, "It really did not matter, at this early stage, what we bombed." The idea was that the crews needed to gain experience before flying into highly defended German airspace.

In an August 1 memo, General Ira Eaker wrote that his VIII Bomber Command had as its role the "destruction of carefully chosen strategic targets, with an initial subsidiary purpose [of determining its] capacity to destroy pinpoint targets by daylight accuracy bombing and our ability to beat off fighter opposition and to evade antiaircraft opposition."

In other words, the secondary mission was to prove that the primary mission was *possible*!

The airpower historian Arthur B. Ferguson of Duke University writes in "Origins of the Combined Bomber Offensive" in Volume II of *Army Air Forces in World War II*, "These early missions were less important for what they contributed directly to the Allied war effort than for what they contributed indirectly by testing and proving the doctrine of strategic daylight bombing. In either instance it was as difficult and dangerous to strive for quick results as it was natural for observers, especially those at some distance from the scene of operations, to look impatiently for them."

These missions, beginning with the one on the fourth of July, marked a timid beginning for a strategic offensive, but even this was about to be interrupted by Operation Torch.

The only major American ground offensive operation against the Germans that was on the drawing boards for the foreseeable future, Torch was the centerpiece of Allied offensive actions against Germany in the second half of 1942. General Erwin Rommel's German Afrika Korps had proven itself to be as successful as the blitzkrieging German armies in Europe in 1940. He controlled Tunisia and Libya, and—in victory after victory—he had pushed the British deep into Egypt. Meanwhile, in his rear, Morocco and Algeria were safe and secure, controlled by the Vichy French, Germany's nominal allies. Planned for early November, Torch was designed to land Allied troops in Morocco and Algeria, and to relieve Rommel of his secure rear.

General Eisenhower, who was in overall command of Torch, and the highest ranking American officer in Europe, was keen to concentrate maximum American firepower in support of this operation. This included the bombers of the Eighth Air Force. He let it be known that he was seriously considering the idea of suspending the Eighth Air Force campaign when it had barely started, in order to concentrate all of the Eighth's bombers under Twelfth Air Force command in the Mediterranean Theater.

While understanding and recognizing the strategic goals of Operation Torch, Spaatz naturally argued in favor of continuing his strategic campaign. Every distraction of Eighth Air Force assets meant a postponement of the validation of the strategic concept that Spaatz and his air commanders sought most feverishly. As Arthur Ferguson recalls, "The delay was the more vexing because from an early stage in war planning the bomber campaign against Germany had been conceived as the first offensive to be conducted by United States forces."

The disagreement between Spaatz and Eisenhower over the use of airpower was more practical than theoretical. Eisenhower may have come from the ground forces, but he understood the potential of airpower. This is why he wanted as much of it as possible to be part of Torch. Spaatz, the airman, wanted no interruption to his aspiration to continue demonstrating airpower's strategic potential. The argument came about because in the autumn of 1942, there were not yet enough USAAF aircraft in Europe to please both men.

It was only because of the fact that Eisenhower was quite fond of Spaatz personally that the strategic air campaign was not suspended indefinitely in September 1942. "From the time of his arrival at London in July [1942] he was never long absent from my side until the last victorious shot had been fired in Europe," Eisenhower recalls in his wartime memoir, *Crusade in Europe.* "On every succeeding day of almost three years of active war I had new reasons for thanking the gods of war and the War Department for giving me 'Tooey' Spaatz. He shunned the limelight and was so modest and retiring that the public probably never became fully cognizant of his value."

Indeed, Spaatz was able to argue the case of the strategic operations convincingly, and on September 5, Eisenhower agreed—but only to allow Spaatz to continue Eighth Air Force heavy bomber operations. Eisenhower diverted personnel, as well as the Eighth Air Force fighters, smaller tactical bombers, and two heavy bomber groups, to the Torch operations. Even the VIII Air Force Service Command was being asked to support aircraft assigned to Operation Torch.

Spaatz's narrow victory was almost pyrrhic. He had won the right to continue his campaign, but he had too few bombers to make it more than a token effort. The loss of half the fighters previously assigned to the VIII Fighter Command also put the VIII Bomber Command in a position of having to become more dependent on RAF Fighter Command for fighter escorts.

This came at the same time that RAF Bomber Command was steadily increasing its ability to conduct strategic missions against Germany, something that the Eighth Air Force had yet to do. While RAF Bomber Command could now muster strike forces of a hundred or more bombers for their nighttime missions against Germany, the Eighth Air Force lagged far behind. As Arthur Ferguson reminds us, "The basic concept of a combined bomber offensive presumed complementary operations of RAF night bombers and AAF day bombers."

However, the two forces were still far from complementary. Most of the Eighth Air Force August missions involved a dozen or fewer Flying Fortresses. As late as mid-September, Spaatz noted in a memo to General George Stratemeyer, Hap Arnold's chief of staff, that the British were in a position to speak with authority on bombing operations and that at the time, the RAF was the only Allied entity persistently engaged in "pounding hell out of Germany."

During September, as the 91st and 301st Bombardment Groups became operational and began flying their first missions, Spaatz and Eaker were able to muster at least 30 aircraft for several missions, but there just weren't as many as they needed. Though 328 Flying Fortresses and 105 Liberators had been deployed overseas by the end of August, preparations for Operation Torch, as well as requirements in the Pacific, had syphoned off much of the flow of equipment that Spaatz might have like to see go to the Eighth Air Force.

On October 9, the Eighth Air Force was at last able to launch more than 100 bombers on a single day. Including two dozen Liberators from the newly operational 93rd Bombardment Group, the Eighth sent out 108 heavy bombers, of which 69 hit their primary target—the industrial complex around the French city of Lille.

Calling the Lille mission a "minor climax," Arthur Ferguson writes enthusiastically that it was "the first mission to be conducted on a really adequate scale and it marked, as it were, the formal entry of the American bombers into the big league of strategic bombardment. Then, for the first time, the German high command saw fit to mention publicly the activities of the Flying Fortresses, although they had already made thirteen appearances over enemy territory. Lille's heavy industries contributed vitally to German armament and transport."

However, Ferguson gives low marks to the bombing precision achieved, noting that it "did not demonstrate the degree of accuracy noticeable in some of the earlier and lesser efforts," although he goes on to say that "despite a scattered bomb pattern and numerous duds, several bombs fell in the target area—enough, in any event, to cause severe damage." He reports Spaatz saying that the "bombing had been accurate in relation to European [RAF] standards rather than according to any absolute standard."

Nevertheless, referring to the VIII Bomber Command study entitled *The First 1,100 Bombers Dispatched*, Ferguson writes that "by early October, the first fourteen missions had been on the whole very encouraging. Targets had been attacked with reasonable frequency, especially during the first three weeks, and hit with a fair degree of accuracy. During the first nine missions, the Germans had evidently refused to take the day bombing seriously. The American forces had been small and the fighter escort heavy, and so the Germans had sent up few fighters, preferring to take the consequences of light bombing raids rather than to risk the loss of valuable aircraft. And when the German fighters did take to the air, they exhibited a marked disinclination to close with the bomber formation."

Citing memos from Eaker to Spaatz, and from Eaker to Hap Arnold, Ferguson goes on to say that "the bombing had been more accurate than most observers had expected. Indeed, it was a tribute of sorts to the accuracy of the Americans that after the ninth mission enemy fighter opposition suddenly increased. And it was a source of satisfaction to the AAF commanders that the B-17s and the B-24s appeared more than able to hold their own against fighter attacks."

RAF Bomber Command planners, who had always been skeptical of the USAAF precision daylight bombing doctrine, were now willing to give the Yanks some measure of credit. As Arthur Ferguson puts it, "British observers in September and October were at least ready to admit that the AAF day bombers and the policy of day bombardment showed surprising promise."

Peter Masefield, the popular aviation journalist and air correspondent for the *Sunday Times*, had written adamantly in August that "there is no doubt that day bombing at long range is not possible as a regular operation unless fighter opposition is previously overwhelmed or until we have something too fast for the fighters to intercept."

On October 18, after the Lille mission, he qualified his stance somewhat, asking in the *Sunday Times*, "Can we carry day air war into Germany?"—which had hitherto been answered in the unqualified negative but was now subject to a new assessment. . . . "The Americans have taught us much; we still have much to learn—and much we can teach."

Originally, Spaatz and Eisenhower had agreed that the loaning of Eighth Air Force assets to Operation Torch would leave the VIII Bomber Command mission substantially intact, but by October, this command had been asked to part with two heavy bomber groups, 1,098 officers, including pilots and navigators, and 7,101 enlisted men.

According to minutes of an Eighth Air Force commanders meeting on November 1, Spaatz had been heard to quip wryly, "What is left of the Eighth Air Force after the impact of Torch?"

In response to this, one might ask, "What might have happened to Torch without the impact of the Eighth Air Force?"

Whatever the answers to these hypotheticals, the fact is that Torch succeeded. Indeed, November 1942 provided a welcome turn of events for the Allies in North Africa. On November 4, the British finally broke Rommel's momentum with a victory at El Alamein, just sixty miles from Alexandria, Egypt, and on November 8, Operation Torch put a one-hundred-thousand-man, mainly American, ground force ashore in Algeria and Morocco against quickly fading resistance. The landings were a big boost to American morale both at home and among the troops overseas.

For the Eighth Air Force, however, November brought only bad weather and a reorienting of its priorities. In late October, Eisenhower ordered another change of direction. The Eighth had not had to relinquish all of its heavy bombers to support Operation Torch directly, but they were now directed to use their range and payload capacity to support Operation Torch *indirectly*.

Eisenhower understood strategic airpower well enough to know that a key principle is cutting off a threat at its source, rather than in the field where it becomes a threat. He had a threat that was in need of being clipped at its source.

One of the most aggravating vexations for Allied planners throughout the war thus far had been the German U-boat campaign. While Britain's Royal Navy had successfully won its campaign against the surface fleet of the German Kreigsmarine, multiple "wolf packs" of submarines lurked beneath the surface of the Atlantic. Since the beginning of the war, they had proven to be the one German naval weapon that most worried the British. They had long been one, preying upon the convoys supplying the United Kingdom from its overseas dominions, and now they were a serious threat to the convoys bringing American men and materiel to the island nation.

As Timothy Runyan and Jan Copes write in their book *The Battle of the Atlantic*, the U-boats sunk 607,247 tons of Allied shipping in May 1942, the month that Dick Hughes came back to England. This was part of the reason that he came by air. The following month, the total tonnage lost was 700,235, and in October, the German submarine fleet sent 619,417 tons to the bottom.

Recognizing that Operation Torch depended on safe passage of troop ships from the United States, Eisenhower ordered Spaatz to use the Eighth Air Force against the U-boat pens, which the Kreigsmarine had constructed along the Atlantic coast of France, at places such as Saint-Nazaire and Lorient, as well as at Bordeaux, Brest, and La Pallice. Because nighttime area bombardment would be ineffective against reinforced concrete submarine pens that required precision strikes, the job could not be done by RAF Bomber Command.

Eisenhower had told Spaatz pointedly that he deemed the reversal of the U-boat threat "to be one of the basic requirements to the winning of the war."

When the Eighth Air Force came to Berkeley Square for a plan, Dick Hughes was pessimistic, telling the generals that "with the size of force and the types of bombs available to us, we could do very little damage to these massive structures, and that I doubted that by such attacks the Eighth Air Force could appreciably affect the outcome of the submarine war. I also pointed out that the anti-aircraft defenses around each of these bases were extremely heavy, and we would probably pay a heavy price for conducting what were virtually training operations over such targets."

Hughes was right. Ultimately the attacks were ineffective against reinforced concrete, and the losses suffered by Eighth Air Force crews were high.

"The crews themselves quickly got onto the fact that the small amount of damage they were doing . . . was in no way affecting the outcome of the war," Hughes writes. "We were proving our point to the British that, with fighter escort, we could operate in daylight over enemy territory with acceptable casualties, but the unfortunate air crews were not, personally, as interested in proving this point, with their own lives, as were the generals, and crew morale began to become a serious problem."

Hughes appealed to both General Spaatz and General Eaker in an attempt to "get these useless attacks abandoned." However, so serious was the U-boat threat that the attacks continued past the successful completion of Operation Torch. It was not until June 1943, by which time the threat had been curbed by more effective naval escorts, that the campaign against the submarine pens was finally discontinued as a priority.

After the premature euphoria of September and early October, the winter brought a maze of difficulties for the Eighth Air Force. The weather, which caused some missions to be canceled, also caused about 40 percent of the missions launched over the ensuing three months to be aborted. This was mainly manifested in targets obscured by cloud cover, which the weather reporting teams had failed to predict. The weather also resulted in mechanical failures. Aircraft taking off in mud and rain often found themselves with frozen guns or with flight deck windows encrusted in frost. According to the Eighth Air Force Operational Research Section (ORS) day raid reports, malfunctioning bomb bay doors were such a problem that some crews took to removing them.

The weather, combined with the inexperience of the crews, also made for navigational errors and impacted bombing accuracy. Sometimes, this involved bombs missing their targets with disastrous results if the bombs hit French civilian residential areas instead of submarine pens. Other times, the errors verged on the almost comical. On November 18, for example, one bomber formation bombed the submarine pens at Saint-Nazaire under the erroneous notion that they were attacking the pens at La Pallice, a hundred miles away.

The ORS reports also indicate that the mounting tempo of battle damage was putting heavy demands on a still-meager maintenance depot infrastructure, which kept a growing percentage of the bombers off the mission-ready list. In September, 13 percent of the aircraft flying missions came back with damage, which could be repaired. In October, this increased to 38 percent, and by December it was above 42 percent. However, the fact that the damage *could* be repaired was only half the story. Hampered by shortages of trained personnel and parts, the depots fell behind to the point where half the fleet was in the shop and any moment.

The issue of damage done to the targets by the bombing eclipsed all other matters, consuming a great deal of the time of the Operational Research Section. The precision that had been promised by the theorists had yet to materialize in 1942. Indeed, when the ORS "crater-counters" studied post-strike photoreconnaissance imagery, they identified the impact points of only about half of the bombs that were known to have been dropped. The other half had either been duds, or bombs that had missed their targets by so wide a margin as to not even appear in the aerial photographs. This raised the obvious concerns about errant bombs striking French civilians.

Of course, in 1942, the art of post-strike analysis was still in its infancy. It was not until after the start of 1943 that a routine for systematic analysis was developed. As with everything pertaining to the as-yet unproven doctrine of strategic airpower, there was a steep learning curve.

Enemy interceptor attacks were second only to bombing accuracy among the operational concerns for the Eighth Air Force planners. Defensive armament aboard the bomber served as a partial deterrent, causing the attackers to adjust their tactics, such as to make quick passes, rather than sustained attacks. A heavy bomber without tail guns, for example, was a doomed airplane. A smaller airplane could have tried to outmaneuver a fighter, but a heavy bomber would be susceptible to having a fighter come up behind and almost leisurely chew it apart.

At the same time, the gunners also claimed their share of downed fighters. Out of the October 9 strike package, gunners aboard the 69 bombers attacking Lille destroyed 21, probably shot down another 21, and damaged 15 German interceptors. The gunners had initially claimed that they shot down 102 German fighters, which would have been more than 15 percent of the estimated Luftwaffe fighter strength in Western Europe. On further scrutiny, it was determined that there were a huge number of multiple claims in which gunners from multiple bombers were shooting at the same fighter.

What this illustrates, other than the obvious need for more careful debriefing of gunners, was the importance of having the gunners from multiple aircraft laying down interlocking fields of fire, thus creating a mutually beneficial defensive zone.

A study conducted by the Eighth Air Force Operations Analysis Section concluded that large numbers of bombers flying in formation would give one another decent protection against fighters. While such a tight formation would then be more susceptible to antiaircraft fire, this would be only in the vicinity of the target, and therefore it would be for shorter duration than the fighter attacks, which took place over a longer duration.

On November 23, the heavy bombers of the Eighth Air Force first met the man who would become their deadly nemesis.

Oberleutnant Egon Mayer was a twenty-five-year-old pilot who was born on the shores of Lake Constance in the penultimate year of World War I. He had joined the Luftwaffe in 1937 and first flew in combat with Jagdgeschwader 2 during the Battle of France in June 1940. Flying against the RAF over southern England, he became an air ace four times over by August 1941, scoring twenty aerial victories, most of them against pilots flying the RAF's best fighter aircraft, the Spitfire. For this, he was awarded the Iron Cross. Within the next year, the young Luftwaffe ace increased his score to fifty, then added two more—both Spitfires—on August 19, 1942, his twenty-fifth birthday.

In November, he was named *Gruppenkommandeur* of III Gruppe of Jagdgeschwader 2. In the meantime, Mayer had studied Eighth Air Force defensive tactics and had observed a critical point of weakness in the Flying Fortresses and Liberators.

On November 23, Egon Mayer first approached the heavy bombers of the Eighth Air Force with the fruits of his observations, and the bombers met Egon Mayer *head-on*. While gun barrels protruded from the top, the bottom, the rear, and the sides of the bombers, their front was their Achilles' heel. Some of the B-17Es and B-17Fs had a single .30-caliber handheld gun, firing through one of four eyelets just off-center of the nose, while B-24Ds had a single .50-caliber center nose gun that was mounted to fire below horizontal only. Both had .50-caliber side-firing nose guns, but all the bombers had a blind spot in front.

As the bombers approached Saint-Nazaire that day, Mayer led III Gruppe up to meet them. His newly developed tactic of attacking the lead aircraft head-on worked to deadly effect. He personally shot down two of the Flying Fortresses and one of the Liberators that the VIII Bomber Command lost that day.

Because of the rapid rate of closure in a head-on attack, it demanded great skill on the part of the fighter pilot, but in the right hands—such as those of Egon Mayer—such a tactic could be deadly. Soon, Luftwaffe pilots across Europe were following Mayer's lead, while in the United States, Boeing and Consolidated engineers responded with the inclusion of powered nose turrets with twin .50-caliber machine guns. These would become standard in the B-17G, as well as the B-24G, B-24H, and B-24J, but these aircraft would not reach the Eighth Air Force in significant numbers until the latter part of 1943.

The legacy of Egon Mayer's brainstorm would be with the Eighth Air Force through to the end of World War II. However, Egon Mayer would not. He was shot down and killed by Lieutenant Walter Gresham, flying a USAAF P-47 fighter, while escorting Eighth Air Force bombers, on March 2, 1944. By this time, however, Mayer had claimed 102 Allied aircraft, 26 of them Eighth Air Force four-engine bombers.

November 1942 brought big organizational changes at the upper levels of command of American forces in Europe. In the wake of the dramatic shift in the strategic situation in North Africa, Eisenhower moved south from England to become commander of the North African Theater of Operations, US Army (NATOUSA), and later commander of the joint Anglo-American Allied Forces Headquarters (AFHQ), the operational command staff for the Mediterranean Theater of Operations (MTO).

When Eisenhower moved, he took Spaatz with him. The man who, as Eighth Air Force chief, had resisted transfer of heavy bombers to the Twelfth Air Force became commander of the Twelfth Air Force in December 1942. Four months later, as Eisenhower became the supreme Allied commander in the Mediterranean, Spaatz was named as commander of the joint Allied Northwest African Air Forces (NAAF), which included the Twelfth Air Force, and which was later a component of the Mediterranean Air Command, headed by RAF Air Marshal Arthur Tedder.

"I had left General Spaatz in England and now I called him forward to take on this particular task," Eisenhower writes in *Crusade in Europe*. "We merely improvised controlling machinery and gave General Spaatz the title of 'Acting Deputy Commander in Chief for Air.' Initially, the commander of the American [Twelfth] Air Force in North Africa was Major General James Doolittle, who had sprung into fame as the leader of the raid on Tokyo. He was a dynamic personality and a bundle of energy. It took him some time to reconcile himself to shouldering his responsibilities as the senior United States air commander to the exclusion of opportunity for going out to fly a fighter plane against the enemy. But he had the priceless quality of learning from experience. He became one of our really fine commanders."

When the USAAF Fifteenth Air Force was created in 1943 to become the strategic equivalent of the Eighth Air Force in the MTO, Doolittle became its first commander.

The plan had been for Eisenhower and Spaatz to return to England after Torch in anticipation of a cross-channel invasion of *Festung Europa* from the United Kingdom. However, as further actions in the Mediterranean that were planned for 1943—specifically the invasions of Sicily and Italy—required their attention, the return would be delayed.

Meanwhile back in England, the post-Torch command shuffle brought Ira Eaker up from VIII Bomber Command to head the entire Eighth Air Force, while Major General Frederick Lewis Anderson Jr., previously Deputy Director of Bombardment at USAAF headquarters, who had been Hap Arnold's representative "on bombardment matters" in the ETO, was named to head the VIII Bomber Command. As Henry Berliner, Dick Hughes's immediate superior, became incapacitated with spinal meningitis, Hughes was promoted to full colonel and took charge of the Eighth Air Force G-5 (operational planning section) and, as such, became an assistant to Eaker.

It was not a marriage made in heaven.

"General Eaker's personality and characteristics were very different from those of General Spaatz," Hughes recalls. "General Spaatz's interest had always been intimately concerned with the conduct of operations, and he very largely delegated day to day administrative problems to others. General Eaker kept even the most minute administrative details in his own hands, and seemed to have very little time, or inclination, for discussing operational plans. For the ensuing year and a half the decision as to which targets our strategic bombers should attack fell squarely upon my shoulders. With no sympathetic intellectual support, or understanding, from my commanding general it was a difficult and heavy burden."

On the other hand, Hughes has high praise for the new chief of VIII Bomber Command.

"Fred Anderson completely understood the problems with which I was confronted, and whenever I was near the breaking point I would drive down to Bomber Command, unburden all my cares and worries on this truly great man, and return again to Eighth Air Force Headquarters, and strong enough to continue ordering out [young American airmen] to their deaths."

SEVEN

CREATING SUBSTANCE FROM PROMISE

Throughout 1942, the Anglo-American Combined Chiefs of Staff had continued to adhere to the strategic airpower principal that had been agreed on at the Arcadia Conference. With regard to the strategic air campaign against Germany, the RAF would continue to fly its nighttime area bombing missions, while the USAAF would endeavor to undertake daylight raids against targets requiring precision attacks.

However, as the year came to a close, the Eighth Air Force heavy bombers had achieved little, despite having been in action since August. Several of the raids on industrial targets had showed promising results, but the attacks on the submarine pens, which had been the primary mission of the American bombers since October, had been a disappointment.

Both Air Chief Marshal Charles "Peter" Portal and Air Marshal Arthur "Bomber" Harris of RAF Bomber Command accepted the idea of the Americans pursuing their daylight precision bombing doctrine, but they did so with serious skepticism. Some British officers who had admitted in October that the American approach had shown "surprising promise" noted in December that the promise was going unfulfilled, and the RAF began to insist that it was time to terminate the American "experiment."

Air Vice Marshal John Slessor wrote in a December 1942 memo to

Archibald Sinclair, the British secretary of state for air, that Americans, like other people, "prefer to learn from their own experience. If their policy of day bombing proves to their own satisfaction to be unsuccessful or prohibitively expensive, they will abandon it and turn to night action. They will only learn from their own experience. In spite of some admitted defects—including lack of experience—their leadership is of a high order, and the quality of their aircrew personnel is magnificent. If, in the event, they have to abandon day bombing policy, that will prove that it is indeed impossible."

The showdown on this issue would come in the new year when Prime Minister Winston Churchill met President Franklin Roosevelt face-to-face on January 14, for the first time since the Arcadia Conference in Washington a year earlier. The place of their meeting, Casablanca in Morocco, was high on symbolism because the city had been in Allied hands for barely two months—and because the fact that it was in Allied hands was directly attributable to the success of Operation Torch, the first major operation planned jointly by the Anglo-American Combined Chiefs of Staff.

They met against the backdrop of numerous strategic concerns. Despite the great potential represented by the United States, the British were impatient with their allies. Not only had the Americans not yet shown substantial results against the Germans in the air, they had yet to confront them in a major land battle.

Churchill and Roosevelt also met against the backdrop of numerous strategic disagreements. The strategic air campaign was only one bone of contention. With Torch having been successful, and the British now having the momentum against Rommel's Afrika Korps, Roosevelt and US Army Chief General George Marshall favored a return to building up forces for the cross-channel invasion of northern France as soon as possible.

Churchill, on the other hand, favored action against what he called the "soft underbelly of Europe." In other words, he wanted to see the next major Allied move in the Mediterranean be an invasion of southern, rather than northern Europe. At the ten-day Casablanca Conference, code-named "Symbol," Churchill was able to convince Roosevelt that the Allies should invade Sicily and Italy in 1943, which effectively delayed the cross-channel invasion until 1944.

The strategic air campaign also emerged as a pivotal agenda item. Anticipating that Churchill would make a move to push the Eighth Air Force into the night, Hap Arnold had ordered Ira Eaker to travel to Casablanca and head off such a decision.

On January 18, Eaker sat down with Churchill himself for a historic half-hour meeting.

"Why," Churchill asked, "has the USAAF flown so few missions, and had so many abortive missions?"

To this, Eaker explained that the crews were inexperienced, coming in at the base of the learning curve. He reminded Churchill of the diversion of Eighth Air Force assets—including service units—to Operation Torch and to the campaign against the U-boats. Finally, he explained that the weather had not favored precision attacks.

Finally, Churchill asked the big question: "Why have the American bombers not yet bombed Germany itself?"

Eaker had known that this was coming and so had his boss. Arnold had told him that the only way to placate the British was to begin operations against Germany as soon as possible.

Cutting to the chase, Eaker told Churchill that the Eighth Air Force would be prepared to routinely send one hundred heavy bombers escorted by one hundred fighters into Germany by the end of the month. Noting that Torch had been successful, he took this opportunity to add that he hoped to have the diverted Eighth Air Force assets returned to Britain.

"Eaker began his defense of the American tactics by maintaining that only one convincing argument had ever been advanced for night bombing over day bombing and that was that it was safer," Arthur Ferguson writes. "But in point of fact the Eighth Air Force rate of loss in day raids had been lower than that of the RAF on its night operations, a fact that was explained in part by the great improvement in German night fighter tactics and in part by the heavy firepower of the American bombers."

Ferguson goes on to say that Eaker estimated that the accuracy of the daylight strikes was about five times greater than "that of the best night bombing, thanks to the excellent [Norden] bombsight they carried. Hence day bombing tended to be more economical than night bombing, for a force only one-fifth as large would be required to destroy a given installation. Eaker of course admitted that the objective of night bombardment was not primarily the destruction of individual targets but the devastation of vital areas, and as such it could not properly be compared to precision bombing on the ground of accuracy."

Acknowledging the persuasiveness of Eaker's arguments, Churchill withdrew his objection to a continuation of the existing doctrine of "around the clock" strategic bombing, assuming that Eaker could make good on his promise to begin operations against Germany within a month.

Three days later, on January 21, the Combined Chiefs of Staff approved what came to be known as the Casablanca Directive. It assumed a continuation of the day-and-night doctrine and delineated a series of priorities for the strategic air campaign, which would later be formally referred to as the Combined Bomber Offensive. Essentially, the Casablanca Directive recognized what had previously existed in practice, while calling for an organizational structure that would coordinate the efforts of the Eighth Air Force and RAF Bomber Command.

In the words of the directive, the primary objective of the Combined Bomber Offensive was "the progressive destruction and dislocation of the German military, industrial, and economic system, and the undermining of the morale of the German people to a point where their capacity for armed resistance is fatally weakened."

The latter phrase echoed the theory repeated by Arthur Harris at every opportunity, that the will of the German people was as valid a target as any factory complex.

In the meantime, Dick Hughes and his EOU team had already been at work behind the scenes, scientifically analyzing the German economy and quietly providing Eaker with the specific *precision* targets.

"Near the end of 1942, after producing some 285 aiming-point reports, Hughes unleashed EOU on the principles and practice of target selection," Walt Rostow recalls. "In the doctrine we evolved, we sought target systems where the destruction of the minimum number of targets would have the greatest, most prompt, and most long-lasting direct military effect on the battlefield. Each of the modifiers carried weight. One had to ask, in assessing the results of an attack, how large its effect would be within its own sector of the economy or military system; how quickly would the effect be felt in front line strength; how long the effect would last; and what its direct military, as opposed to economic, consequences would be.

"The application of these criteria was serious, rigorous intellectual business. In part, it required taking fully into account the extent to which the military effect of an attack could be cushioned by the Germans by diverting civilian output or services to military purposes or buying time for repair by drawing down stocks of finished products in the pipeline. In all this, our knowledge as economists of the structure of production, buttressed by what we had learned from the aiming-point reports, converged with the classic military principles Hughes and his best senior colleagues brought to the task. The EOU view was, then, a doctrine of warfare, not of economics or politics."

Though the formal Combined Bomber Offensive plan would not be worked out until June, orders issued to operational units on February 4 contained a hierarchy of general targets, "subject to the exigencies of weather and tactical feasibility."

In order of priority, these were to be German submarine construction yards, the German aircraft industry, the German transportation system, and German petroleum facilities, with "other targets in enemy war industry," added to round out the list.

In addition to the list of general targets, the Combined Bomber Offensive would continue to be tasked with attacking U-boat bases on the west coast of France, as well as the city of Berlin. The latter was included "for the attainment of the especially valuable results unfavorable to the morale of the enemy or favorable to that of the Russians."

Specific to the Eighth Air Force and the second item in the list of priorities, the Casablanca Directive stated that the American bombers should "take every opportunity to attack Germany by day, to destroy objectives that are unsuitable for night attack, to sustain continuous pressure on German morale, to impose heavy losses on the German day fighter force and to contain German fighter strength away from the Russian and Mediterranean theaters of war."

As Allied air planners debated the merits of various hierarchies of target priorities within the German economy, the latter was not static. If Egon Mayer personified the nemesis of Allied aircrews, the man who played that role for the planners at Berkeley Square and Bushy Park was Albert Speer, a thirty-seven-year-old architect and gifted technocrat. A member of Adolf Hitler's inner circle, he had been named by the Führer as the Third Reich's minister of armaments in February 1942, upon the death in a plane crash of his predecessor, Fritz Todt. The post gave Speer immense powers in organizing the German economy, especially industrial production. As such, it was his job to build and expand upon the same entity that Dick Hughes and others were committed to tearing down.

"We formed 'directive committees' for the various types of weapons and 'directive pools' for the allocation of supplies," Speer explains in his memoirs. "Thirteen such committees were finally established, one for each category of my armaments program. Linking these were an equal number of pools. Alongside these committees and pools I set up development commissions in which army officers met with the best designers in industry. These commissions were to supervise new products, suggest improvements in manufacturing techniques even during the design stage, and call a halt to any unnecessary projects. The heads of the committees and the pools were to make sure—this was vital to our whole approach—that a given plant concentrated on producing only one item, but did so in maximum quantity."

As Speer bragged, "Within half a year after my taking office we had significantly increased production in all the areas within our scope. Production in August 1942, according to the *Index Figures for German Armaments End-Products*, as compared with the February production, had increased by 27 percent for guns, by 25 percent for tanks, while ammunition production almost doubled, rising 97 percent. The total productivity of armaments increased by 59.6 percent. Obviously we had mobilized reserves that had hitherto lain fallow."

As summarized in the report of the postwar US Strategic Bombing Survey, directed by the economist John Kenneth Galbraith, "Speer set about replacing the existing machinery of control with a new organization (the 'Rings' and 'Committees'), manned by people selected from among the production managers and technicians of industry. They were charged with the task of increasing production by rationalizing German war industry; that is, by simplifying designs, standardizing components, concentrating production in the most suitable plants, reducing the number of different armaments orders given to a single firm, exchanging patents and secret processes, and generally adopting, throughout industry, the most efficient processes of production. The result of this policy was a more than three-fold increase in Germany's munition production."

Such was the challenge faced by the EOU, as well as by the Combined Bomber Offensive. They were not attacking an economy that remained static, but one that was rapidly expanding and one which had a great deal of expansion potential.

In the meantime, as the economists were analyzing the substance of target systems, the operational units were still coordinating the form of their operations.

While the Combined Chiefs of Staff saw the day and night missions carried out under the Combined Bomber Offensive as complementary, they were never really coordinated in a strict sense of the word.

As Arthur Ferguson explains, "It was assumed that the 'area' bombing of the RAF would be complementary to the daylight campaign, but, owing mainly to differences in tactics and operating potentialities, the two forces in fact seldom achieved more than a general coordination of effort. The Combined Bomber Offensive was thus a combined offensive but not a closely integrated one."

Back at 40 Berkeley Square, Dick Hughes welcomed the news from Casablanca and noted that Eaker's lack of interest in operational details gave the EOU a unique opportunity.

In his memoir, Hughes writes that the Casablanca Directive "had furnished us with a list of target priorities, but the directive was purposely so loosely phrased that, in practice, we had virtually complete freedom to conduct operations as we saw fit. Air Marshal Sir Charles Portal, also, with complete wisdom, kept his hands completely off attempting to direct, or control, Eighth Air Force operations, and all decisions were ultimately made by myself, with the cooperation and backing of General [Fred] Anderson at VIII Bomber Command."

Echoing Hughes's assessment, Arthur Ferguson writes that "the Casablanca Conference did much to clear the strategic atmosphere, especially in regard to the use of air power. It was thereafter possible for Allied strategists to plan with new assurance and to think with new clarity. But the work of the conference was done on the level of general policy; although it laid down guiding principles, it did not entertain specific plans."

Anderson and Hughes, the airman and the analyst, developed a unique and effective working relationship of the sort that is so desirable within an organization, but often not achieved. As Hughes has written, "Fred Anderson completely understood the problems with which I was confronted," and Hughes understood the issues that Anderson faced.

While Hughes had gone to Sandhurst, Anderson was a 1928 graduate of the US Military Academy at West Point. He had earned his wings a year later and had worked his way through the Air Corps to a position on General Arnold's staff as deputy director of bombardment before going overseas as Arnold's personal representative for bombardment matters in both North Africa and England.

Anderson's right-hand man at the VIII Bomber Command, meanwhile, was a fellow West Pointer, class of 1929, named Charles Glendon Williamson. In the *Howitzer*, the West Point yearbook, it had been said of Cadet Williamson that "his ambitions in life are to make an airplane, do things never before imagined and to make better drawings. May he be successful in both, and any other activities he may undertake in his career as an Army officer."

If he had not *made* an airplane, he and Anderson now commanded lots of them, and they were doing things that had never—at least not before Billy Mitchell—been imagined.

As in his relationship with Hughes, Anderson worked well with Glen Williamson, though the two were recalled as an odd couple by many who interacted with them. For example, Charles J. V. Murphy, a well-connected Harvard dropout turned freelance journalist—who later authored biographies of Winston Churchill as well as of the Duke and Duchess of Windsor—colorfully described the contrast in a 1944 article for *Life* magazine.

"Anderson is tall, rawboned and supple, temperamentally a well-anchored man, a good talker and an easy mixer," writes Murphy. "Only seldom will a stranger catch the gleam of purpose beneath the affability. Williamson is short and stumpy and given to long spells of moodiness.

Logical, erudite in the details of his profession, uncompromising, he is one of the foremost theoretical thinkers of the Army Air Forces."

An odd couple who were a good fit, both with each other and in their interactions with Berkeley Square, they were both devotees of the sixth-century B.C. Chinese warrior-philosopher Sun Tzu. The author of the seminal *The Art of War*, Sun Tzu is today even more fashionable in military and business leadership circles than he was in mid-century.

One of Sun Tzu's more memorable maxims tells the reader that "if you know your enemies and know yourself, you can win a hundred battles. . . . If you only know yourself, but not your opponent, you may win or may lose. . . . If you know neither yourself nor your enemy, you will always endanger yourself."

Knowing the enemy was exactly why Fred Anderson deliberately cultivated a close working relationship with Dick Hughes and the EOU.

EIGHT

DEFINING THE MISSION

When General Ira Eaker had promised Winston Churchill a demonstration of American action against targets inside Germany by the end of January, Dick Hughes delivered the plans, Fred Anderson and Glen Williamson delivered the bombers, and the crews of the Eighth Air Force delivered the bombs.

On January 27 the Eighth Air Force made its first attack on targets within Germany, albeit with fewer than the one hundred bombers promised by Eaker. The primary target, plucked from the top item in the hierarchy of targeting priorities, the naval yard at Wilhelmshaven, would be hit by fifty-three heavy bombers while two others diverted to Emden.

Hughes and others may have been impatient with the ineffectiveness of the attacks on U-boat pens, but the strikes against shipyards within Germany meant hitting the insidious submarines at their more vulnerable source. On February 2, an attempted second attack on Germany was aborted because of weather, but the Eighth Air Force returned to Wilhelmshaven on February 26. Thus began the off-and-on campaign against the shipyards that would continue through 1943.

The German shipbuilding industry, which was in the midst of increasing the proportion of its resources devoted to U-boats, was far more vulnerable to attack than the reinforced concrete pens. Reconnaissance photos showed that the attacks on the shipyards were reasonably effective. They were also a good example of cooperation between the Combined Bomber Offensive partners, as the RAF carpet-bombed the same areas that the Eighth Air Force struck during the day.

As the American bombers began reaching targets within Germany, they met more determined Luftwaffe resistance. While Luftflotte 3 (Air Fleet 3), charged with the air defense of occupied Belgium and France, had fewer than two hundred interceptors, attacks against Germany brought the Eighth Air Force into contact with the Luftwaffenbefehlshaber Mitte (Air Command Central), an organization with substantially greater resources for *Reichsverteidigung* ("Defense of the Reich") operations. Inside the Reich, targets were well defended, and losses would often be heavy.

Over the coming weeks and months, Luftwaffenbefehlshaber Mitte used a variety of weapons and tactics against the bombers. The standard Luftwaffe single-engine fighters, such as the Messerschmitt Bf 109 and the newer Focke-Wulf Fw 190, were encountered, but so too were twin-engined Messerschmitt Bf 110s, which were more commonly used as night fighters against RAF Bomber Command raids.

These interceptors used Egon Mayer's head-on attack tactic, but also another method, pioneered by *Oberleutnant* Heinz Knoke in March 1943, that of dropping bombs on the bombers, even as the Americans were lining up to bomb ground targets. Indeed, the Luftwaffe's Jagdgeschwader 11, formed in 1943 as a *Reichsverteidigung* air defense unit, routinely used air-to-air bombing with 250kg bombs. Meanwhile, larger aircraft, such as Ju 88 bombers, started attacking the Americans from beyond the range of their defensive machine guns, using Werfer-Granate 21 rocket launchers to lob 21cm Nebelwerfer 42 air-to-air rockets.

One of the simplest and most effective Luftwaffe tactics was to gang up on individual bombers. They often picked the low-hanging fruit of aircraft that had strayed out of formation, but frequently they beset the lead aircraft, ganging up on them with a dozen or more fighters, under the theory that this would disrupt the formation. Sometimes it did, but the American pilots were drilled repeatedly to maintain the integrity of their formations no matter what.

The experience of being attacked by the Luftwaffe was hellish. As one Flying Fortress pilot mentioned in a debriefing, "The German fighter raked us the length of the Fortress's belly. It was like sitting in the boiler of a hot-water heater and being rolled down a steep hill. The right wing was shot to hell. There were holes everywhere. A lot of them were 20mm cannon holes, and they tear a hole you could shove a sheep through. The entire wing was just a goddamn bunch of holes."

At the same time, anti-aircraft fire from the 88mm long-range guns in flak batteries near the targets in both France and Germany was improving in its accuracy and effectiveness, and also began exacting a toll on the bomber formations, which strictly maintained their tight box formations during their bomb runs. While the close formations made the bombers easier targets for the flak batteries, they actually served to protect the bombers from interceptors by allowing the bomber gunners to use interlocking fields of defensive fire against the Germans. Bomber pilots frequently used the phrase describing the black puffs of exploding shells as a carpet "thick enough to walk on."

During March, there were further raids against the shipyards in Wilhelmshaven, as well as in Vegesack, a northern suburb of Bremen, forty miles to the south, on the Weser River, both of which built U-boats.

These missions continued to alternate with strikes against the facilities in France that housed and serviced the U-boats. Though electricity and water supply into the U-boat pens was interrupted, the damage done in the latter attacks was primarily to the surrounding cities, impacting the French civilian population and the workforce employed at the pens, rather than the pens themselves.

As the Kreigsmarine's Grand Admiral Karl Doenitz, the man in charge of the U-boat operations, told a meeting of the *Reich Zentrales Planungsamt* (Central Planning Office for War Production) on May 4, "The Anglo-Saxons' attempt to strike down the submarine war was undertaken with all the means available to them. You know that the towns of Saint-Nazaire and Lorient have been rubbed out as main submarine bases. No dog nor cat is left in these towns. Nothing but the submarine shelters [into which all essential facilities had been moved] remain."

During the first five months of 1943, American bombers put 70 percent of their anti-U-boat tonnage on yards rather than pens, inflicting serious damage on the yards in seven out of a dozen major attacks. Post-strike analysis of the effectiveness of the raids showed that they had cut the monthly output of the shipbuilding industry from sixteen U-boats to fewer than eight, although the shipyards were able to repair the damage more quickly that the photo interpreters realized.

When weather obscured the U-boat targets, the Eighth Air Force alternated with attacks on the rail network across northern France and northwestern Germany. These were not done in sufficient volume, with large enough numbers of bombers, to do any lasting damage, but they did disrupt rail transportation for short periods of time. Though construction crews were able to repair the damage and get trains running within a few days of the attacks, the work did tie up considerable manpower, which could not be used elsewhere. Naturally, any locomotive or railcar that needed to be replaced would divert resources away from building tanks or other vehicles.

Despite apparently good results, the Eighth Air Force was still not operating up to the levels that Eaker had promised at Casablanca. They were still unable to put one hundred bombers out on any given day during February or March. The numbers of mission-ready aircraft were not increasing as quickly as anticipated. Through April, the Eighth Air Force operated six heavy bombardment groups, four of Flying Fortresses and two of Liberators. Meanwhile, two Flying Fortress groups, the 2nd and the 99th, which had been earmarked for the Eighth Air Force, were diverted to the Twelfth Air Force, while the Liberators of the 308th Bombardment Group were sent to the Fourteenth instead of the Eighth.

The total number of Flying Fortresses and Liberators listed as being on hand in the ETO in February were 186 and 69 respectively. Because of combat losses and other damage, the numbers of B-17s was actually less than the total of 234 that had been on hand in October 1942. At the same time, the average daily combat strength of the Eighth Air Force stood at only 74 "operating combinations" (combat crews and aircraft).

Naturally, the number of crews was as important as the number of aircraft, and even the limited operations during the dead of winter had taken a toll. Through January, only twenty replacement crewmen arrived to take the places of sixty-seven who had been lost, and at the same time the Combined Bomber Offensive was taking the Eighth Air Force into Germany, some of the heavy bombardment groups were reporting that attrition had reduced their total crew strength by half, a fact that had a detrimental effect on operations—as well as on the morale of other crews.

As General Anderson wrote in a March 2 memo to General Stratemeyer at USAAF headquarters, until the total number of heavy bombers and crews reached six hundred, the best that the VIII Bomber Command could do was "nibble at the fringes of German strength."

The RAF still viewed the sluggish buildup of American heavy bombing capacity with as much, or more, alarm as their Combined Bomber Offensive partners. In a series of memos to Hap Arnold, Air Chief Marshal Portal tactfully described the Eighth Air Force operations as having been "strikingly successful," but complained in an understated way that "my one fear is that their efforts may be curtailed or even brought to a standstill by lack of numbers."

Numbers not seen by Portal, or indeed by most operational people at the front-line fields in East Anglia, were the huge numbers of aircraft entering the pipeline at the source. The American aircraft industry was growing exponentially, and the flow of new aircraft was on the verge of suddenly becoming a torrent. Having produced 1,412 Flying Fortresses and 1,164 Liberators in 1942, Boeing, Consolidated, Douglas, and Vega would build 4,179 and 5,214 of these respective heavy bombers in 1943. This flow would hit East Anglia in early summer and become a tidal wave by the end of the year.

As Arthur Ferguson points out, "It was not until May that the Eighth Air Force began to acquire the strength appropriate to its mission." The total of six heavy bombardment groups that were operational with the Eighth Air Force doubled by the end of May. During that month, the arrival in England of the 94th, 95th, 96th, 351st, and 379th—and the reversion of the 92nd from training status—greatly enhanced to Eighth Air Force's ability to get large numbers of aircraft over the target. The total number of heavy bombers in the ETO increased from 255 in February to 705 by the end of May.

At the same time, the numbers of fighter escorts also increased. Through most of April, only the 4th Fighter Group, flying Republic P-47

Thunderbolts, had been available, but two additional groups were on line by the end of the month and capable of routinely escorting the bombers.

On April 17, the Eighth Air Force had finally been able to put more than one hundred heavy bombers over Bremen. This mission marked a milestone of another sort as well. By May, the wheels were in motion for a major shift in strategic direction, specifically a gradual refocusing of the Combined Bomber Offensive from the U-boat campaign to the German aircraft industry.

When he went to work at the EOU on Berkeley Square in March, Charlie Kindleberger's primary function had been to study the German aircraft industry and to plan missions against it. The April 17 Bremen mission targeting the Focke-Wulf Flugzeugbau facility was significant insofar as the Eighth Air Force had sent its largest mission to date to target the aircraft industry.

It was also with a certain irony that the specific product being targeted was the Focke-Wulf Fw 190 fighter, when the mission saw the bomber force badly mauled by those same German fighters. Though the bombers left the enemy factory half-destroyed, the Eighth Air Force lost sixteen aircraft shot down and forty-six damaged.

The heavy American losses on April 17 stemmed from the enemy's having come to expect Bremen as a repeat target, and from improved coordination and intensity of defensive action, both on the ground and in the air. Initially, Luftwaffenbefehlshaber Mitte put up as many as 150 interceptors, flying through their own anti-aircraft fire to attack the American lead bombers head-on in an effort to break up the formations as they entered the target area.

When it came to fighting the heavy bombers, the Luftwaffe assigned points to fighter pilots for disrupting the formations. While only the actual destruction of an enemy aircraft, an *abschuss*, counted toward a fighter ace's aerial victory tally, points assigned for breaking up a formation, a *herausschuss*, and for *endgueltige vernichtung*, the "final destruction" or "finishing off" of a damaged enemy aircraft, also counted toward awards and decorations. A pilot might receive a single point for the *abschuss* of a fighter plane and three points for shooting down a four-engine bomber. It took three points for an Iron Cross First Class, and forty points for a Knights Cross.

Under the practice that existed in 1943, but which was phased out later, a *herausschuss* involving a four-engine bomber netted two points.

Though breaking up the formations on the final bomb run was usually unsuccessful, the fighters always regrouped and hit the bombers again as they emerged from the target area and headed toward England. Employing the usual tactic of picking stragglers from the periphery of the formation, the interceptors harassed the formations all the way to the North Sea.

Within a month, the Eighth Air Force fighter groups were able to put up a sufficient number of P-47 Thunderbolts to successfully defend against such situations. The bomber crews came to appreciate, rely upon, and praise their "little friends," as they called the escorting fighters. The only limiting factor was the range of the fighters. Even with auxiliary fuel tanks, the Thunderbolt could only accompany bombers to targets in northern Germany that were no farther than 475 miles from their bases, but they could always cover them on their way out or for the last leg of a trip home.

Also during May, the large influx of new USAAF crews and aircraft changed the complexion of the Combined Bomber Offensive. The Eighth was gradually beefing up its numbers in the face of RAF criticism. Whereas it had taken the Eighth Air Force eight months from its first mission to finally mount a hundred-plane mission, it took less than a month to go from that point to launching two hundred bombers on a single day. In a memo to Hap Arnold, Eaker called it "a great day for the Eighth Air Force. Our combat crew availability went up in a straight line from 100 to 215. . . . If the groups prove to be superior in combat to the old ones, it will scarcely be a fair fight!"

One may assume that Arnold understood that Eaker was speaking with irony.

Also worth an exclamation point by this time was the improved bombing accuracy, which had long been promised, but which had been slow to develop. Since March, the Eighth Air Force had been using automatic flight-control equipment (AFCE) to increase precision through the use of an autopilot to control the aircraft during the bomb run.

As Arthur Ferguson points out, "The few seconds immediately before the bombardier released his bombs obviously constituted the critical moment in the entire mission, for it was then that the bombardier performed his final sighting operation. So it was essential that the aircraft should be held as nearly as possible to a steady course without slips, skids, or changes in altitude, and that the pilotage be as free as possible from the influence of flak and of attacking fighters. Perfection of this sort was impossible even with the best of pilots. With those produced by the hasty training program into which the AAF had been forced it could not even be approximated."

AFCE had been tested in 1942 to mixed reviews, but by the spring of 1943, the bugs had been worked out. During the attack on Vegesack on March 18, a lead bombardier using the AFCE successfully led the 305th Bombardment Group to drop 76 percent of its ordnance within a radius of one thousand feet of the aiming point.

Meanwhile, even as the decision makers were finally considering the suspension of the attacks on the U-boat pens for which Dick Hughes and others had been lobbying, these targets were the recipients of hundred-plane raids during May. On May 17, 118 heavy bombers targeted Lorient, while on May 29, the Eighth Air Force ended the month with a 147-bomber mission against Saint-Nazaire.

The May 17 mission contained a milestone moment for the Eighth Air Force. In one of the B-17s flying that day was the first Eighth Air Force heavy bomber crew to complete their full quota of twenty-five missions, and hence to be qualified to return home. The aircraft was the famous B-17F commanded by Captain Robert Morgan and nicknamed *Memphis Belle*. Assigned to the 324th Bombardment Squadron of the 91st Bombardment Group, the aircraft had been the subject of a USAAF documentary film entitled *The Memphis Belle: A Story of a Flying Fortress*. The film was directed by William Wyler, who had just won the Best Director Oscar for the 1942 film *Mrs. Miniver*. During filming of the documentary, Wyler flew a number of live combat missions aboard the *Memphis Belle* and other aircraft, and his cinematographer had been killed when another Flying Fortress was shot down.

Morgan and his crew subsequently flew the *Memphis Belle* back to the United States, where they would participate in war bond tours, and where Wyler's film—released in 1944 by Paramount—would dramatically publicize the dangerous work being done by Eighth Air Force crewmen.

NINE

POINTBLANK

Since January 1943, as William Wyler had been gathering footage for his film, the Eighth Air Force was building up its strength and testing the waters of operations inside Germany. They had been doing so under the general outlines of the preliminary Combined Bomber Offensive targeting plan that was contained in the Casablanca Directive. Meanwhile, the Combined Chiefs of Staff had been developing a more formal plan that would succeed the Casablanca Directive and be implemented on June 10, marking the "official" beginning of the Combined Bomber Offensive.

The origins of this official plan dated back to December 9, 1942, when Hap Arnold decided to have someone in his office come up with a document that went beyond AWPD-42 in addressing the issue of strategic targets, and which addressed targeting scientifically and systematically.

Arnold had ordered Colonel Byron Gates to empanel a "group of operational analysts under your jurisdiction to prepare and submit to me a report analyzing the rate of progressive deterioration that should be anticipated in the German war effort as a result of the increasing air operations we are prepared to employ against its sustaining sources. This study should result in as accurate an estimate as can be arrived at as to the date when this deterioration will have progressed to a point to permit a successful invasion of Western Europe."

Originally called the Advisory Committee on Bombardment, it was later known more vaguely as the Committee of Operations Analysts (COA). Its form and function were similar—arguably duplicative—to those of Hughes, Kindleberger, Rostow, and the EOU team, but while the EOU was in a secret location in London, the COA was located within reach of Arnold's own headquarters. While the EOU existed for ongoing operational requirements, the COA theoretically existed to provide Arnold with a onetime single USAAF plan that could ultimately be integrated into the joint directive succeeding the temporary Casablanca Directive.

The function of the COA, like that of the EOU but more general in nature, was to identify "industrial targets in Germany the destruction of which would weaken the enemy most decisively in the shortest possible time."

The form of the COA was modeled after the EOU paradigm insofar as civilian analysts, in this case mainly bankers and industrialists, were brought in to study the goals of a strategic air campaign against Germany. The most prominent were Edward Earle, of the Institute for Advanced Study at Princeton, Thomas Lamont of J.P. Morgan & Company, and investment banker Elihu Root Jr., of the New York firm of Root, Clark, Buckner, and Ballantine and the son of the former US senator and secretary of state to Theodore Roosevelt. Also included were Fowler Hamilton from the Board of Economic Warfare, Edward Mason of the OSS, and Boston attorney Guido Perera. Malcolm Moss represented the EOU.

The COA also tapped the expertise of OSS, the Bureau of Economic Warfare, and the State and Treasury departments—as well as the War Production Board, roughly America's equivalent to Albert Speer's Armaments Ministry. At the end of January 1943, members of the COA even flew to England to meet with the British Ministry of Economic Warfare and to visit 40 Berkeley Square.

The COA had submitted its report to General Arnold on March 8, 1943, six weeks after Casablanca. "It is better to cause a high degree of destruction in a few really essential industries or services than to cause a small degree of destruction in many industries," the COA concluded, echoing what Hughes had previously determined. "Results are cumulative and the plan once adopted should be adhered to with relentless determination."

As Edward Earle told Arthur Ferguson in November 1945, the committee "refrained from stating a formal order of priority for the target systems considered . . . for reasons of security. . . . But it is clear from the arguments presented that the systems were listed in descending order of preference."

With this understanding, the first "system" on the COA list was the German aircraft and aircraft engine industry, which had been third on the priority list in AWPD-1 and second in the list contained in the Casablanca Directive, and which had been Charlie Kindleberger's assignment at the EOU since March. The petroleum industry also made the top four on all the lists.

The reason that aircraft production—especially single-engine fighter aircraft production—moved up the list was certainly the fact that Eighth Air Force operations were now being seriously impacted by Luftwaffe opposition. It was now clear to all that in order to work through the other items on the list, something would have to be done to lessen Luftwaffe effectiveness.

The notion that the Combined Bomber Offensive should concentrate against the Luftwaffe over all other targets, was underscored by the planners on the Combined Operational Planning Committee (COPC). In an April 9 memo, the British planners summarized this by declaring that "the most formidable weapon being used by the enemy today against our bomber offensive is his fighter force—his single engined fighters by day and his twin engined fighters by night—and the elimination or serious depletion of this force would be the greatest contribution to the furtherance of the joint heavy bomber offensive of the RAF and AAF."

With this having been agreed, Eaker delegated the operational details to General Anderson at the VIII Bomber Command and General Hansell, who would work with RAF Air Commodore Sidney O. Bufton to come up with a target list. At the EOU, Walt Rostow was assigned as a liaison to the British Air Ministry, with an eye toward making sure that the Americans and the British each knew what the other was doing with regard to the aircraft industry mission.

Second to the aircraft industry in the COA target hierarchy, and to a certain extent related to it, were ball bearings. A simple component, ball bearings, and other anti-friction bearings, were essential not only to fighter aircraft and aircraft engine production, but to a broad spectrum of industrial production, from military vehicles to factory machine tools. Indeed, anti-friction bearings, including roller bearings and ball bearings, were seen as a "bottleneck" industry, one which, if removed from the supply chain, would negatively affect a myriad of industries.

In third place came the petroleum industry, which had topped the AWPD-1 list and had come in at fourth in the Casablanca Directive. Also considered by many to be a bottleneck industry, petroleum was downplayed by other analysts who felt that Germany had adequate standby refining capacity. Nevertheless, Ploeşti in Romania, from which the Reich derived—by some estimates—about 60 percent of its refined petroleum, would be an important future objective for Allied bombers flying from bases in the MTO.

As the postwar Strategic Bombing Survey would later demonstrate, the COA report missed the boat in downplaying the importance of Germany's synthetic petroleum and rubber industries—but in the spring of 1943, these seemed less important than they actually were. Writing with the benefit of 20/20 hindsight, Ferguson observed that the COA was "handicapped by a faulty understanding of the German chemical industry. Synthetic rubber, synthetic oil, nitrogen, methanol, and other important chemicals formed interdependent parts of a single industrial complex. The production of nitrogen and methanol, both of extreme significance in the manufacture of explosives, was heavily concentrated in synthetic oil plants. The attack on synthetic oil, when it finally came, in fact succeeded in producing, as a fortuitous by-product, a marked drop in the production of nitrogen, which in turn contributed to the shortage of explosives experienced by the Wehrmacht in the closing campaigns of the war."

The COA report was favorably received by British authorities when it was sent across on March 23. Representatives of the Air Ministry, the Ministry of Economic Warfare, and the RAF concurred with the major recommendations, agreeing that the principal targets should be related to the aircraft, anti-friction bearing, and petroleum industries.

The principal point of contention was the U-boat campaign. The Americans had greatly downgraded its importance, but the British, so fully dependent on the safety of the sea lanes connecting the United Kingdom to the outside world, still insisted that attacks on shipyards building U-boats remain on the list for Combined Bomber Offensive operations.

Though the U-boat campaign would remain as part of the Combined Bomber Offensive Plan, the problem was being overtaken by events, as naval antisubmarine warfare weapons and tactics began to prove themselves to be a more effective solution to the problem. After victories in the North Atlantic in May 1943, it was clear that detecting and sinking U-boats at sea was far more effective than bombing submarine pens. However, as a compromise, shipyards building U-boats, which were more vulnerable than the heavily reinforced concrete pens, retained a priority on the target lists.

Although the Combined Bomber Offensive was addressed at the May 12–27, 1943, Trident Conference in Washington, the third wartime meeting between Roosevelt and Churchill, it was not a controversial issue, as it had been at Casablanca. It was now a foregone conclusion in which the basic premise had been proven. What did emerge from Trident was the understanding by Roosevelt, Churchill, and the Combined Chiefs of Staff that the Combined Bomber Offensive was an integral and significant part of the overall strategic plan for the cross-channel invasion of *Festung Europa*. This massive operation, to be code-named Overlord, was now tentatively scheduled for May 1944.

On May 18, after considerable discussion, the Combined Chiefs of Staff approved the *Plan for the Combined Bomber Offensive from the United Kingdom*—as presented. This document, in turn, formed the basis for the detailed Pointblank Directive, which was issued on June 10.

The target list contained within the plan retained U-boat building and included the petroleum industry (which Dick Hughes had placed on his first list of priorities back in the summer of 1941), notably synthetic fuels and synthetic rubber. Mention was made of aluminum, which was one of the top three target categories—along with the aircraft industry. There was also attention given to the anti-friction bearing industry, which was appealing to target planners because of its being a bottleneck industry that served so many other industries.

As Walt Rostow wrote for the *War Diary* of the OSS Research and Analysis Branch, "The ball bearing industry appeared to offer the most economical and most operationally feasible method of impinging by air attack on the whole structure of German war production."

However, the line that was arguably the most significant in the Combined Bomber Offensive Plan was the one that described the Luftwaffe fighter threat as "second to none in immediate importance" and stated that "if the growth of the German fighter strength is not arrested quickly, it may become literally impossible to carry out the destruction planned and thus to create the conditions necessary for ultimate decisive action by our combined forces on the Continent [Operation Overlord]."

Bearing this in mind, the COPC had formulated the Pointblank Directive, as a corollary to the Combined Bomber Offensive Plan. This directive initiated the operation of the same name, the campaign against the Luftwaffe and against the German aircraft industry, which would culminate eight months later in Big Week.

Of this, Rostow adds, "In the course of the war, no aspect of intelligence received wider, more continuous, and more devoted attention than the [Luftwaffe], and within it, German aircraft production. It was recognized early that aircraft production bore a more immediate and direct relationship to fighting at the front than other forms of armament manufacture."

Rostow credits Dick Hughes with being notable in bearing "the brunt of the salesmanship at higher levels that led to [the] acceptance" of the recommendations that formed the Pointblank Directive.

The importance of Operation Pointblank to continued strategic bomber operations was illustrated almost immediately—ironically in missions directed at shipyards.

On June 11, the day after the Pointblank Directive was formally adopted, almost on cue, the bad weather that had prevailed over the continent for several weeks finally lifted. On that "opening day," the Eighth Air Force launched 252 heavy bombers against Bremen. Upon encountering cloud cover over the primary target, 168 bombers diverted to attack Wilhelmshaven, while another 30 bombed Cuxhaven.

Because these targets lay beyond the range of Eighth Air Force P-47s or RAF Spitfires, the bombers flew the mission without fighter escort. As was expected, based on past experience, the Luftwaffe interceptors struck as the formations began their bombing run. The tactic, as usual, was a head-on attack against the aircraft and the front of the formations. This greatly interfered with the lead bombardiers' ability to accurately sight their targets, and most of the bombs dropped by the force missed their targets.

Two days later, 102 Eighth Air Force heavy bombers struck Bremen, the missed primary target from two days before, while 60 went to the shipyards at Keil. The Luftwaffe attacked the bombers bound for Keil over the North Sea coast, and hammered them all the way to their final run on the target. In this action, the Luftwaffe doctrine of utilizing over-whelming force came into play. The Eighth would report them as the heaviest attacks encountered to date. In addition to the usual Bf 109s and Fw 190s, the crews saw German night fighters, painted black all over.

Black indeed was the unlucky thirteenth of June. While only 8 aircraft had been lost by the Eighth Air Force two days before, there were 26 heavy bombers shot down on that day, including 22 from the force that had attacked Keil.

Trying to put lipstick on a particularly unsightly pig, the Eighth Air Force press people focused on the probable claims that the American gun-ners had shot down nearly 40 German fighters. To this, Arthur Ferguson writes that "although hailed by both British and American air commands [in Tactical Mission Report 62] as a great victory, the 'Battle of Kiel' can be so considered only in terms of the bravery and determination with which the shattered force of bombers did in fact reach the target and drop its bombs. In terms of the cold statistics which ultimately measure air victories, it was a sobering defeat."

The Battle of Keil provided a painful demonstration of why the Luft-waffe threat was "second to none," and why Operation Pointblank was of vital importance if the Combined Bomber Offensive was ever to succeed.

A week after the "sobering defeat" at Keil there came the story of a successful mission wrapped in an interesting paradox. On June 22, 183 bombers flew deep into the Ruhr industrial area, the deepest penetration yet by the Eighth Air Force, to strike Chemische Werke Hüls, a synthetic rubber works at the city of Hüls. Operated by I.G. Farben, and sprawling across 541 acres, the plant was one of the largest, most modern, and most efficient in the world, providing 30 percent of Germany's styrene and synthetic rubber needs.

The success story was that the bombers took the Germans by surprise and succeeded in doing enough damage to shut the facility down for a month—and to reduce Germany's total reserves to just a six-week supply. Indeed, full production would not be back on line until the end of the year. To this achievement, one might add that the bomber formation lost just a single aircraft in this unanticipated strike, compared to a third of the force shot down at Kiel, a location where the Luftwaffe was used to seeing Allied bombers.

The paradox in the story was that despite the vulnerability of the fragile factory, which was illustrated by the success, the Eighth Air Force never returned. Neither the COA nor the EOU fully appreciated the importance of synthetic rubber to the German war machine. As Arthur Ferguson writes, the postwar Strategic Bombing Survey later determined that "three to five strong attacks would have effectively eliminated Hüls as a producing plant. To the amazement of German officials it received no major attack after 22 June 1943, and in March 1944 it reached peak production."

In another instance, on July 24, the Eighth Air Force again broke out of the usual targeting parameters to run an extremely long-distance attack on German aluminum facilities at Herøya in Norway. The Nordische Aluminium Aktiengesellschaft aluminum and magnesium plant in Herøya, which had been built by the Germans after they occupied Norway in 1940, was operated jointly by the Norwegian aluminum and hydroelectric company, Norsk Hydro, in partnership with the Luftwaffe, making it a prime Operation Pointblank target.

In contrast with the attack on Hüls, where the plant recovered, the plant complex at Herøya was so badly damaged that the Germans boarded it up and walked away, costing the German aircraft industry a major new state-of-the-art supplier. However, Allied photoreconnaissance interpreters mistook the boarding up for repairs and did not realize that the plant had been abandoned. Nevertheless, like Hüls, it was not the subject of a follow-up attack. Postwar surveys showed that the bombers had scored 151 direct hits, three times the number observed in the reconnaissance imagery.

Even as the precision bombing sought by the Eighth Air Force was finally beginning to materialize, RAF Bomber Command's Air Marshal Arthur Harris was mounting larger and larger nocturnal area raids. As these attacks, which were by their nature imprecise, grew in scale and ferocity, it was inevitable that substantial areas of civilian residences would be hit. These operations became one of the most controversial legacies of the Combined Bomber Offensive. This was especially the case as increasing numbers of bombers became available.

Most often cited today as examples of such attacks are those against Dresden in February 1945, but the 1943 attacks on Hamburg involved a more sustained campaign and resulted in even greater loss of life. In five nighttime attacks between July 24 and August 3, most of them involving more than seven hundred four-engine bombers, the RAF decimated Germany's largest port and second largest city. In the 1961 United Kingdom government publication *The Strategic Air Offensive Against Germany, 1939–1945*, Noble Frankland and Charles Webster note that 42,600 civilians were killed that week in Hamburg, as opposed to 25,000 in Dresden in 1945.

"Rash as this operation was, it had catastrophic consequences for us," Albert Speer later observed. "The first attacks put the water supply pipes out of action, so that in the subsequent bombings the fire department had no way of fighting the fires. Huge conflagrations created cyclone-like firestorms; the asphalt of the streets began to blaze; people were suffocated in their cellars or burned to death in the streets. The devastation of this series of air raids could be compared only with the effects of a major earthquake. Gauleiter Kaufmann teletyped Hitler repeatedly, begging him to visit the stricken city. When these pleas proved fruitless, he asked Hitler at least to receive a delegation of some of the more heroic rescue crews. But Hitler refused even that."

Speer went on to comment cynically that "Hamburg had suffered the fate Göring and Hitler had conceived for London."

Having leveled a square mile of central Rotterdam in May 1940 in order to bully the people of the Netherlands into surrender, Hitler had indeed intended to do the same to the British capital, and to a certain extent, he did so during the Blitz of 1940.

"Have you ever looked at a map of London?" Hitler crowed at a dinner party in his chancellery in 1940. "It is so closely built up that one source of fire alone would suffice to destroy the whole city, as happened once before, two hundred years ago [actually in 1666]. Göring wants to use innumerable incendiary bombs of an altogether new type to create sources of fire in all parts of London. Fires everywhere. Thousands of them. Then they'll unite in one gigantic area conflagration. Göring has the right idea. Explosive bombs don't work, but it can be done with incendiary bombs— total destruction of London. What use will their fire department be once that really starts!"

As Harris had pointed out, Hitler had been operating "under the rather childish delusion that they were going to bomb everyone else, and nobody was going to bomb them." In Harris's biblical analogy, his RAF Bomber Command had just caused Hamburg to "reap the whirlwind."

As Speer had observed, Hitler's plan and Harris's whirlwind had now been inflicted on the Reich's largest port. Luckily, Hitler now demanded that Hermann Göring, the commander in chief of his Luftwaffe, take the steps necessary to build a fleet of four-engine bombers for the Luftwaffe.

The Eighth Air Force passed through the smoke from Hamburg's smoldering ruins twice during this period, on July 25 and again the next day, as part of a series of precision daytime strikes on shipyards building U-boats, which also included another round of strikes against Keil. Much of the American attention during these early days of Pointblank was focused on aircraft factories in Germany. Included were those of Heinkel and Focke-Wulf in Warnemünde, and of Feisler and Focke-Wulf near Kassel.

Through June and July, as the weather improved, the Eighth Air Force had been spending a great deal of time alternating between aircraft-related targets in Germany and aircraft-related targets in France. The latter, less enthusiastically defended by the Luftwaffe than those in the Reich, provided a welcome break for the crews and a case study in the importance of fighter escorts.

As Operation Pointblank oriented the Eighth Air Force toward the German aircraft industry, it is worth a reminder that *French* aircraft factories had been on the Eighth Air Force target list off and on since October 1942, when thirty Flying Fortresses first hit the Avions Potez plant at Méaulte in the Picardy region of northern France.

One of the most overlooked aspects of German aircraft acquisition during World War II is the important part played by the *French* aircraft industry. Under the terms of a July 1941 agreement, plane makers in France were allowed to continue operating, so long as two-thirds of their production was for Germany.

As Julian Jackson writes in *France: The Dark Years*, "The total contribution of the French aircraft industry to Germany was not insignificant: 27 percent of Germany's transport planes in 1942, 42 percent in 1943, and 49 percent in 1944 had come from France. Planes produced in France supplied Rommel's African army in 1942 and German troops at Stalingrad in 1943. If Vichy had not collaborated in this matter, the Germans would probably have dismantled French aviation factories and reassembled them in Germany. But there were more positive motives for cooperation. German orders kept the French aircraft industry going, allowed France to envisage building up an air force again, and provided employment to the aircraft workers who had been laid off after the Armistice. Their number had dropped from 250,000 in May 1940, to 40,000 in June; by 1942 it was back to 80,000; by 1944, 100,000. The aircraft industry embodied a paradox which applied to French industry as a whole: the Germans posed a threat to the French economy, but they also provided the only prospect of its [postwar] recovery."

Allied attacks on French factories would continue through 1943 and into 1944, although the bulk of the attention given to aircraft manufacturing would naturally target combat aircraft—made mainly in Germany—rather than factories building transports.

During the last week of July, when the Eighth Air Force was concentrating mainly on targets inside Germany, Luftwaffe action cost the Americans a loss rate of roughly 8.5 percent of the bombers dispatched. American fighters could escort the bombers to any target in northern France, but it was not until late July that the P-47s received the jettisonable auxiliary fuel tanks that would give them the range to accompany the bombers to *some* of the targets in Germany.

The remarkable North American P-51 Mustang long-range fighter, then in development back in the United States, would be a game-changer of the highest order when it arrived in substantial numbers, but this would not happen until late in the year.

Though the arrival of the Mustang would completely alter the balance of power in air-to-air combat over Europe, the Germans also feared the P-47. They feared it for what it represented. Scarcely had the Americans started operating their four-engine bombers over the heart of the Reich, then they audaciously sent their *fighters* over Germany. The P-47s could not penetrate much farther than Aachen or Emden, but they *were* in German skies.

General Adolf Galland, the Luftwaffe's *general der Jagdflieger*, or inspector general of fighter units, was deeply troubled by this and understood that this was only the beginning. A fighter pilot himself, Galland had commanded Jagdgeschwader 26 in 1940–1941, and had scored nearly one hundred victories flying against the Royal Air Force before being put in charge of the entire fighter force in November 1941. As soon as he became aware of there being American fighters over Germany, he informed his boss, Hermann Göring, as well as Hitler himself.

Göring reacted not merely with disbelief, but with a *refusal to believe!* Albert Speer, who was present at a meeting between Göring and Galland when the topic came up, paints a picture of a conversation that borders on the surreal.

"What's the idea of telling the Führer that American fighters have penetrated into the territory of the Reich?" Göring snarled accusatorially at Galland.

"Herr *Reichsmarschall*," Galland replied calmly, "they will soon be flying even deeper."

"That's nonsense, Galland, what gives you such fantasies?" Göring said emphatically. "That's pure bluff!"

"Those are the facts, Herr *Reichsmarschall*!" Galland explained. "American fighters have been shot down over Aachen. There is no doubt about it!"

"That is simply not true, Galland," Göring insisted. "It's impossible."

"You might go and check it yourself, sir; the downed planes are there at Aachen."

"Come now, Galland, let me tell you something. I'm an experienced fighter pilot myself," Göring said, although that had been a quarter of a century earlier, during World War I. "I know what is possible. But I know what isn't, too. Admit you made a mistake. What must have happened is that they were shot down much farther to the west. I mean, if they were very high when they were shot down they could have glided quite a distance farther before they crashed."

"Glided to the east, sir?" Galland asked impassively. "If my plane were shot up . . ."

Göring seethed. "Now then, Herr Galland. I officially assert that the American fighter planes did not reach Aachen."

"But, sir, they were there!"

"I herewith give you an official order that they weren't there!" Göring said with finality. "Do you understand? The American fighters were not there! Get that! I intend to report that to the Führer. You have my official order!"

"Orders are orders, sir!" Galland smiled wryly.

The delusional Göring still had half a year before he would be compelled to issue an order to the effect that the Mustangs did not exist. For those six months, bombers reaching past Emden or Aachen would do so without their "little friends." It was something they would rather not have had to do, but there were Pointblank targets outside the range of the USAAF fighter escorts that just could not wait. Topping that list, of course, were those of the Pointblank Directive and the campaign against the German aircraft industry.

To date, these attacks had focused on the Focke-Wulf facilities, which were located in northern Germany, closer to the Allied bases, and in places where fighter escort was available for most of the mission.

Not yet struck by precision attacks, however, were the large Messerschmitt facilities building the Bf 109. Two Messerschmitt complexes, located at Regensburg in Bavaria and Wiener Neustadt, near Vienna, were then producing 48 percent of the Luftwaffe's single-engine fighters. However, Regensburg was deeper inside Germany than the Eighth Air Force had yet flown, while Wiener Neustadt was an equally grueling hike for bombers based in the Mediterranean. Messerschmitt's headquarters factory at Augsburg in Bavaria was even farther from either England or the Mediterranean, and would not be on a list for USAAF missions until the end of the year.

The ink on the Combined Bomber Offensive Plan had been dry for about a month when the Eighth Air Force prepared to mount its first attack on the German anti-friction bearing industry. To the men on the COA staff who had studied this industry in the abstract, it was a very straightforward target, because the vast majority of Germany's ball bearing factories, or *kugellager*, were located in or near a single city, Schweinfurt. The two largest of the anti-friction bearing factory complexes in the area were those belonging to the firms of Kugelfischer and Vereinigte Kugellagerfabriken (VKF), a subsidiary of the Swedish Svenska Kullagerfabriken (SKF) company.

However straightforward the ball bearing industry as a bottleneck industry may have appeared on paper, it was far from an easy target. Like Regensburg, Schweinfurt was located in Bavaria, more than four hundred miles from Eighth Air Force bases in Britain. This put both cities at the limits of the effective range of bomb-laden American aircraft, and substantially beyond the range of fighter escorts. It was like a tempting piece of fruit hanging on a limb beyond a precipice, just out of reach, easily seen, but untouchable without considerable peril. Regensburg and Schweinfurt presented a level of danger beyond what had yet been experienced by the Eighth.

Yet, with every passing day, more and more ball bearings flowed forth from Schweinfurt to Regensburg and to factories across the Reich, just as Regensburg was churning out increasing numbers of the single-engine fighters to challenge the bombers. As with the rivers of bearings, the fighter threat could not be allowed to grow and grow.

By the beginning of August 1943, the men of the COA had rolled down their sleeves and gone home, but at 40 Berkeley Square, the hard decision making for the EOU was in full swing.

"Almost in despair," Dick Hughes recalls painfully, "General Anderson and I decided to 'go for broke,' and attempt to destroy the ball bearing factories at Schweinfurt—without regard for casualties. It was one of those horrible decisions. On the information available to us at the time, it appeared that we were damned if we did, and that we were doubly damned if we did not."

TEN

GOING DEEP AT GREAT COST

Four clusters of pins appeared on the target map. August 1943 was shaping up to be a big month for USAAF strategic operations. In terms of coordinated planning, it was an important precursor to Big Week. The pins were backed by a plan to organize missions to all four of these target clusters as part of a rapid series of maximum effort attacks under the mantle of Operation Pointblank.

What distinguished these clusters of pins from earlier clusters was that they were situated mainly in parts of the map that were closer to the heart of Hitler's Reich, in places where such pins had not previously been placed.

Richard Hughes and the EOU had been busy. As it was conceived, the plan for August was to correlate strikes against the Reich's economy made by the Eighth Air Force from bases in England with missions flown by Ninth Air Force bombers flying from the Mediterranean. While the Eighth would fly south to the clusters of pins ringing Schweinfurt and Regensburg, the Ninth would fly north to Wiener Neustadt, as well as to Ploeşti. It had been fourteen months since the great Romanian refinery complex had been touched by the USAAF.

Of the four missions delineated by the four clusters of pins, one would attack bearings, one would attack petroleum, and two missions would be mounted against Messerschmitt factories.

This stratagem had evolved as Dick Hughes was contemplating maps that stretched across the floor of his office, from East Anglia in the north to Benghazi, Libya, in the south.

"As I casually studied [the maps] I was suddenly struck with a flash of inspiration," he recalls. "Why should not our newly formed 3rd Bombardment Division, now being equipped with long range fuel tanks, attack Regensburg from England, and then, instead of flying back under heavy fighter attack all the way across Germany to England, fly straight from their target over the Alps, cross the Northwest corner of Italy and the Mediterranean Sea and land at airfields in Africa?"

Hughes further theorized a simultaneous attack on Schweinfurt by the other Eighth Air Force air divisions, which would compel the Luftwaffe to split its interceptor resources between the two targets. Having hastily sketched the plan on a map, he took it immediately to General Eaker's office.

"General Eaker was completely disinterested," Hughes recalls. "I sorrowfully returned to my office and filed the map away in my safe."

Four days later, the Eighth Air Force received a message that Secretary of War Henry Stimson would be arriving in London the following day. Unknown to anyone at Berkeley Square, or anyone at the Eighth Air Force headquarters, was that Stimson and Dr. Vannevar Bush, director of the Office of Scientific Research and Development, were visiting London in July 1943 to draft an agreement with Winston Churchill defining the terms for future collaboration on the atomic bomb program. The visit to Eighth Air Force headquarters was secondary to Stimson's unannounced primary mission.

Before he visited, Stimson had let Eaker know that he wanted to discuss a solution to the problem of high casualty rates on the Eighth Air Force missions into Germany. Eaker decided that he should probably show Stimson something dramatic in relation to Operation Pointblank. Remembering Hughes's proposal, Eaker ordered him to prepare a large-map briefing for the secretary of war, and this was done.

When Stimson had departed, Eaker ordered Hughes to drive to VIII Bomber Command and outline the plan to General Fred Anderson. When Hughes arrived, Anderson was conferring with Colonel Curtis LeMay, the commander of the 4th Bombardment Wing (later a component of the 3rd Bombardment Division, which would then be commanded by LeMay).

"I was able to go over [the plan] with both of them simultaneously. Even the usually phlegmatic LeMay caught fire at the idea, and both he and General Anderson immediately grasped its immense possibilities."

Hughes writes that he and LeMay then flew to North Africa in a Flying Fortress to "sell the idea" to General Tooey Spaatz and Air Marshal Arthur Tedder, who were the air commanders in the Mediterranean under Eisenhower. Historian Arthur Ferguson goes a step further, writing in the official history of the USAAF that their mission was actually "to arrange for necessary maintenance and base facilities" for an already "sold" operation.

Hughes reports that Spaatz and Tedder "agreed to cooperate in every possible way." They sent for General Lewis Brereton, who headed the USAAF Middle East Air Forces (MEAF) under Spaatz's command, and "instructed him to make all preparations to attack Wiener Neustadt simultaneously with the Eighth Air Force attack on Regensburg and Schweinfurt."

Brereton expressed concerns about casualties that would result from such a deep penetration mission.

"In front of General Spaatz and Air Marshal Tedder, he asked me how many planes I thought he might lose," Hughes recalls. "I told him that our information on the German fighter defenses in Austria indicated that opposition would be slight, and that in my opinion I did not think that his whole force would lose more than two bombers."

Hughes and LeMay then flew to the fields, notably Telergma Airfield in northeastern Algeria, near the Tunisian border, which Spaatz had promised to put at their disposal to receive the bombers from the Regensburg mission. They informed the base commanders of the mission and asked them to secretly stockpile sufficient fuel to get the strike force back to England.

Flying over the Atlantic on the way back to England, Hughes thought about Brereton's pointed questions and did some soul searching.

"This plan, a risky one, was particularly my own," he reflected. "Over the previous months I had been strictly chair-borne while sending, maybe two or three thousand young men to their deaths. Day by day it had preyed on my mind more, until it seemed absolutely necessary personally to make some expiation."

When he had returned to Britain, Hughes went to see Eaker to request permission to personally accompany the bomber force on the Regensburg attack.

"Eaker turned me down cold, telling me that, informed as I was on all our future operational plans, I was the last person whom he could possibly permit to fly over enemy territory. That ended that."

Hughes then asked Eaker whether the EOU should draw up a plan for targets that could be bombed on the way back to England from North Africa. Eaker told him that he didn't want them to do this. The bombers would just fly out over the Atlantic on the way back.

Hughes suggested that Hap Arnold would probably like to see them bomb *something* on the return, "but General Eaker disagreed."

The Ploeşti mission, designated as Operation Tidal Wave, designed as the first of the package of four deep penetration missions planned for August, was launched on the first day of the month. Generals Eisenhower and Spaatz, as well as Air Chief Marshal Portal, had favored an attack on Wiener Neustadt *before* Tidal Wave, but from Washington, George Marshall and Hap Arnold both insisted that the operation against Ploeşti should come first.

The force included the 98th "Pyramiders" Bombardment Group and the 376th "Liberandos" Group of the Ninth Air Force, as well as three bombardment groups on loan from the Eighth Air Force (the 44th, 93rd, and 389th). A total of 177 Liberators took off from Benghazi, Libya, crossed the Mediterranean, and attacked the source of most of the Third Reich's refined petroleum.

The cost to the USAAF, on what came to be known as "Black Sunday," was staggering. There were 53 aircraft shot down, more than 300 crewmen killed, and more than 100 captured. Among those killed in action was the commander of the 93rd, Lieutenant Colonel Addison Baker, who earned a posthumous Medal of Honor for his heroic leadership in the inferno of Ploeşti.

Worth mentioning is that Major George Scratchley Brown, West Point class of 1941, who took command of the leaderless 93rd Group during the air battle, earned a Distinguished Service Cross for leading it over the target and later went on to serve as chief of staff of the postwar US Air Force and as chairman of the Joint Chiefs of Staff in the 1970s.

It would be nice to say that the price paid at Ploeşti on August 1 was worth the results, but the massive complex of multiple refineries there suffered minimal damage, and this was repaired within weeks.

Black Sunday cast its shadow across the other three clusters of pins on the map and added to the sense of despair at Berkeley Square. Still, those charged with the remaining missions in this maximum effort inside the Reich pressed on, knowing that they were, as Dick Hughes had said, damned if they did, but *doubly damned* if they did *not*.

The idea was for the other three targets to be attacked on August 7, with a week's delay to allow the Tidal Wave crews, tasked with the Wiener Neustadt mission, a chance to rest. However, bad weather that blew in over Britain effectively grounded the Eighth Air Force, and the plan to coordinate the three missions was scrapped.

The Ninth Air Force went ahead with a one-two punch against Wiener Neustadt on August 13 and 14, using Liberators that had survived Tidal Wave, including sixty-one of its own the first day and another sixty-one comprised of those on loan from the Eighth Air Force on the second. The attack reduced the output from the facilities of Wiener-Neustadter Flugzeugwerke AG, a Messerschmitt subcontractor, by about a third, but the factory was far from being put out of business.

In the meantime, the Eighth Air Force was refining its battle plan for its deepest strikes yet into Germany.

On August 16, the crews were briefed for the mission the following day, which was the first anniversary of the first Eighth Air Force heavy bomber mission over continental Europe. The Regensburg strike force, led and commanded by LeMay personally as 4th Bombardment Wing commander, consisted of seven bombardment groups totalling 146 Flying Fortresses. They were to take off at 5:45 A.M., fly 430 miles into *Festung Europa*, bomb their targets, cross the Alps, and continue on to the fields in North Africa.

Heading to Schweinfurt simultaneously would be the 1st Bombardment Wing—formerly commanded by Laurence Kuter and Haywood Hansell, now led and commanded by General Robert B. Williams—which was comprised of a force of 230 Flying Fortresses. They were to take off immediately after LeMay's force, attack targets 320 miles inside Europe, and return to England.

As Hughes recalls, "The weather reports over Germany were satisfactory, but those over England were not so good. General Anderson, however, decided to carry out the attack and things immediately got off to a bad start."

All of East Anglia was blanketed by a thick ground fog, which delayed the takeoff for LeMay's contingent by ninety minutes. Knowing that further delay would put them over Algeria in the dark, LeMay ordered an instrument takeoff, something for which Williams's crews had not trained. Delayed for five hours, Williams did not get his bombers airborne until LeMay was practically to Regensburg.

The delay meant that two elements of the original plan were no longer possible. First, Williams had planned to strike his wing's targets from east to west with the sun at their backs, but when they arrived at nearly 3 P.M., he reversed direction, causing some measure of confusion.

Second, the idea of overwhelming the German interceptor force with two simultaneous attacks had obviously not worked out. The Luftwaffe fighters that attacked LeMay in the morning had the opportunity to land, refuel, and even to eat lunch, before Williams arrived.

On top of this, among the three hundred interceptors that met the Schweinfurt strike force was the Luftwaffe's Jagdgeschwader 11, whose Bf 109G-6 fighters had coincidentally just been armed with Werfer-Granate 21 air-to-air rocket launchers.

"Scarcely did one group of enemy fighters withdraw before another took its place," Arthur Ferguson writes. "The Luftwaffe unleashed every trick and device in its repertoire. . . . In some instances entire squadrons attacked in 'javelin up' formation, which made evasive action on the part of the bombers extremely difficult. In others, three and four enemy aircraft came on abreast, attacking simultaneously. Occasionally the enemy resorted to vertical attacks from above, driving straight down at the bombers with fire concentrated on the general vicinity of the top turret, a tactic which proved effective."

As Thomas Coffey writes in his book *Decision Over Schweinfurt*, so many Flying Fortresses were shot down so quickly that some American airmen thought that their whole wing would be annihilated before anyone reached a target.

The losses at Schweinfurt were not quite *this* severe, but they were sobering to say the least. LeMay's force lost twenty-four aircraft, fifteen of them before they reached the target, while Williams lost thirty-six, twenty-two before reaching the target. The total losses amounted to sixty aircraft and more than five hundred crewmen, the highest number of losses suffered by the Eighth Air Force in a single day thus far. The 100th and 381st Bombardment Groups each lost nine Flying Fortresses, nearly half their complements.

"The very essence of my plan to reduce losses had been nullified to a large extent by those fogged-in fields," Dick Hughes lamented. "Under the circumstances I consider the whole operation should have been postponed, but that decision, of course, was entirely out of my hands, and in fact, up at Eighth Air Force headquarters I did not know until several hours later that everything had not gone as scheduled."

However, the Eighth Air Force could take some solace in knowing that at Regensburg, the six primary aircraft factories were destroyed or seriously damaged.

At Schweinfurt, even accounting for the confusion resulting from the change in direction, the results were good. Thomas Coffey reports that the two largest factory complexes, Kugelfischer and Vereinigte Kugel-lagerfabriken, took eighty direct hits and that 380,000 square feet of factory structures were destroyed.

Albert Speer, the Reich's armaments minister, estimated a 34 percent loss in production, forcing the German war machine to fall back on reserve stocks of anti-friction bearings of all types. Production dropped from 140 tons in July to 69 in August and 50 in September.

Commenting on the Regensburg-Schweinfurt dual mission from a tactical perspective, Speer was disparaging—albeit thankful—that the Eighth Air Force failed to launch a near-term follow-up attack on Schweinfurt, which he'd expected and which would have been devastating to German bearing production.

"We barely escaped a further catastrophic blow on August 17," the armaments minister recalls in his memoirs. "The American air force launched its first strategic raid. It was directed against Schweinfurt where large factories of the ball bearing industry were concentrated. Ball bearings had in any case already become a bottleneck in our efforts to increase armaments production. But in this very first attack the other side committed a crucial mistake. Instead of concentrating on the ball bearing plants, the sizable force of 376 Flying Fortresses divided up—146 of the planes [by German estimates] successfully attacked an airplane assembly plant in Regensburg, but with only minor consequences. Meanwhile, the British air force continued its indiscriminate attacks upon our cities. After this attack the production of ball bearings dropped by 38 percent. . . . We were forced back on the ball bearing stocks stored by the armed forces for use as repair parts. We soon consumed these, as well as whatever had been accumulated in the factories for current production."

Apropos the ongoing debate between the Anglo-American partners over area bombing versus precision targeting, one statistic stands out. Compared to the 42,600 civilians believed to have been killed in the RAF area raid on Hamburg three weeks earlier, 203 civilians were killed in the precision attacks on Schweinfurt.

As for the aftermath of the Regensburg mission, it turned out that Dick Hughes had been correct when he surmised that General Arnold would like to have LeMay's force bomb *something* on their way back to England, and he had sent word to Eaker to that effect. Eaker then called Hughes in and sheepishly ordered him to pick out a target and fly down to Telergma with maps and briefing materials.

"I chose the easiest target in France which I could possibly select—and yet have some semblance of a military target," Hughes recalls, realizing that this was a last-minute addition to the program and bombs had not been stockpiled in Algeria for a major effort. "It was the Fw 200 airfield outside Bordeaux [from which these aircraft attacked convoys in the Atlantic]. This meant that the force could fly over the Mediterranean Sea, cut across the narrow neck of southwest France just east of the Pyrenees, bomb the airfield, and then fly sufficiently far out over the Bay of Biscay to be safe from German fighter interference all the way back to England. In their 12-hour flight they would be exposed to the possibility of fighter attack for about one hour, and information showed that there were few German fighters based in the Bordeaux area."

As Hughes collected his maps for the trip south, he asked Eaker for permission to fly with the strike force. This time, the Eighth Air Force commander acquiesced.

When Hughes reached Telergma with news of the Bordeaux mission, LeMay told him to wait at Spaatz's headquarters in Tunis until the weather over the target was suitable. Informed of Arnold's desire for the Eighth Air Force to undertake more "shuttle" missions like the present one, LeMay, who was standing at Telergma watching fuel being hand-pumped into his bombers, disagreed.

In an August 29 memo to Fred Anderson, which was passed up the chain of command, LeMay would explain that it was "difficult to operate heavy bombers without their ground crews, especially if maintenance and base facilities were insufficient, as in Africa, where the changing nature of operations demanded that the supplies and equipment be constantly moved. Moreover, landing away from their bases put an additional strain on combat crews and affected their efficiency adversely."

Nevertheless, the mission was on. It had been ordered by Hap Arnold.

On August 24, the weather cleared and the bombers took off for Bordeaux. The contingent was comprised of 84 Flying Fortresses, which had survived the aerial battle over Regensburg. Others that had been damaged would linger behind for repairs, which were slow to come. In England, the Eighth Air Force had access to an increasingly sophisticated depot network. In Africa, things were still quite spartan.

"The runways were just dry packed dirt and the dust kicked up by the takeoff ascended to something like 2,000 feet," Hughes explains. "As we circled, waiting for the remaining bombers to take off and fit themselves into their respective formations, it was quite impossible to see the field at all under the dust cloud. Plane after plane popped out of the dust and by some miracle all took off safely."

The force crossed the Mediterranean, and headed into Bordeaux at twenty-three thousand feet, with the Pyrenees under their left wings. They passed through minimal anti-aircraft fire, but noticed the contrails of German fighters high above. These attacked the rear of the formation, claiming four of the Flying Fortresses. The "easiest target in France" turned out not to be so easy for those four crews.

As they passed over the Bay of Biscay, LeMay ordered the bombers down to five hundred feet so that they could fly under the German radar and avoid a second fighter interception.

They returned to England late, so LeMay invited Hughes to spend the night at his headquarters at Camp Blainey. "Both of us were still considerably hopped up from oxygen [used at high altitude for most of the day] and found difficulty sleeping," Hughes writes. "Suddenly this grim, taciturn character began to talk, and I don't think he stopped talking for two or three hours. All the pent up feelings from his terrible raid on Regensburg, and from all the tough missions that he had invariably led, came spilling out of him in a gush. I doubt whether any person in the world, except perhaps his wife, ever heard the great Lieutenant General LeMay, presently [circa 1950s] commander of the Strategic Air Command, express himself so freely."

It was not until September that the Eighth Air Force undertook another maximum effort against Germany on the scale of the August 17 missions. On September 6, there were 407 bombers launched, the largest number to date, though, as on August 17, it was a split force, with 69 Liberators flying a diversionary sweep over the North Sea, while the main force flew south to bomb Stuttgart, home to Daimler-Benz, manufacturer of everything from military vehicles to the DB601 aircraft engines used in Messerschmitt Bf 109s. When they found the city obscured by cloud cover, the formations broke up and 262 bombers attacked "targets of opportunity."

Once again, as on August 17, and indeed on every mission flown thus far by the Eighth Air Force inside Germany, Luftwaffe interceptors took a terrible toll. A total of 45 bombers were shot down, for a loss rate of 17 percent of those that dropped bombs.

Losses such as these, on top of the losses suffered on August 17, took a severe toll on Eighth Air Force effectiveness—not to mention the toll on morale.

The nemesis of the bombers this day was II Gruppe of the Luftwaffe's veteran Jagdgeschwader 27, which had redeployed from the Mediterranean in August for *Reichsverteidigung* operations, and which was based at Wiesbaden's Erbenheim Airfield. Four of the bombers were claimed by Werner Schroer, II Gruppe's leader, an ace who increased his total of aerial victories to 88 on September 6, and who would eventually shoot down 26 four-engine bombers.

It was days like this that underscored the fact that bomber crews over Germany were more likely to be killed in action than front-line marines in the terrible fighting in the Pacific.

In the aftermath of the September 6 mission, the Eighth Air Force initiated what amounted to a three-week intermission in Operation Point-blank, and a diversion of resources to two other activities, both over northern France—within the range of fighter escort. Of the two, Operation Starkey was part of the long-term Combined Bomber Offensive Plan, while Operation Crossbow was undertaken as an emergency measure.

Operation Starkey involved a series of attacks on the road and rail transportation network across northern France. These missions had several purposes. First, they were seen as a rehearsal for the types of operations that the Eighth Air Force would be called upon to conduct immediately ahead of Operation Overlord, the cross-channel invasion of northern France. Though this was not planned to take place until May 1944, a secondary purpose of Operation Starkey was to give the Germans the suggestion that it might take place sooner.

If the enemy were to be lured into believing this, they would divert resources to northern France from elsewhere. In turn, such a diversion of ground assets would please the Soviets, who were fighting a ground war against the Germans. Meanwhile, a diversion of Luftwaffe assets from the air defense of Germany would reduce the number of fighters that they could throw against Eighth Air Force bombers flying Pointblank missions.

Beginning in August, and continuing into September, VIII Bomber Command heavy bombers, as well as VIII Air Support Command medium bombers, conducted extensive Starkey operations against transportation and port facilities, as well as industrial targets and Luftwaffe bases. As Arthur Ferguson writes, "No pains were spared to stage a heavy air attack and to create the illusion of an impending major amphibious assault."

Operation Crossbow was put together as a response to an entirely unanticipated threat. Allied photoreconnaissance aircraft had discovered that the Germans were constructing fixed launch facilities for V-1 cruise missiles and V-2 ballistic missiles in northern France. Knowing that these weapons would be used against England, Crossbow was organized to take out the launch facilities. The first of several Crossbow missions was flown by 187 B-17s against a site at Watten on August 27. Because Allied knowledge of the "V Weapons" was still classified, the target was officially referred to as an "aeronautical facilities station."

Attacking the sites proved ineffective because, like the U-boat pens, the V-1 sites were protected by thick reinforced concrete. Most V-2s, meanwhile, were launched from hard-to-locate mobile launchers. As it was, for reasons unrelated to Crossbow raids, the Germans would not start launching V-1s against England for another ten months, and the first operational V-2 launch was still more than a year away.

Operations against Germany resumed on September 27 and October 2 with two major efforts involving 246 and 339 heavy bombers respectively. These were not deep penetration missions like those of August. The target was the port city of Emden, the closest German target to the Eighth Air Force bases in England, and well within the range of escort fighters.

The missions did mark the first operational use by the Eighth of the H2S airborne ground-scanning radar that had been developed in Britain for use by the RAF in night missions. The H2S provided a crude—by today's standards—image of cities and urban areas on a radarscope, thereby allowing a bombardier to conduct his bomb drop as though he could actually see his target. First used operationally by the RAF in January 1943, the H2S system was installed in one or two pathfinder aircraft that flew ahead of each bomber formation.

Meanwhile, the H2S concept was seen as a possible solution to the single most limiting factor in Eighth Air Force daylight bombardment operations—the weather. When a target was obscured by clouds, which seemed to have been the case more often than not, precision bombing was impossible, so bombers had to forgo an attack on their primary target to search for targets of opportunity. Though the RAF was acquiring H2S equipment as fast as it could be manufactured, the Eighth Air Force managed to get its hands on a small number of sets and began installing them in its bombers. Flying Fortresses thus equipped formed the nucleus of the 482nd Bombardment Group at Alconbury, which was specifically designated as a Pathfinder group.

In the meantime, because supplies of the H2S sets were so limited, the USAAF decided to seek development of a homegrown H2S analog. It so happened that the Massachusetts Institute of Technology Radiation Laboratory, known as the "Rad Lab," had been doing substantial research on the same technology. They were able to develop an improved variation on the H2S, which they called H2X, and which the USAAF later designated as AN/APS-15. The H2X used a shorter frequency than the H2S, and therefore provided imagery with higher resolution.

By the third week of September 1943, the Rad Lab had installed a dozen H2X sets in a dozen Flying Fortresses, and the aircraft were on their way to England. Here, they joined the H2S-equipped bombers in the 482nd Bombardment Group. General Eaker was already making plans for a squadron of bombers equipped with the H2S, and two with the H2X system.

Aside from an experimental flight of a single H2S-equipped bomber in August, the September 27 mission marked the first use of Pathfinders at part of a bomber formation. Emden was picked in part because it was a port city, and the ground-scanning radar displayed especially high contrast between land and sea.

More than 300 Flying Fortresses from the 1st and 2nd Bombardment Divisions took part in the raid, with a pair of Pathfinders assigned to lead each division. It was customary for bombardiers in the formations to follow the example of the lead bombardier, and such was the case here, except that in this case, the lead bombardier "saw" his target only on a radarscope.

On October 2, the VIII Bomber Command launched another mission to Emden, this time with 339 bombers led to the targets by Pathfinders.

"Although by no means completely successful, these two initial attempts at radar bombing gave room for restrained optimism regarding the new techniques," Arthur Ferguson writes, summarizing the ORS report on the Emden "blind bombing" missions. "Three of the four combat wings that bombed on an H2S plane achieved the reasonably small average circular error of from one-half to one mile. Difficulty in the fourth sighting resulted in an abnormal error of two to three miles. Results were less encouraging for the combat wing that attempted to bomb on flares dropped by the Pathfinder planes. Confusion [at the beginning of the bomb run] during the first mission and a high wind during the second, which blew the smoke of the markers rapidly from the target area, help to account for an average error of more than five miles. One of the leading combat wings did considerable damage. . . . More encouraging than the bombing was the fact that the enemy fighters, since they had to intercept through the overcast, fought at a distinct disadvantage. Overcast bombing was obviously a safer type of bombing than visual."

Promising results had been achieved by formations that were led directly by a Pathfinder, but it was determined that the smaller the number of bombers led by a Pathfinder, the more condensed and more accurate the bombing pattern would be.

There was also a good deal of optimism with regard to improving technology in aircraft armament. By the autumn of 1943, the Eighth Air Force was beginning to receive new-model Liberators and Flying Fortresses equipped with the long-awaited powered nose turrets, each armed with a pair of .50-caliber machine guns, to counter the nagging and serious threat of head-on attacks by Luftwaffe interceptors.

An improvement over the first generation B-24C and B-24D Liberators, which had been in USAAF service around the world in 1942 and early 1943, the second generation, which started arriving in the field by the autumn of 1942, all had powered nose turrets. Most of the Liberator nose turrets themselves were based on the design of the tail turrets, which had been developed for the Liberator by Emerson Electric.

There were three major second generation Liberator variants, which were similar to the point of being hard to distinguish visually. These included the B-24G, built by North American Aviation in Dallas; the B-24H, built by Ford at Willow Run, Consolidated, in Fort Worth or by Douglas in Tulsa, using Ford subassemblies; and the B-24J, initially built only by Consolidated in Fort Worth and San Diego, but later by the other manufacturers. Of a total of more than 18,000 Liberators, 6,678 were of the B-24J variant.

The new B-17G Flying Fortress, meanwhile, retained the same Plexiglas nose as the previous B-17 variants, but had a powered Bendix "chin" turret located beneath the nose. The nose of the B-17G also retained the "cheek" guns that had been introduced on the sides of the nose in late-production B-17Fs. Aside from the chin turret, the B-17F and B-17G were largely similar, including improved Pratt & Whitney R1820-97 engines, and had the same Boeing model number (299P). Seventy percent of all Flying Fortresses were of the B-17G variant, of which 2,250 were built by Lockheed Vega, 2,395 by Douglas, and 4,035 by Boeing.

The B-17Gs began arriving in England for Eighth Air Force assignments in August and September, 1943, with the second generation Liberators coming on line over the next few months. Many of these newer Liberator variants would also go to the Fifteenth Air Force, formed in the Mediterranean Theater in November.

With the promise of such a technological marvel as blind bombing now a reality, and with more and better aircraft flooding into the bases in East Anglia, those who had theorized and prophesied the validation of the daylight strategic doctrine were optimistic. Against a technologically static foe, all of this would have added up to a decisive turning point.

However, the Germany of 1943 was not a technologically static foe. Though they had been slow to exploit radar technology, they now had an increasingly effective radar early warning system to track incoming Eighth Air Force and RAF bombers. The Luftwaffe had also gotten its hands on a British H2S set, taken from a downed bomber, and they were learning how to direct interceptors to attack Pathfinders by homing in on their radar.

Meanwhile, just as the bombers were increasingly better armed, the Luftwaffe was matching the Allies move for move with other weapons and tactics of their own.

If the enlarging and improving Eighth Air Force was cause for optimism in the fall of 1943, that feeling was tempered by the knowledge that the Luftwaffe still controlled German airspace, and nose turrets alone would not change that. The German interceptor pilots would remain the masters of the skies in the heart of the Reich until there were American fighter pilots to challenge them in those skies. Until the P-51 Mustang arrived, no American fighter pilots could go there.

ELEVEN

BLACK WEEK

On August 1, the Luftwaffe had painted Black Sunday black, and they had painted August 17 with paint from the same bucket.

No matter how the Eighth Air Force went about its business and structured its missions, there would continue to be days like this so long as the bombers went deep into the Reich without fighter escort. Ira Eaker knew this. Fred Anderson knew this. Dick Hughes knew this, and it was why he continually tormented over "sending young men to their deaths."

However, to suspend the Combined Bomber Offensive, or to limit Eighth Air Force participation to easier targets in France, would have been no option. Operation Overlord was coming, and work needed to be done before D-Day arrived. If the Combined Bomber Offensive and Operation Pointblank were unsuccessful, or if those who planned them threw in the towel, then tens of thousands of young lives could be lost in the cross-channel invasion. If Overlord failed, all those lives would have been lost in vain. With weather and sea conditions what they were in the English Channel, and with the time needed to regroup from a failed Overlord, it would be 1945 before it could be tried again.

There was nothing to do but press on.

There would continue to be days like Black Sunday on the road to Big

Week and Overlord. Beginning on October 8, there would be a whole *week* like Black Sunday. The week that came to be called "Black Week" was, on the planning papers, a miniature prototype of what was to come in Big Week. In other words, it was planned as a sustained series of maximum efforts.

It had not been long since a three-hundred-plane raid was an isolated milestone, but this week was planned to be a series of back-to-back missions comprised of numbers in excess of three hundred. Normally, the force would be compelled to stand down after such a mission. By October, the Eighth Air Force had enough resources to keep going—despite the losses. The latter phrase contained the darkest implications of the week.

On Friday, October 8, a record number of heavy bombers, one shy of four hundred, went out from East Anglia. The targets were familiar, the Focke-Wulf plant and the shipyards in Bremen, and the Bremer Vulkan shipyard, which built U-boats in Bremen's northern suburb of Vegesack. Of the planes that took off, 357 made it through to bomb their targets.

The Luftwaffe and the flak batteries on the ground had seen them coming, though not as well as they might have. Just as the Yanks had borrowed H2S radar bombing technology from the Brits, so too had they borrowed technology for *confusing* radar. The British called it "Window," and today we call it "Chaff." In 1943, the Eighth Air Force, who first used it on October 8, called it "Carpet."

The concept was as brilliant as it was simple. Just as metal foil reflects light, so too it reflects radar, creating false echoes. The RAF had been studying the concept since 1937 but did not use it operationally until the summer of 1943, out of fear that the Germans would start using it against England. By that time, British air defense radar had improved toward a point where the value of using Window outweighed the potential negatives.

Window, which consisted of metallic coated sheets of paper, was successful in fooling the Luftwaffe at night, because the night fighters depended on their radar to find the bombers. The Eighth Air Force, whose Carpet consisted of narrow strips of aluminum foil, would not foil the German interceptors when they could *see* the bombers visually, but it was harder for the flak batteries to target them.

Nevertheless, the flak batteries over major targets, such as Bremen, were now so many and so concentrated that they could fill the entire sky with the dirty black layer of bursting 88mm shells, coincidentally described by bomber crews as a "carpet" so thick that you could walk on it.

The flak took a heavy toll on October 8, even though two bombardment groups of the 3rd Bombardment Division, who led the attack that day, were using Carpet. There were thirty bombers shot down that day, and twenty-six of those that limped back to England were heavily damaged, and many of these had to be written off. The two numbers together accounted for 16 percent of the number of bombers that got through to the target. Even if new aircraft were flooding into the East Anglia bases from the Arsenal of Democracy back home, planners and commanders from Eaker to Anderson to Hughes wondered how long such losses could be sustained.

Flak took its share of young American lives, but so too did the Luftwaffe, although the young American gunners also exacted a price from the defenders of the Reich. They claimed that they got 167 German fighters, which was good for sagging morale, even though everyone knew the numbers were exaggerated by multiple reports of the same kills. Postwar reviews of the Luftwaffe's own records reveal losses of 33 fighters destroyed and 15 damaged through "enemy action" on October 8. This is still a testament to good shooting by the young Americans who were tracking airplanes flying as fast as 200 mph through crowded skies, and who were able to sight on their targets for a few seconds at best.

The next day, it was a maximum effort to the maximum distance yet flown by the Eighth Air Force to a target. On Saturday—despite Friday's losses—378 bombers took off and headed east, some of them flying as far as 780 straight-line, one-way miles, compared to a mere 570 in the Regensburg missions. The targets were divided between Pointblank operations against the German aircraft industry and the continuing war on U-boat yards.

Having flown over the North Sea, and the narrow neck of Denmark, the strike force divided into three parts over the Baltic Sea. The first to attack were 106 bombers that struck an Arado Flugzeugwerke factory at Anklam on the Baltic coast, which manufactured subassemblies for Focke-Wulf Fw 190s.

The remaining force continued eastward for yet another two hundred miles. Of these, 96 bombers flew to Marienburg in East Prussia (now Malbork in Poland). It was here, nearly eight hundred miles from England, that Focke-Wulf had established an assembly plant under the assumption that it was reasonably safe from the Allied Combined Bomber Offensive.

At the same time, another 150 bombers targeted what was probably the largest port and shipbuilding complex east of Hamburg. Like the plane makers in Marienburg, the shipbuilders of Danzig imagined themselves, being nearly eight hundred miles from England, to be safer than their brethren in Hamburg or Bremen.

In 1980, the shipyards of Danzig—Gdansk in Polish—would be the birthplace of the Solidarity movement that accelerated the end of Polish Communist rule, but in 1943, the shipyards were part of the German Reich and building U-boats for the German Kreigsmarine. On October 9, the shipyards of Danzig, as well as those at Gdingen (Gdynia), a dozen miles to the north, were the targets of the Eighth Air Force.

Given the distance, there was certainly no chance of an VIII Fighter Command escort all the way to any of Saturday's targets, but the distance also stymied the defenders, who had not seen USAAF bombers over their cities before. The force striking Anklam lost eighteen bombers, but the defenders farther east were taken by surprise. Compared to 17 percent losses over Anklam, where the Bf 109 and Fw 190 interceptors attacked with air-to-air rockets, the Danzig and Marienburg attackers suffered only a 4 percent loss.

The Luftwaffe scrambled everything they had, which was less than they would have had farther west, and found it costly. By their own records, the Germans lost fourteen fighters destroyed and nine damaged.

Except for the 2nd Bombardment Division, whose work at Danzig and Gdingen was judged as poor, the mission results were extraordinary. Given the anticipated element of surprise, the bombers went in at ten thousand to fourteen thousand feet, relatively lower altitudes than would have been used at more heavily defended targets, and this improved their precision considerably. Nearly every building at the Anklam factory complex was hit, and heavy damage was rendered by other units at Danzig and Gdingen.

"It was at Marienburg that the most brilliant bombing was done," Arthur Ferguson writes. "There, the Focke-Wulf plant was almost completely destroyed by high-explosive and incendiary bombs dropped with unprecedented accuracy."

As Dick Hughes and others studied subsequent photoreconnaissance imagery, they could see that 286 of the 598 five-hundred-pound general purpose bombs that had been dropped at Marienburg had landed within the factory complex, and that 35 had achieved direct hits on buildings. As late as July, the bombers were putting 12.7 percent of their ordnance within one thousand feet of the aiming point, and 36.7 percent within two thousand feet. In October the accuracy numbers had increased to 27.2 percent and 53.8 percent, respectively.

In a letter to Robert A. Lovett, Henry Stimson's assistant secretary of war for air (and future secretary of defense), Eaker called Marienburg and Anklam "the classic example of precision bombing."

In his own analysis of Eighth Air Force operations, Arthur Ferguson credits experience and enhanced training for the improvements. He also mentions changes in tactics. Citing Eighth Air Force monthly reports, he notes that the earlier practice of having formations follow lead formations over the target resulted in the accuracy of the following formations falling off very rapidly. He notes that when this was changed, the results for the third and fourth formations improved by 58 and 105 percent, while "formations in positions still farther back showed improvement amounting to as much as 178 percent. This improvement, which more than anything else raised the average of accuracy, resulted from separating the bombing formations with great care, especially as they approached the target."

Of course for the October 9 missions, not having the sky clogged with the Luftwaffe probably improved accuracy immeasurably.

As it was, that day was the only day during the week on which one might find anything but a black lining in the clouds.

The next day, the "maximum effort" mustered fewer bombers, of which 236 reached their target, which was the great complex of rail and highway interchanges in and around the city of Münster. In stark contrast with Danzig and Marienburg, Münster was in the heart of the Ruhr industrial region, one of the most heavily defended targets in *Festung Europa*.

Indeed, the fighters were out in force. As was often the case over the Ruhr, the Luftwaffe matched an Eighth Air Force maximum effort with a maximum effort of their own. There were fast, single-engine Bf 109s and Fw 190s, as well as larger, twin-engine aircraft, such as Bf 110 and Me

210 night fighters and Ju 88 light bombers, which were now doubling as rocket-launching night fighters. There were even Dornier Do 217 bombers lobbing rockets into the bomber formation from just outside the range of the Eighth Air Force gunners.

While the gunners would claim 183 German aircraft shot down, the Luftwaffe's own loss records put the number at a more plausible 22 destroyed and 5 damaged.

The bomber stream first met the Luftwaffe at their IP (initial point), the start of the bomb run, and were followed by them as they entered the target area and as they withdrew and headed for home. As Arthur Ferguson writes in the official history, the fighters "flew parallel to the bombers, out of range, in groups of twenty to forty, stacked in echelon down. They then peeled off, singly or in pairs, in quick succession to attack the lowest elements of the formation."

The 100th Bombardment Group, flying in the lead position that day, was the first to feel Luftwaffe wrath. The Germans knew that the Eighth Air Force had traditionally organized missions so that subsequent groups "bombed on" the lead group, so it was customary for the Luftwaffe interceptors to hit the lead group hard to knock them off course. The 100th, which had also flown in the Saturday and Sunday missions, launched 18 Flying Fortresses of their own on Monday from their base at Thorpe Abbots, as well as two that were "borrowed" from the 390th Bombardment Group to round out the complement to 20 bombers. Of these, six aborted over the North Sea for mechanical reasons, so there was an unlucky 13 that reached the initial point.

There began seven minutes of hell. The lead bomber was hit and was engulfed in burning aviation fuel as he began to fall. Lieutenant Jack Justice, the pilot of *Pasadena Nena*, later recalled in a document preserved on the 100th veterans' website, that "his wing man, according to procedure, should have taken over the lead formation, instead, all five ships in his squadron followed him down, leaving our squadron with three aircraft and the high squadron with three aircraft. The Germans immediately came in at all of us and split the remaining formation all over the sky. We found ourselves completely alone."

Justice joined another formation but was hit by a German fighter attempting to attack the lead in this formation, taking out the number four engine of *Pasadena Nena* and sending it into a fast spin. As the plane fell from twenty thousand to five thousand feet, Justice and copilot John Shields finally managed to bring it under control. Most of the crew promptly abandoned ship, while the two pilots decided to try to fly back to England.

However, another German fighter attacked, and they too decided to bail out. Shields did not make it, but Justice did. Once on the ground, Justice evaded capture and walked to the Netherlands, where he luckily happened upon members of the Dutch resistance. The story of his amazing escape, which took him across France to the Pyrenees, across Spain to Gibraltar, and to Christmas dinner in London, is now on the 100th Bombardment Group veterans' website, 100thbg.com.

Most of the 100th Bombardment Group's crewmen were not so lucky. One aircraft from the group, *Royal Flush*, piloted by Lieutenant Robert "Rosie" Rosenthal, made it back to England limping in on two engines, with two men badly injured. Except for Jack Justice, everyone else who survived crashing over Europe wound up as a prisoner of war. Because of a staggering series of losses going back even before Regensburg on August 17, the group earned the sobriquet "Bloody Hundredth."

The 3rd Bombardment Division, of which the 100th was a component, lost 29 of its 119 aircraft. However, the 1st Bombardment Division, which followed them over Münster that day, lost only 1 of their 117 bombers, because of the Luftwaffe practice of throwing everything at the lead formation or stragglers.

After three consecutive days of maximum efforts, the Eighth Air Force did stand down, but only until Thursday, when the target for the day would be the long anticipated return to the ball bearing factories of Schweinfurt.

Like Dick Hughes and the EOU, Minister of Armaments Speer had long recognized the precarious nature of a bottleneck industry like bearings. As noted earlier, he was both pleased and mystified by the failure of the Allies to return to Schweinfurt soon after the August 17 raid.

"As early as September 20, 1942, I had warned Hitler that the tank production of Friedrichshafen and the ball bearing facilities in Schweinfurt were crucial to our whole effort," Speer recalls. "Hitler thereupon ordered increased antiaircraft protection for these two cities. Actually, as I had early recognized, the war could largely have been decided in 1943 if instead of vast but pointless area bombing the planes had concentrated on the centers of armaments production."

Historians with the benefit of access to German files and the luxury of 20/20 hindsight have often joined Speer in criticizing the Eighth Air Force for having not come back sooner to finish the job at Schweinfurt. Speer goes on to recall that "we anxiously asked ourselves how soon the enemy would realize that he could paralyze the production of thousands of armaments plants merely by destroying five or six relatively small targets."

How soon? The answer was two months.

However, one need look no further than the fate of the Bloody Hundredth on October 10 to understand how difficult it was to fly so deep into the increasingly defended industrial heartland of the Reich. It seemed that with each mile the bombers flew, the perils mounted exponentially. Each mile placed them farther from fighter escort support and exposed them to more opportunities for detection and tracking by German defenses, and for Luftwaffe attack.

For the attack on October 14, the Eighth Air Force planned another maximum effort, intending—and hoping—that the very mass of the attack would serve as its own protection.

The plan for August 17 had called for simultaneous attacks on Regensburg and Schweinfurt, while the October 14 plan called for two bombardment divisions to hit only Schweinfurt, in two coordinated, parallel attacks. While the two contingents in the August mission had reached the target hours apart, every effort was made to ensure that this problem would not recur in October.

On Thursday morning, 351 bombers took off from England. The 1st and 3rd Bombardment Divisions contributed 149 and 142 Flying Fortresses respectively, while the 2nd Bombardment Division launched 60 Liberators. After the Flying Fortresses attacked abreast, the Liberators would circle in from the south to deliver a coup de grâce.

One group of P-47 Thunderbolts was assigned to each division, escorting them as far as possible on the run to the target, landing to refuel, and picking them up on the way back. Longer range Lockheed P-38 Lightnings, assigned to the 55th Fighter Group, were arriving in England around this time, but they were, unfortunately, not yet operationally available. This was only the first of many things that would go wrong that day.

As had been the case on the first Schweinfurt mission, poor weather proved to be the curse of the best laid plans. While the Flying Fortresses managed, with a great deal of difficulty and using radar in the thick cloud cover, to sort themselves into proper formations, the Liberators did not. When twenty-nine of the Liberators finally did form up, it was decided that they were too few for a deep penetration, and they were redirected to what was essentially a diversionary attack on the port of Emden.

The Flying Fortresses headed south, more or less on the same schedule as planned. At least the two divisions were not five hours apart as had happened to the best laid plans of August. As might have been expected, the Luftwaffe attacked just as the P-47 "little friends" turned back over the German city of Aachen. The tactics were familiar. Leaders and stragglers bore the brunt of their fury.

"Like good duck hunters they fired at the leading element," Arthur Ferguson colorfully explains, "knowing that the normal spread of bursts would be likely to give them hits."

As in the Münster mission, the Germans attacked in waves, using every weapon imaginable, including rockets and air-to-air bombing. Rockets, like flak, had often proven useful in breaking up the formations, which led to inaccurate bombing—as well as the creation of stragglers, which were so readily plucked by the Luftwaffe's single-engine fighters. Leading the 1st Bombardment Division, the 40th Combat Wing lost seven of its forty-nine aircraft before even reaching the initial point.

"Most of the tactics used by the German fighters that day had been used before," Ferguson observes. "But never before had the enemy made such full and such expertly coordinated use of these tactics. Indeed so well planned was the counterattack that it gave rise to the suspicion that the German fighter control had received advance warning of the timing and objectives of the mission."

Indeed, General Eaker himself expressed this same idea in a memo to Hap Arnold five days later. If true, the idea was never proven conclusively.

The 1st Bombardment Division approached the target already badly mauled.

"We are approaching the Initial Point, the point at which we commit ourselves directly to the bomb run on the target," observes Colonel Budd Peaslee, who led the 384th Bombardment Group. "Schweinfurt, here we come! As we turn, I take a hasty reading on our formation. I have eight aircraft left and my other group has been reduced to six. Fourteen planes left, and we still have so many miles to go! I call the captain leading the other bombers, and tell him to close in on me and to drop on my command, 'Bombs away.' He does not respond, but his formation moves in near to ours as we start the sighting run. The fighters know what our intentions are and they come at us like tigers. . . . We are right behind the leading formation as the bomb run starts. They are in good order, but one of their groups of 21 bombers has been reduced to two! The unit has been devastated, and it's more than a little pathetic to see those two lonesome guys plugging along as though all were intact."

The 1st Division began releasing bombs over Schweinfurt at 2:39 P.M., and emerged from the hellstorm of flak protecting the target area just six minutes later. There was a break in the cloud cover, and visibility was considered good for precision strikes. Even the battered 40th Wing bombardiers were able to line up their Norden bombsights on their intended targets and to put more than half their bombs within one thousand feet of the aiming point.

Captain James McClanahan, the bombardier aboard the Flying Fortress *Battle Wagon*, commanded by Major George Harris, noted that "the visibility was good over the target. I saw our bombs hit and I can say we knocked hell out of it. The bombs burst and the smoke rolled up, then there was a big explosion and all of a sudden there was a great splash of fire right in the center of everything. We got even with them today."

The 2nd Bombardment Division followed six minutes later, at 2:51 P.M., and emerged at 2:57. A few clouds had drifted over the target, and the bombardiers were also somewhat hampered by the columns of smoke from the earlier attack. From beginning to end, the second Eighth Air Force raid on the *kugellager* of Schweinfurt had lasted eighteen minutes, and the survivors were on their way back to East Anglia by 3 P.M.

It would be a terrible ride home.

The same fighters that had mauled them so mercilessly during the hours coming in were refueled and ready to reprise their actions on the way out. First came the ubiquitous Bf 109s and Fw 190s, and then came the waves of twin-engine defenders who turned to heavy-caliber cannons when their rockets had been expended.

Damaged bombers strayed from their formations, becoming sitting ducks, which became losses.

When the surviving Flying Fortresses finally stumbled into East Anglia at the end of a long day, the numbers of those losses became manifest. The 305th Bombardment Group had taken off from Chelveston that morning with 16 bombers, lost one to an abort, and suffered 12 shot down before reaching Schweinfurt. Only two made it back to Chelveston after the mission. Of the 291 Flying Fortresses that had taken off that morning, 60 had failed to return. Another 17 were damaged so badly that they had to be written off, and 121 suffered serious damage, which could be repaired, although each of those aircraft would be off the active list for some time.

Though 186 German fighters were claimed by the gunners, the actual number was 38 shot down and 20 damaged in combat.

For Adolf Hitler, the terrible mauling suffered by the Americans was a glass half-full. Speer was with him that night at his field headquarters, the Wolfsschanze ("Wolf's Lair"), near Rastenburg in East Prussia, when he received the news.

"The Reich Marshal urgently wishes to speak to you," Hitler's adjutant said, entering the room to report that Hermann Göring was on the phone. "This time he has pleasant news."

As Speer reports, "Hitler came back from the telephone in good spirits. A new daylight raid on Schweinfurt had ended with a great victory for our defenses, he said. The countryside was strewn with downed American bombers."

Not sharing in Hitler's jovial reaction, and admitting to a certain queasiness about potential damage in Schweinfurt, Speer attempted to phone the city.

"All communications were shattered," he writes. "I could not reach any of the factories. Finally, by enlisting the police, I managed to talk to the foreman of a ball bearing factory. All the factories had been hard hit, he informed me. The oil baths for the bearings had caused serious fires in the machinery workshops; the damage was far worse than after the first attack. This time we had lost 67 percent of our ball bearing production. . . . Our reserves had been consumed; efforts to import ball bearings from Sweden and Switzerland had met with only slight success. Nevertheless, we were able to avoid total disaster by substituting slide bearings for ball bearings wherever possible. But what really saved us was the fact that from this time on the enemy to our astonishment once again ceased his attacks on the ball bearing industry."

Indeed, a great deal of damage *had* been done in Schweinfurt that day.

"The entire Works are now inactive," Fred Anderson reported cheerfully after he had seen the post-strike photoreconnaissance imagery. "It may be possible for the Germans eventually to restore 2.5 per cent of normal productive capacity, but even that will require some time. A tremendous amount of clearance, repair work, and rebuilding will be necessary before plants can again be operative. Fires raged throughout three of the plant areas, burning out not only factories, but stores and dispatch buildings as well."

The postwar US Strategic Bombing Survey report, *The German Anti-Friction Bearings Industry*, notes "a high concentration of bombs in all the target areas . . . on and about all three of the big bearing plants. Of the 1,122 high-explosive bombs dropped, 143 fell within the factory area, 88 of which were direct hits on the factory buildings. . . . Strategically it was the most important of the sixteen raids made during the war on the Schweinfurt plants. It caused the most damage and the greatest interference with production, and it led directly to a reorganization of the bearing industry. The raids of 14 October, coming upon the still fresh damage of 17 August, alarmed the German industrial planners to a degree that almost justified the optimistic estimates made by Allied observers in the fall of that year."

Citing German records, and a postwar debriefing of Speer, the Strategic Bombing Survey goes on to say that had the attack been followed promptly by another one, the ball bearing industry would have been seriously crippled. Indeed a November 18 memo from the British Ministry of Home Security stated that the bearing plants at Schweinfurt "are ready for practically immediate reattack."

The "re-attack" would not come "immediately" in October, or November, or indeed, before Big Week.

Indeed, "the re-attack" that Speer both feared and expected was postponed because of the success that *appeared* to have been achieved. In Washington, General Arnold proudly told the media that "now we have got Schweinfurt," but he was only partly right, and trying to spin the good part. In Arnold's defense, his remarks to the media were made against the backdrop of great apprehension on the home front about the casualties that were being endured by the Eighth Air Force—especially over Schweinfurt.

In a memo to Secretary of War Stimson, which exaggerated even the reconnaissance evidence, Arnold wrote, "All five of the works at Schweinfurt were either completely or almost completely wiped out. Our attack was the most perfect example in history of accurate distribution of bombs over a target. It was an attack that will not have to be repeated for a very long time, if at all."

His concluding sentence, which bought valuable time for Albert Speer, could not have been further from the truth.

As Speer himself recalls in his memoirs, "In June 1946 the General Staff of the Royal Air Force asked me what would have been the results of concerted attacks on the ball bearing industry. I replied: Armaments production would have been crucially weakened after two months and after four months would have been brought completely to a standstill.

"This, to be sure, would have meant: One: All our ball bearing factories (in Schweinfurt, Steyr, Erkner, Cannstatt, and in France and Italy) had been attacked simultaneously. Two: These attacks had been repeated three or four times, every two weeks, no matter what the pictures of the target area showed. Three: Any attempt at rebuilding these factories had been thwarted by further attacks, spaced at two-month intervals."

Ironically, the damage that Fred Anderson, Hap Arnold, and others observed, celebrated, and *misinterpreted* resulted in the industry being "reorganized"—i.e., dispersed away from Schweinfurt. This made it much less efficient but spared it from total annihilation.

"In the two months following the first attack [in August] on Schweinfurt nothing had been done," Speer writes of the decentralization effort.

"There was resistance on all sides, The Gauleiters did not want new factories in their districts for fear that the almost peacetime quiet of their small towns would be disturbed."

Speer goes on to say that after the second heavy raid on October 14, "we again decided to decentralize. Some of the facilities were to be distributed among the surrounding villages, others placed in small and as yet unendangered towns in eastern Germany."

The official armaments ministry office journal entry for October 18 reveals that "the minister [Speer] forcefully expressed his dissatisfaction with the measures previously taken, asserting that the urgency of the matter required all other considerations to be put aside. Deeply impressed by the damage and by the minister's account of the potential consequences for the armaments industry, everyone readily offered all assistance, even the neighboring Gauleiters who would have to accept the unwelcome intrusions into their domains that would accompany the transfer of operations from Schweinfurt to their territories."

In the Schweinfurt aftermath, the results of the attack were of less concern to the Eighth Air Force than the losses it had suffered. It has been written in numerous accounts that if the Eighth Air Force had continued to sustain losses on this level, it would have soon been out of business.

October 14 was dubbed "Black Thursday," with good cause. Including those Flying Fortresses shot down or written off, the Eighth Air Force had suffered a staggering loss rate of 26 percent, or 28 percent of those that reached the target. Meanwhile, nearly six hundred airmen were killed, and more than fifty who bailed out became prisoners of war. Schweinfurt marked the most severe losses suffered by the Eighth Air Force to date.

As Ferguson writes of Black Week, "The Eighth Air Force was in no position to make further penetrations either to Schweinfurt or to any other objectives deep in German territory. The Schweinfurt mission, bad enough in itself, had climaxed a week of costly air battles. Within the space of six days the Eighth lost 148 bombers and crews, mostly as a result of air action, in the course of four attempts to break through German fighter defenses unescorted."

Walt Rostow, who worked on the plan that Hughes had presented to the secretary of war in July, credits Fred Anderson with great heroism in pursuing the Pointblank objectives against steep odds and criticism from higher quarters. He celebrates Anderson for taking "the bold initiative of attacking aircraft production, then concentrated in central Germany, before long-range fighters were available to protect the bombers."

Martin Caidin, in his book about that day, writes that "the battle fought on Black Thursday stands high in the history of American fighting men. It will be long remembered, like the immortal struggles of Gettysburg, St. Mihiel and the Argonne, of Midway and the Bulge and Pork Chop Hill. Tens of thousands of our airmen fought in desperate battles in the sky during World War II. From China to the Aleutians, from Australia through the Philippines and across the Southwest Pacific, through the Central Pacific, in Africa and the Mediterranean, and across the length and breadth of Europe, American fliers engaged in combat with the Germans, the Japanese, the Italians. In all these battles one stands out among all the others for unprecedented fury, for losses suffered, for courage. This was the battle on Black Thursday. . . . It is an aerial struggle remembered with great pride, for it demanded the utmost in courage, in skill, in carrying on the fight in the face of bloody slaughter."

Because of how deeply this bloody slaughter cut into the total bomber fleet—not to mention the morale of surviving crewmen—the Eighth Air Force deliberately opted against any further deep penetration raids for the time being. By the time that the force was built up through newly arrived equipment and personnel, it was December, and winter weather hindered operations. Without adequate fighter escort, the Eighth was essentially finished when it came to missions such as Schweinfurt.

"The severe casualties suffered in these successive raids into Germany, without fighter escort, convinced us all that such losses could no longer be sustained or the Eighth would cease to exist as a fighting force," Dick Hughes laments explicitly. "Operations beyond fighter cover were sharply curtailed, and every effort was made to have long range P-51s and P-47s sent to us as soon as possible. It had been a most gallant effort, but many, too many, had paid with their lives in disproving the Air Corps pre-war theory that the Flying Fortress could defend itself, unaided, against enemy fighters."

TWELVE

GRASPING FOR A TURNING POINT

By the time of Black Thursday, four months had passed since the Pointblank Directive, and lamentably little had been done to impede the Luftwaffe, or to damage German single-engine aircraft production—*and* the Luftwaffe still maintained air superiority over Europe.

On August 17, ironically the same day as the first costly raid on Schweinfurt, the Combined Chiefs of Staff had sat down in Quebec for the Quadrant Conference, the fourth high-level wartime meeting involving Winston Churchill and Franklin Roosevelt. During that meeting, complaints and concerns had been aired about the slow pace of the Combined Bomber Offensive, and of addressing the Pointblank objectives. Two months, a Black Thursday, and numerous other costly missions later, the same concerns continued to be met with the same optimistic prognostications from the Eighth Air Force—and the same perceived lack of results.

On October 14, ironically the same day as the *second* Schweinfurt debacle, Hap Arnold had sent a wire to Ira Eaker, asserting that it was the opinion of analysts in *his* office that the Luftwaffe was on the threshold of collapse. The following day, Eaker wrote back, agreeing with his boss and telling him that "there is not the slightest question but that we now have our teeth in the Hun Air Force's neck," and that the actions of a robust Luftwaffe over Schweinfurt had actually been "the last final struggle of a monster in his death throes."

Upon reflection, and upon examination of the damage done to his Eighth Air Force on Black Thursday, Eaker wrote again to Arnold on October 21, telling him that there was, in fact, *no* reason for such optimism. The monster was *not* in his death throes. Not even close.

Having bubbled positively in his initial comments to the media, Arnold also did some rethinking. In his memoirs, he candidly writes of Black Thursday that "no such savage air battles had been seen since the war began. Our losses were rising to an all-time high, but so were those of the Luftwaffe, and our bombers were not being turned back from their targets. Could we keep it up? The London papers asked the question editorially. To this day, I don't know for certain if we could have. No one does. We had the planes and replacement crews by then to maintain the loss-rate of 25 percent which I had originally determined must be faced; but obviously there were other factors. To obscure the argument forever, in mid-October the weather shut down foggily on southeast Germany for most of the remainder of the year."

For nearly a year, certainly ever since the Casablanca Conference, air superiority over the continent had been a presumptive precursor to the cross-channel invasion. However, during that year, the Luftwaffe, far from being degraded, had actually grown *stronger*.

In the summer, Allied analysts had correctly ascertained that the Luftwaffe fighter strength for Defense of the Reich operations was more than five hundred, and by October, it exceeded seven hundred. These numbers were partly attributable to increasing production, but also to redeployment from the Eastern and Mediterranean fronts. During the summer, 30 percent of total German fighter strength was over the Reich, and by October the proportion had increased to 56 percent, although Allied planners overestimated this at 65 percent.

Just as the Luftwaffe had grown stronger, it had grown stronger *faster* than the Allies had imagined.

Indeed, the Reichsluftfahrtministerium (RLM), the German Air Ministry, had twice, in December 1942 and again in October 1943, moved to greatly ramp up single-engine fighter production. Analysts guessed that the monthly average for such aircraft was 595 during the first half of 1943, increasing to 645 in the second half. However, the postwar Strategic Bombing Survey revealed that the figures were actually 753, increasing to 851.

"By mid-October 1943 the daylight bombing campaign had reached a crisis," Arthur Ferguson admits, echoing the pessimism expressed by Dick Hughes. "Its cost had risen alarmingly while its successes remained problematical. The assumptions underlying it therefore came up for reexamination. The Combined Bomber Offensive had by October come to the end of its second planned phase, and it became a matter of the utmost concern to all those in charge of the operation to determine whether or not it had accomplished its objectives. It was of particular importance to examine the work done by the American daylight force, for around it there still tended to gather certain doubts and questions."

When planners pointed to serious damage that had been done to the German industrial infrastructure—from bearings to petrochemicals—the listing and detailing of such accomplishments was always followed by the word "but." This word was, in turn, followed by recountings of the tenacity of the Luftwaffe, and of the resilience and dispersal of German industry. Even though they were aware of this, Allied planners consistently underestimated the adaptability and resourcefulness of German industry throughout this stage of the war.

After the war, the full backstory of the great difficulties and delays faced by the Germans in doing this would be known. So too would be the grisly stories of their extensive use of slave labor. In November 1943, though, the planners focused only on the *results* of the resilience and the dispersal, and the high cost of trying to stop it.

After Black Week, it was time for reflection.

The Combined Chiefs of Staff ordered a review of the Combined Bomber Offensive. The Combined Operations Planning Committee grappled with the big picture and the future of the relationship of the Combined Bomber Offensive to Operation Overlord.

While the RAF nighttime raids were focusing on area attacks on cities and on the dense concentrations of industrial targets in the Ruhr, the aircraft factories, by their nature, required precision daylight attacks. Therefore, the entire mission of Operation Pointblank as the necessary precursor to Overlord lay on the shoulders of the Eighth Air Force, which appeared to have little to show for all its efforts.

As Arthur Ferguson so perfectly summarized, the USAAF strategy for the ETO in the autumn of 1943 "rested upon the assumption that the full resources of the Eighth Air Force must be concentrated on the successful completion of the Combined Bomber Offensive against Germany's war potential and particularly against the German Air Force as an indispensable preliminary to the invasion."

To date, that successful completion was nowhere in sight. Indeed, the Combined Chiefs of Staff decision makers were starting to question whether it was even *possible* for the Eighth Air Force to achieve superiority over the Luftwaffe in the six months remaining before the scheduled launch of Operation Overlord.

The Combined Chiefs of Staff review determined that in the nine months from February through October 1943, RAF Bomber Command had flown 45,844 night sorties with a 3.9 percent attrition rate, while the VIII Bomber Command had flown 15,846 daylight sorties with losses at 4.4 percent. At the same time, it was determined that only 65 percent of the forces originally scheduled for Pointblank were on hand by that date. On December 3, the RAF's Air Chief Marshal Charles "Peter" Portal told the Combined Chiefs of Staff in a memo that Operation Pointblank was "a full three months behind schedule."

Nevertheless, when Roosevelt, Churchill, and their Combined Chiefs of Staff met at the Sextant Conference in Cairo in late November, there was virtually no opposition expressed to the continuation of the Combined Bomber Offensive. It continued to be an assumed part of the overall strategy for Overlord. Portal's bleak characterization notwithstanding, the Combined Chiefs of Staff confirmed in a directive on December 6, that "the present plan for the Combined Bomber Offensive should remain unchanged except for revision of the bombing objectives which should be made periodically."

And so, as the shadows lengthened, the days shortened, and winter overcast moved in to shroud the continent, the Combined Bomber Offensive ground on. Despite the divergence of opinions over tactics and targeting, the basic strategy to which Roosevelt, Churchill, and their respective staffs had committed at Casablanca continued. Of course, if the Luftwaffe threat was to be muzzled before Overlord, there was *no other weapon* in the Allied arsenal other than strategic airpower that could even attempt to meet the challenge.

And the Combined Bomber Offensive was not operating in a vacuum. The Allies were fighting an increasingly extensive global war in 1943. It had been a year of expanding American operations in the Pacific, as well as a time of major Allied ground operations in the Mediterranean Theater. The Operation Husky invasion of Sicily in July–August had gone relatively smoothly, but the Operation Avalanche invasion of mainland Italy in September was meeting stiff German resistance—aided by favorable terrain—and sucking up considerable Allied resources. Indeed, the Eighth Air Force had been called on to divert resources to the Mediterranean for these operations, just as it had been required to do so in support of Operation Torch in 1942.

However, the bitter taste of the diversion of resources to the operations in Italy also presented the Combined Bomber Offensive with an opportunity to make lemonade.

The idea of launching strategic bombing operations against Germany from the sunny Mediterranean had long been on the wish list of strategic planners, especially when they considered the long weeks in which weather interfered with missions flown from Britain. As the August mission against Wiener Neustadt had demonstrated, the Reich was at the far limit of the range of Allied bombers flying from North Africa. However, now that southern Italy was in Allied hands, the picture changed considerably.

Even as Black Week was unfolding in northern Europe, bulldozers were at work in the area between Bari and Foggia, on the heel of the Italian boot. By November, a complex of bomber bases was starting to emerge from the swirling dust. On the first day of November, the USAAF activated the Fifteenth Air Force under the command of General Nathan Twining, previously the commander of the Thirteenth Air Force in the Pacific. Within a month, missions were being flown from new bases more than five hundred miles closer to Germany than those in North Africa.

The Fifteenth Air Force offered the potential of striking targets in southern Germany and Austria that were beyond the effective reach of the Eighth Air Force. Among those on the Operation Pointblank target list that were reachable from the bases in Italy was the Messerschmitt factory complex at Wiener Neustadt, as well as the one at Augsburg that had thus far been considered too deep inside the Reich for an Eighth Air Force mission.

Amid the sweetness of the lemonade, there were, of course, certain drawbacks to operations from Italy. These ranged from the mundane issue of building up an adequate depot and maintenance infrastructure from scratch, to the dramatic difficulty of flying across the Alps, especially in the winter, or with battle-damaged aircraft.

Though the Fifteenth was able to launch a sizable mission against Wiener Neustadt on November 2, the day after its formal activation, and a 150-plane mission to Augsburg in December, weather and lack of equipment limited the Fifteenth mainly to targets south of the Alps through the end of the year.

While the Fifteenth Air Force was being organized for a prominent role in Operation Pointblank and a significant role in strategic operations over Europe, Portal and Bomber Command's "Bomber" Harris changed gears. They veered away from Operation Pointblank to focus not on the German aircraft industry, or indeed on *any* German industry, but back on the concept of attacking German morale. Continuing to cite the theory that a collapse of morale had pushed the German surrender in the First World War, the RAF revisited the approach long advocated by Harris that the war could be won by exhausting and dispiriting the German people through the burning of their cities.

While some RAF officers continued to insist that area bombardment was directed at industrial areas rather than civilian areas, Harris was very unambiguous that area bombardment was used primarily as a weapon against civilian morale. As quoted by Henry Sokolski in a Strategic Studies Institute study published by the US Army War College, Harris famously said "the destruction of houses, public utilities, transport and lives, the creation of a refugee problem on an unprecedented scale, and the breakdown of morale both at home and at the battle fronts by fear of extended and intensified bombing, are accepted and intended aims of our bombing policy. They are not by-products of attempts to hit factories."

However, as Walt Rostow disagreed in the OSS Research and Analysis Branch *War Diary*, this perspective represented what the "EOU regarded as a misconception concerning the breakdown of Germany during 1918. It was felt to be important that romantic notions not be entertained about the vulnerability of the German political and social structure to internal collapse."

Rostow's ideas represented those of the Americans at the EOU. Arthur Harris governed the direction taken by RAF Bomber Command.

During the summer, Harris had run a five-day series of area attacks against Hamburg. Now he took the war home to Germany's symbolic target number one, in what he would call the "Battle of Berlin."

The German capital had been bombed before, but Harris now planned to take the "maximum effort" approach, involving four-hundred-plane raids on the nights of November 18–19 and November 22–23.

The second mission proved to be the most damaging against Berlin to date. Even Albert Speer recalled it in his memoirs. In his objective assessment of the strategy, he was critical of the British having deviated from the practical objectives of the strategic mission, but personally, the attack absolutely got his attention.

"Instead of paralyzing vital segments of industry, the Royal Air Force began an air offensive against Berlin," Speer writes. "I was having a conference in my private office on November 22, 1943, when the air-raid alarm sounded. It was about 7:30 P.M. A large fleet of bombers was reported heading toward Berlin. When the bombers reached Potsdam, I called off the meeting to drive to a nearby flak tower, intending to watch the attack from its platform, as was my wont. But I scarcely reached the top of the tower when I had to take shelter inside it; in spite of the tower's stout concrete walls, heavy hits nearby were shaking it. Injured antiaircraft gunners crowded down the stairs behind me; the air pressure from the exploding bombs had hurled them into the walls. For 20 minutes, explosion followed explosion. . . . My nearby Ministry was one gigantic conflagration. . . . In place of my private office I found nothing but a huge bomb crater."

Arthur Harris famously remarked about the Battle of Berlin, "It will cost us between 400 and 500 aircraft. It will cost Germany the war."

Harris was wrong and Albert Speer was right. The war would be won, not through frightening Berliners but through paralyzing vital segments of industry. Indeed, historians have also often pointed out that the Luftwaffe had erred strategically in 1940, when it shifted its target priority from attacking RAF fighter bases to the less practical, more spiteful, Blitz of London.

For the Eighth Air Force, on whose shoulders rested the primary responsibility for taking down the German industrial economy, November and December were a time of building up to fulfill potential, rather than of the dramatic action of more deep penetration missions.

The Eighth put 350 bombers over Bremen on November 26, and 154 over the same city three days later. On December 11, 437 heavy bombers hit factories near Emden with 15 losses. Two days later, port facilities farther east were targeted, with 171 heavies hitting Bremen again, and 379 bombing Kiel. The Eighth was also flying against easier targets in France and the Netherlands, but deep penetration operations against Pointblank targets, the backbone of German aircraft production, were deferred for the time being.

However, the buildup was evident in how fast the numbers of bombers had been growing in December. Whereas the Eighth had managed to launch 400 bombers only once prior to the second Schweinfurt mission, they were now beginning to send out forces in excess of 600 heavy bombers. On December 13, the Eighth launched 710 heavy bombers, of which 649 bombed Bremen, Hamburg, and Keil, while 658 bombed Ludwigshafen on December 30.

American industry, with its almost limitless potential, was gearing up to unprecedented levels as a resource of weapons and aircraft. In 1942, American industry had rolled out 47,836 total warplanes. In 1943, that number would be 85,898, and for 1944, even higher.

Production of both Flying Fortresses and Liberators increased greatly in 1943, although, for most of the year, operational numbers had lagged far beyond the number being produced. Factory acceptances of Flying Fortresses increased from 1,412 in 1942 to 4,179 in 1943, and of Liberators from 1,164 to 5,214. However, as the aircraft flowed into the global USAAF, the numbers on hand in the ETO were reactively smaller. Flying Fortress inventory increased from 175 at the start of 1943 to 907 in October. For Liberators, the number increased from 39 to 197. By the end of 1943, the Eighth Air Force possessed 1,307 Flying Fortresses and 308 Liberators, while the newly formed Fifteenth Air Force had 289 Flying Fortresses and 268 Liberators. One Eighth Air Force heavy bomber group had been added in November, but four were activated in December, bringing total strength to twenty-five groups by the end of the year.

And then there were the fighters. By December, there were more than 1,200 P-47 Thunderbolts in the European Theater, double the number that had been present in August. Meanwhile, the remarkable P-51 Mustang had started to reach the Eighth Air Force fighter groups. In August, there had been none. By December, there were nearly 300, and this number would double during January.

The increase in aircraft was one thing, but another part of the story was the increasing numbers of crews who were arriving in Britain.

As typical as any among these men were David and Archie Mathies, the brothers from the coal patch town of Finleyville, Pennsylvania. Archie had enlisted at the end of 1940, when the USAAF was still the Air Corps. David, being four years younger, joined the USAAF on June 20, 1942, half a year after Pearl Harbor, and wound up going overseas as part of the Eighth Air Force buildup while Archie was still stateside. By the spring of 1943, David had been in England for a year as a ground crewman with the 4th Fighter Group at Debden in Essex, while Archie was still a flight engineer attached to the 28th Bombardment Squadron of the 19th Bombardment Group at Pyote Field in Texas.

Anxious to get overseas, Archie volunteered for aerial gunnery school at Tyndall Field in Florida, but was still trapped in a "hurry-up-and-wait" career track while David was in Britain drinking warm beer and sleeping in cold, drafty Quonset hut temporary barracks.

The bomber crews assigned to the Eighth Air Force were generally formed and trained as a crew in the United States, then assigned a bomber, which they would, in turn, fly to England. By October 1943, Archie Mathies was at Alexandria Army Airfield, near Alexandria, Louisiana, assigned as part of a bomber crew.

The pilot and aircraft commander was Second Lieutenant Clarence

Richard Nelson Jr. from Riverside, Illinois, who had enlisted in the US Army as a private and had been a pilot only since May 1943. Second Lieutenant Joseph Martin from Burlington, New Jersey, was the bombardier, and Second Lieutenant Walter Edward "Wally" Truemper had joined Nelson's crew as the navigator in September. Like Nelson, Truemper was twenty-four years old, and from Illinois, specifically Aurora. Also like Nelson, he had enlisted in the regular US Army but had applied for flight school and wound up in the USAAF.

The copilot was Flight Officer Ronald Bartley, from Underwood, North Dakota. The vast majority of the men with a pilot's rating in the USAAF were officers, but enlisted men who had completed flight training could be assigned as "flight officers," noncommissioned pilots with a rank equivalent to warrant officer. Though the lowest ranking men on the flight deck, they were also the most experienced. In 1942, Bartley had flown his first tour of duty with the 12th Bombardment Group in North Africa as a radio operator aboard a B-25 medium bomber.

Ron Bartley had come home, married his girlfriend, Bernice, and signed up for flight school. Having earned his wings at the end of August 1943, he volunteered to go back overseas to fly with the Eighth Air Force.

There were six sergeants assigned to Nelson's crew. Working just aft of the flight deck were the radio operator, Joe Rex, from Defiance, Ohio, and Carl Moore, from Williamsport, Pennsylvania, the flight engineer. An Arkansas-born Texan named Thomas Sowell was the left waist gunner, while Russell Robinson, from Springfield, Colorado, stood across from him at the right waist position. Robinson had been in the midst of flight training when he had his twenty-seventh birthday. In those days, the USAAF required that pilots earn their wings at age twenty-six or earlier, so Robinson became a gunner.

Magnus "Mac" Hagbo, a Norwegian kid from Seattle, was the tail gunner, and Archie Mathies rounded out Dick Nelson's crew as the man who crawled into the tight confines of the Sperry ball turret on the bottom of the Flying Fortress.

Having trained to fly and function as a crew, they were assigned the B-17G that they would take overseas. In World War II, nearly every bomber had a name, and this one was named *Mizpah*, from a biblical reference suggested to Nelson by his mother. In Genesis 31:49, Laban speaks the word "Mizpah" and says, "The Lord watch between me and thee when we are absent one from another."

Florence Nelson wanted her twenty-four-year-old boy to come home safely.

The young crew flew *Mizpah* out of the recently completed Kearny Army Airfield in Buffalo County, Nebraska, on the last day of November, bound for England by way of Bangor, Maine, and Goose Bay, Labrador. After an icy, hair-raising midwinter crossing of the Atlantic, they reached Northern Ireland on December 16.

It was here that *Mizpah* herself became the first casualty of Dick Nelson's wartime saga. On the night before the crew was about to make the last, short hop to Britain, a winter storm blew in and the wind pushed several Flying Fortresses together, damaging their control surfaces.

Without a plane, the crew made that last leg of their journey by boat, and the next day, Archie Mathies found himself in Scotland, the land of his birth. Within a week, *Mizpah*'s crew found themselves assigned to the Eighth Air Force Replacement Depot Casual Pool, waiting for further orders, and for whatever came next.

As Christmas came and went, and as the new year arrived, these men were just ten of the tens of thousands who were accumulating in England in anticipation of the year that promised to be the make-or-break one for the Eighth Air Force, the Combined Bomber Offensive, and the realization of the full potential of strategic airpower.

THIRTEEN

OPERATION ARGUMENT

Just as young Americans like Archie Mathies had come to crew the bombers, young Americans had been flooding into England by the tens of thousands also to form the waves of ground troops who would battle their way into *Festung Europe* with Operation Overlord and begin the long and difficult march into Hitler's Reich. There were so many that it was almost like an invasion.

Some British people referred, with both tongue in cheek and a certain accuracy, to the Yanks as "oversexed, overpaid, and over here." It was a culture shock for both sides.

Others simply, and more charitably, referred to the invasion of England by the young Americans as "the Friendly Invasion."

To command these young Americans, indeed to command *all* the Allied forces, there would be an American—General Dwight David Eisenhower.

In 1942, the British, by right of their experience and their relative numbers, had held sway in the decision making within the Combined Chiefs of Staff. By the end of 1943, it was the Americans, by right of their growing experience and their growing numbers, who had earned the right to command Operation Overlord. As early as the Quadrant Conference in Quebec in August, even Winston Churchill had agreed.

The Allied command structure underwent a substantial reorganization during December. On December 7, Eisenhower was formally confirmed as the supreme allied commander in Europe, heading the Supreme Headquarters, Allied Expeditionary Force (SHAEF) and turning over the supreme Allied command in the Mediterranean Theater to British General Henry Maitland Wilson.

Meanwhile, Air Chief Marshal Sir Arthur Tedder, who had previously commanded the joint Mediterranean Air Command (MAC), now went back to England to sit at the right hand of Eisenhower as his deputy supreme Allied commander, in charge of air operations for Operation Overlord. Another RAF man, Trafford Leigh-Mallory, was named to command the joint Allied Expeditionary Air Force (AEAF), which was an umbrella for all of the American and British *tactical* air operations in connection with Overlord. This included the USAAF Ninth Air Force, commanded by General Lewis Brereton, which was relocated from the Mediterranean to England for tactical operations. Theoretically, the AEAF umbrella did not cast its shadow over the strategic Eighth Air Force—at least not for the moment.

Concerning this arrangement, Arthur Ferguson later wrote that "General Eisenhower had expected Spaatz to manage heavy bomber operations for Operation Overlord, and he was a little surprised that Tedder, who he had hoped would serve as his 'chief air man,' was in a vague position as officer without portfolio in air matters while 'a man named Mallory' was titular air commander in chief [for Overlord air operations]."

With respect to American air operations, the USAAF announced, and the Combined Chiefs of Staff approved, the creation of a new *strategic* air command, the United States Strategic Air Forces in Europe (USSAFE, later USSTAF and referred to as such herein), as an umbrella organization for both the Eighth and Fifteenth Air Forces. To command this new organization, and as the highest ranking American air officer in Europe, Hap Arnold picked Tooey Spaatz.

Spaatz then returned to his former headquarters, and that of the

Eighth Air Force, at Widewing (Bushy Park), near London, which now became the headquarters of the USSTAF. Technically, the Eighth was redesignated as the USSTAF, and the VIII Bomber Command was then redesignated as the "new" Eighth Air Force, with its headquarters still at the air base at High Wycombe, west of London, that also served as headquarters of RAF Bomber Command.

As had the Eighth previously, the USSTAF would coordinate its operations with RAF Bomber Command through the Combined Bomber Offensive organization. In a somewhat confusing arrangement, the USSTAF would also maintain administrative control of the Ninth Air Force, while operational control of the Ninth for Overlord rested with the AEAF.

Meanwhile, the Mediterranean Allied Air Forces (MAAF) were created as a successor to MAC and as an umbrella organization for all American *and* British tactical air forces in the Mediterranean Theater of Operations (MTO).

In the musical chairs shake-up of the USAAF command staff in the ETO and MTO, as Spaatz went back to England, General Eaker went south to command the MAAF and General Doolittle was transferred from command of the Twelfth Air Force in the Mediterranean to replace Eaker as commander of the Eighth Air Force in England.

General Fred Anderson, formerly commander of the VIII Bomber Command, became Spaatz's deputy commander for operations at USSTAF. While USSTAF was theoretically a "supervisory and policy-making" organization, Anderson would become the most influential operations man within the new strategic air command.

"Just before departing [for his new post at MAAF], General Eaker asked me whether I would accompany him to the Mediterranean Theater and take charge of his new plans division there," Dick Hughes recalls. "I thankfully, but respectfully, declined the offer."

Eaker now commanded a *tactical* air organization, and for the time being, Hughes was anxious to continue what he had started with respect to the *strategic* air war against the Reich.

Indeed, while the Eighth and Fifteenth Air Forces had been building up their strength and flying relatively limited endurance missions through most of December, the next phase of that strategic campaign had been shaping up on drawing boards from Bushy Park to Berkeley Square.

On November 29, 1943, the Combined Operational Planning Committee (COPC) of the Combined Bomber Offensive had issued a highly classified memo describing the general outlines for the maximum effort code-named Operation Argument. Essentially, Operation Argument was to be the intensely focused capstone of Operation Pointblank, the climactic moment in the campaign against the Luftwaffe and the German aircraft industry that Peter Portal had complained was behind schedule.

Ironically, while there had been numerous arguments about strategic airpower policy over the preceding year, as November faded into December, those on the COPC were of like mind over the singular objectives of Operation Argument.

Though specific details bounced back and forth between Berkeley Square and Bushy Park through December, the general plan for Argument called for a *weeklong* series of daylight precision bombing missions against high-priority aircraft industry targets in southern and central Germany— such as Augsburg, Leipzig, and Regensburg—that would have an immediate effect on frontline Luftwaffe fighter strength.

As had long been envisioned by Dick Hughes, Charlie Kindleberger, and everyone who had understood the German economy as an integrated organism, the plan called for a systematic assault not merely against final assembly plants, but on component plants and, once again, ball bearings. In a conversation with Arthur Ferguson a month later, Dick Hughes gave a series of examples.

He explained that attacks on the Erla-Maschinenwerk GmbH plant in Leipzig, which assembled Messerschmitt Bf 109s, would be complemented by strikes on factories in the Leipzig suburb of Heiterblick where components and subassemblies were manufactured. The Junkers Flugzeug-und-Motorenwerke AG factory at Bernburg, which assembled Ju 88 aircraft, would "share" an attack with the Ju 88 fuselage works at nearby Oschersleben and the Ju 88 wing plant at Halberstadt.

The huge Messerschmitt plant at Augsburg contained both subassembly and final assembly in one complex, but at Regensburg, the final assembly was done in the suburb of Obertraubling, and subcomponents were made in another suburb, Prüfening. Hughes said that both targets would get equal consideration from the Eighth Air Force.

Operations would be coordinated between the Eighth and Fifteenth Air Forces, with the RAF attacking the same areas on many of the intervening nights during this weeklong effort. The Ninth Air Force, recently relocated to England to manage all the tactical bombing operations in France ahead of Overlord, would cooperate with the heavy bomber units by running diversionary attacks over northern Europe with fighters and medium bombers. The idea would be to lure the Luftwaffe into dividing its forces, pulling fighter strength away from its strategic mission.

Because of this coordination between several commands and separate air forces, Fred Anderson would be integral to planning for Operation Argument. Indeed, the operational direction of Operation Argument would be Anderson's responsibility in his role as Spaatz's deputy for operations.

Hughes writes of a visit to General Spaatz's residence one night, during which he and Anderson laid out the dimensions of their proposal for the specifics of the Argument operations, complete with pages of lists, and maps unrolled across the floor.

"My target list included German fighter assembly plants scattered virtually over the whole of Germany, and many called for very deep penetrations," he recalls. "Understandably, General Spaatz was most concerned, lest this operation result in tragic casualty percentages similar to those we previously had suffered in our attacks on Schweinfurt and Regensburg."

On everyone's mind was the last time the Eighth Air Force mounted a *weeklong* maximum effort. That week, Black Week, had culminated in the debacle over Schweinfurt, when the attacking force had suffered the worst casualty rate of any major mission ever. Their minds' eyes were filled with images of the faces of hundreds of young men who would never go home.

Meanwhile, everyone's mind then turned to images of the faces of *thousands* of young men who would be coming ashore in Normandy in just a few short months, and what their lives would be like as they staggered for safety under skies filled with the vengeful wrath of the determined and efficient Luftwaffe.

As Dick Hughes explains, each man in the room knew that, as painful as it would be, Operation Argument was absolutely indispensable to Operation Overlord. Each man knew that "only from its results could we possibly determine whether or not we could gain air superiority before D-Day, and whether or not by the exercise of strategic airpower on decisive German industrial target systems, we could appreciably shorten the length of time for which the Germans could resist. Moreover, we now, for the first time, had a very strong strategic bomber force and an adequate supply of long range fighter escorts. If we failed, this time, we would probably never have any more forces than we now had, with which to succeed."

As the Christmas decorations began appearing around London, and in the Mayfair shops Dick Hughes passed on his way to Berkeley Square, he presented Fred Anderson with the details and nuances of the specific Operation Argument objectives. As he recalls, "General Anderson agreed with me completely, and we sent the target priorities over to Eighth Air Force and told them to get ready for a maximum effort."

It was make-or-break time for the Eighth Air Force, and indeed for the entire Anglo-American Combined Bomber Offensive, for Operation Argument was to be its climactic moment, a moment that could *not* end in failure.

Everything that the Combined Bomber Offensive, and especially the Eighth Air Force, had been *trying* to do, at least since the Pointblank Directive of June 1943, would now be funneled into this single "maximum effort" for which the Eighth Air Force now finally seemed to have the resources.

"Strategic heavy bomber groups were now piling into England at a much faster rate for the buildup for the invasion, and several [fresh] groups of long range P-51s and P-47s had also arrived," Hughes writes of the turning point that was coming with the turn of 1943 to 1944. "In my opinion, for the first time, we finally had the real opportunity of breaking the back of the German fighter defenses, and all my time was spent planning just how to do this as soon as weather conditions became favorable for operations over Germany."

Favorable weather conditions?

In northern Europe—in *January*?

Favorable weather conditions, in northern Europe, in January for an *entire week*?

Operation Argument could not go forward until the maximum effort could be sustained for a week. As Anderson later observed, "It was the business of getting in and out of Germany that was going to be costly. I was not prepared to accept such risks for anything less than a clear shot at the targets."

It was not just weather over the targets that worried Anderson, it was the weather in East Anglia, where ground fog is common in the winter months. Because of the short days of winter, and the distance to the targets deep inside Germany, the bombers would be taking off and returning in the dark. Adding thick ground fog to nighttime landings with damaged aircraft was a prescription for disaster.

Until they were sure of a week of favorable weather, the Combined Bomber Offensive would just be biding time with routine missions to routine targets. The first month of 1944 began with Eighth Air Force operations on a scale that would have been impressive just four months earlier, but was *not* so impressive when it was recognized that the Eighth's part of Operation Argument was now *four* months behind schedule.

On the fourth of January, the Eighth managed to launch more than five hundred heavy bombers, and followed with more than four hundred the next day, and again on January 7. However, as with the operations in December, the primary targets were still relatively close—the port of Keil and the I.G. Farben factory at Ludwigshafen—and attacking them did nothing toward the mission of hitting the strength of the Luftwaffe at its source.

Each day, and several times each day, Tooey Spaatz, Fred Anderson, and Dick Hughes were not alone among the men of the Eighth Air Force who craned their necks and looked into the sky for anything favorable about the damnable winter weather. More often than not, their gaze was met with raindrops, which they knew would exist as ice and sleet at the altitudes where the Flying Fortresses and Liberators were flying.

An indication of the poor weather conditions during the month came on January 24, when 857 B-17s and B-24s were launched, but all but fifty-eight had to be recalled because of the weather.

Favorable weather conditions, in northern Europe, in January for an *entire week?*

It would not happen.

January came and went, and it had not.

Time was running out. The campaign against the Luftwaffe was another month behind, and Operation Overlord was another month *closer*.

If they looked skyward and saw the clouds part, how would they know how long it would last?

Even today, in an era of satellite imagery and computer analysis, most people still consider meteorology to be as much art as science, in which the weatherman hedges his bets with percentages. In the 1940s, weather forecasting, especially long-range weather forecasting, was much more art than science.

As Arthur Ferguson writes, during January, "Argument had been scheduled repeatedly—every time, in fact, that early weather reports seemed to offer any hope; but each time deteriorating weather had forced cancellation."

Just as Fred Anderson was growing impatient, so too was his boss. On February 8, Tooey Spaatz told Anderson emphatically that Argument *must* happen by the end of the month.

"By February the destruction of the German fighter production had become a matter of such urgency that General Spaatz and General Anderson were willing to take more than ordinary risks in order to complete the task," Ferguson continues, "including the risk of exceptional losses that might result from missions staged under conditions of adverse base weather."

Just as Tooey Spaatz was growing impatient, so too was *his* boss. Finally, to aid the men of the Eighth Air Force, Hap Arnold, the commanding general of the USAAF, sent his *own* weatherman.

Arnold had first met Dr. Irving P. Krick in 1934, when he was stationed at March Field near Riverside, California, and Professor Krick had just founded the Department of Meteorology at California Institute of Technology at Pasadena. Krick had recently leapt to national attention when he explained the cause of the 1933 crash of the US Navy airship USS *Akron*. Arnold called his first meeting with the professor "unforgettable," and, in his memoirs, he lists numerous almost uncanny long-term predictions made by Krick.

"Naturally, I watched Dr. Krick's work eagerly after that," Arnold writes. "Weather is the essence of successful air operations."

Krick's method, which was considered unorthodox by the meteorology establishment in those days, used modeling of past events to predict the future. Krick studied weather patterns going back decades in order to determine patterns. According to Kristine Harper in her book *Weather by the Numbers*, Francis Reichelderfer, the head of the federal Weather Bureau, derided Krick as a "smug, supremely self-confident self-promoter."

Though his "weather typing" was nontraditional, it seemed to work, and Hap Arnold believed in him. Indeed, the USAAF chief was so taken with the professor that he had him commissioned as a major and brought him into the service when the war started.

The arrival of the maverick meteorologist to prognosticate weather for Operation Argument was almost like a scene from a motion picture, and indeed, he would have been at home in such a scenario. Krick was no stranger to Hollywood. In fact, David O. Selznick had hired him to predict the weather in advance of filming the burning of Atlanta scene for the 1939 film *Gone with the Wind*.

Looking thoughtfully at the leaden overcast, Krick told Anderson and Spaatz that they would need to wait for a stable, high-pressure pattern to move in over southern England and the continent and linger for several days.

They asked him to tell them when, and he asked for historical weather maps. Fortunately, they had been creating weather maps in England and northern Europe since the middle of the nineteenth century. Sitting down with data on winter weather patterns going back to the 1890s, Krick calculated what to look for as the harbinger of such a stationary high.

At last, on the afternoon of Friday, February 18, Krick came to see Anderson and Spaatz with a guardedly optimistic expression on his face.

"A good-looking sequence," he said, "is in the making."

This was an understatement.

He explained that not one, but two extensive pressure areas were developing. One would be centered in the Baltic, the other just west of Ireland.

If the area over the Baltic moved southeast across Europe as Krick predicted, the resulting winds would break up the cloud cover and leave most of Germany under clear skies or scattered clouds for at least three days beginning on Sunday, February 20.

The only problem was that there would be thick cloud cover over England when the bombers launched. The aircraft would have to climb above the clouds before assembling into their formations, but the crews were used to this.

Anderson was ecstatic, but other weather forecasters were unconvinced. There were arguments on the very eve of the operation of the same name when the data was presented to the Eighth and Ninth Air Force weathermen on Saturday. They insisted that the scenario that Krick projected was extremely rare in this area for this time of year.

In the upper echelons of command Jimmy Doolittle of the Eighth and Lewis Brereton of the Ninth were inclined to believe the weather reporting of their own meteorologists, who considered Krick's hypothesis to be impossible. As Anderson's right-hand man, Glen Williamson, later explained to Arthur Ferguson, neither man shared Anderson's confidence in Krick's predictions.

The USAAF meteorologists assigned to the operational units were of the traditional school who were extremely skeptical of Krick and his methodology. He was well known, and not very well respected, within the small world of forecasting. His reputation for unorthodox methods had preceded him, and so too had the controversy.

However, as John Cox reports in his book *Storm Chasers*, Krick had the confidence of Hap Arnold, and within the USAAF, that was the last word on which weatherman would be Operation Argument's final authority.

When Anderson then cabled Ira Eaker, now in command of the MAAF in Italy, to tell him that Operation Argument was on, and that the Fifteenth Air Force was needed, it could not have been more inopportune timing.

As noted, the Combined Bomber Offensive was not happening in a vacuum. Operation Overlord, the big show for the troops gathering in England, was still months away. However, in the Mediterranean Theater, home of the Fifteenth Air Force, Anglo-American ground forces were already engaged. Indeed, Operation Shingle, the big Allied invasion of Italy at Anzio, had taken place less than a month earlier, on January 22. Things had not gone as hoped. The German resistance was much tougher than anticipated, and the Allied troops had been tenuously clinging to their beachhead with bloody fingernails.

When Anderson's alert reached Eaker and Nathan Twining of the Fifteenth Air Force, they were then in the midst of discussions with General Mark Clark of the US Fifth Army, planning air support for a breakout from the Anzio beachhead. The Fifteenth Air Force was to be a key component of what was being planned for February 20.

Eaker told Anderson and Spaatz that he could not participate in Operation Argument on Sunday. As Glen Williamson later revealed, Eaker did not want to press the point with the Mediterranean Theater commander, General Henry Maitland Wilson, for fear that Wilson would take over direct command of the Fifteenth Air Force and *also* prevent Eaker from participating in Argument later in the week. Spaatz took the question to the RAF commander in chief, Peter Portal, who trumped everyone by telling Spaatz that Churchill himself wanted all the Allied airpower in the Mediterranean available over Anzio.

This turn of events, on top of an almost universal distrust of Dr. Krick's weather reporting, marked a very ill-omened beginning for Operation Argument.

Even as the airmen across the length and breadth of East Anglia who would fly the biggest mission of the war to date were bedding down early on Saturday evening, the command staff was preparing for a long night, and a very long day.

Before dawn, Sunday morning, Fred Anderson issued the order, which he dutifully recorded in his official journal:

"Let 'em go."

FOURTEEN

BEFORE SUNDAY'S DAWN

More than eleven thousand young American airmen arose to eat breakfast when the sunrise of the first day of Big Week was still hours away. It was biting cold that morning, but that was nothing new. This was February in East Anglia. Every day, in the wee hours of the morning, was monotonously cold in February. What made this Sunday different was that the weather was supposed to be clear over Germany.

Nobody got to sleep in.

"The week of good bombing weather was over Germany," Derwyn Robb of the 379th Bombardment Group recalls of Big Week in his memoir, *Shades of Kimbolton.* "In no way could anyone say that about the weather conditions in England during the same period of time. Snow covered the ground, runways were sheets of ice, and the wind whipping across the base froze everything and everyone in its path. . . . It all started on the dreary afternoon of the 19th when Division sent down the usual alert with the usual notation 'maximum effort.' Again the planes were loaded with bombs, again the gas was put in, and again completely readied for a mission. Cooks again prepared chow and S-2 again prepared the briefing. No one really expected the mission to go out but preparations went on anyway with the usual griping."

But Big Week had already started. At about 3:15 A.M., as the Yanks were mustering for breakfast, 921 bombers from RAF Bomber Command were beginning an hour-long bombardment of Leipzig, Germany's fifth largest city.

When General Fred Anderson said "Let 'em go," the Eighth Air Force would proceed to launch more bombers than it ever had. For the first time, more than a thousand bombers wearing American stars would be headed toward Germany.

At Eighth Air Force bases all across East Anglia, those eleven thousand young American airmen, nearly four times the number who mustered here on Black Thursday, finished their coffee and headed for their briefings.

Held simultaneously in dozens of Quonset huts all across East Anglia, the briefings were always a dramatic affair, whether it was your first, or your twenty-fifth—and last. The temperature went from the cold and damp of the night outside to hot and muggy as dozens of warm bodies crowded inside, each sweating his immediate future.

The briefings were the unveiling of "your target for today," which was a little like waiting for your name to be drawn in a lottery. The men who had been through the Selective Service lottery understood this well. Until the target was announced, there could only be guesses.

"More than one pair of sleepy eyes popped open when they saw the routes stretching into Germany to twelve different targets, and heard that over a thousand heavies with fighter escort would be crowding the skies on this one mission," Derwyn Robb recalls of the briefing at the 379th that morning.

"There probably will be icing conditions at altitude, and you may have a little difficulty with contrails," the briefing officer cautioned.

"This remark was generally made for every mission during the winter months," Robb explains. "It was usually a very gross understatement."

"A neat major steps on the platform at the front of the room and begins roll call," recalls Colonel Bud Peaslee, who had led the 384th Bombardment Group to Schweinfurt in October. "He sings out only the names of the plane commanders. Each answers for his crew. There is some screwing around in the front rows as a few commanders turn to scan the faces in the back for their men. All are present. The major moves to the rear of the platform and rips aside a black curtain hanging against the wall. A large-scale map appears with the usual length of black yarn crossing it. There is no noise now as all lean forward, looking at the eastern end of the yarn."

The black curtains were drawn back, and at RAF Polebrook, about sixty-five miles northeast of London, Second Lieutenant Dick Nelson of the 351st Bombardment Group, took in the eastern end of *his* piece of yarn. It was Leipzig, the same target that the RAF was just finishing as the Americans watched the curtain.

The 351st was part of the 1st Bombardment Division, which would have the biggest role to play on Day One of Big Week, and they would go the deepest into Hitler's Reich. About 80 miles southwest of Berlin, Leipzig is around 527 miles from East Anglia, farther than Regensburg or Schweinfurt.

This morning, Dick Nelson was about to embark on his second combat mission. He glanced around at the officers in his crew—Joe Martin, the bombardier; Wally Truemper, the navigator; and Flight Officer Ron Bartley, his copilot. Their attention was on the yarn, the destination, and the lecture being delivered by the briefer.

After having lost their first Flying Fortress, *Mizpah*, in mid-December, Nelson and his crew had passed their first month and their first Christmas overseas, biding their time in the Replacement Depot Casual Pool, before going to the 1st Training and Replacement Squadron, all the while waiting to be given a home, and an airplane to fly.

On January 19, they had finally been assigned to the 510th Bombardment Squadron of the 351st Bombardment Group, based at Polebrook.

Nelson's whole crew, minus Ron Bartley, flew their first mission on February 6, against German targets near Caen in northern France, with Nelson flying copilot to Harold Peters, a pilot with seven missions under his belt. Their aircraft was a nearly new B-17G named *April Girl II*. Bartley had sat out the mission so that Nelson could fly with a more experienced pilot on his first outing.

The briefing officer explained that Operation Argument was all about the German aircraft industry, and Leipzig was the home of the Junkers Flugzeug-und-Motorenwerke and the Erla Maschinenwerke. The Junkers factories were where they made the versatile, twin-engined Ju 88, which was used by the Luftwaffe both as a tactical bomber—mainly on the eastern front—and as a rocket launching interceptor against the Eighth Air Force. Erla, meanwhile, built components for Messerschmitt aircraft, and they were also one of the principal final assembly sites for the Bf 109G fighter, especially the newer, enhanced-range Bf 109G-10 variant.

The crews were told that Leipzig was ringed by twelve hundred anti-aircraft guns, and the city would be ferociously defended by the Luftwaffe.

Most of the 1st Division's Flying Fortresses were tasked with the Erla and Junkers plants in the Leipzig suburbs of Heiterblick and Abtnaundorf, as well as at Leipzig's Mockau airfield, which was home to the Junkers engine works, where they made Jumo 213 engines for Fw 190s. In addition to the Erla and Junkers facilities, the galaxy of targets arrayed around Leipzig also included numerous aircraft component subcontractors, including Allgemeine Transportanlagen Gesellschaft (ATG). A smaller number of 1st Division B-17s were assigned targets among the Junkers facilities at Bernberg, about fifty miles northwest of Leipzig.

Like the flight crew, the sergeants were up at around three-thirty for breakfast, and the gunners picked up their guns. These they loaded into trucks along with their flak suits. As described by Wright Lee of the 445th Bombardment Group, the suits were "cushioned, steel panel enclosed jackets covering the front and back of your body from neck to groin." The suits weighed more than twenty pounds and were awfully uncomfortable, but they served a definite purpose. If they had extra flak suits, crewmen sat on them to protect themselves from beneath. For additional protection, the men also often wore regular M1 GI steel helmets over their aviator's helmets.

The flak, like the Luftwaffe, was greatly dreaded, but the antagonist most feared by the men in bombers was the cold, the searing, painful subzero cold.

The crewmen, officers, and sergeants alike dressed in sheepskin-lined leather, from their jackets—of the style known to this day as a "bomber jacket"—to their ungainly sheepskin-lined flying boots.

Russell Robinson and Tom Sowell, the waist gunners on Dick Nelson's crew, picked up their .50-caliber Brownings and caught a lift to the flight line. In combat, they had the dangerously cold and unenviable task of aiming their single machine guns through open windows in the frigid stratosphere where a man could lose his fingers to frostbite. They wore thick, lined gloves, tight-fitting leather helmets, and leather pants. With their goggles, and the oxygen masks they wore at high altitude, no skin was exposed to the air—although the rubber of the oxygen mask was hardly adequate protection. Contemporary descriptions often referred to the waist gunners as looking like "men from Mars."

As Jerry Penry recalls in his memoir, *Sunrise Serenade*, named for his 452nd Bombardment Group Flying Fortress, the ambient temperature above twenty thousand feet was often around forty degrees below zero, which made it very difficult for the airmen to function inside the unheated planes.

"The airmen wore heated flying suits, but they were not able to keep every part of their body covered to avoid getting frostbite," Penry explains. "One area that was susceptible to frostbite was the face, particularly the cheeks. A bare hand touched against the side of any metal surface would adhere itself to the metal at these extreme temperatures. The instinctive reflexes needed by the gunners to shoot at enemy fighters were considerably slowed due to the often bulky clothing. Under the large gloves worn by the gunners was a nylon glove that closely fit the contour on the hand. These gloves allowed the gunners to work on their equipment without getting their hands stuck to the bare metal. Often the guns turned white due to the extreme cold temperature. Many airmen realized that it was indeed possible to both freeze and sweat at the same time during a tense mission."

Though not every man carried one, every combat crew member was issued a Colt .45 semiautomatic pistol, along with two clips. As John O'Neil recalls in Marshall Thixton's anthology about the 482nd Bombardment Group, "Around this period of the European air war, US fighters began making ground-level attacks on airdromes, airplanes, trains, military vehicles and other potential targets. The Eighth fighters would do their strafing on the way back to England after escorting bombers, or as direct ground-level missions. This in effect threw out some of the unwritten ground rules under which the old air war was carried out. German broadcasts to England stated that captured Allied airmen would be dealt with

as murderers. Many German civilians were attacking downed Allied airmen, if possible, before German military arrived on the scene. If an Allied
airman had a firearm when captured, it could be an excuse to kill the
airman on the spot. It was also never clear what a handgun could accomplish for a downed airman in any case. For these reasons and others, a
number of US airmen did not carry their Colt .45s on missions."

Mac Hagbo, the tail gunner in Dick Nelson's crew, took his place with
his twin .50-calibers in the distant rear of the aircraft. His glassed-in perch
had some protection from the elements, but he had the worst of the wild
gyrations of turbulence and the dubious distinction of defending against
German fighters who could park themselves in the bomber's wake and
pour 20mm and 30mm cannon shells into the aircraft—and the gunner—
for long durations.

Archie Mathies would be flying in the cramped position as the ball
turret gunner. This would be Archie's second combat mission, the first
having been the February 6 mission to France—although on February 11,
he and bombardier Joe Martin had filled in with another crew aboard *April
Girl II* on a mission to Frankfurt that had been aborted. Having just been
promoted to staff sergeant, Archie had the distinction of being the senior
enlisted man aboard.

Aviation author Martin Caidin called the Sperry ball turret "unques-
tionably the loneliest position in the Flying Fortress—or the Liberator."

"The turret," wrote Caidin, "is like some grotesque, swollen eyeball
of steel and glass and guns that seems to hang precariously from the belly
of the B-17. It is a hellish, stinking position in battle; the gunner must
hunch up his body, draw up his knees, and work [himself] into a half ball
to meet the curving lines of the turret. The guns are to each side of his
head, and they stab from the turret eyeball like two even splinters. Jailed
in his little spherical powerhouse, the ball turret gunner literally aims his
own body at enemy fighters, working both hands and feet in deft coordination, spinning and tilting and then depressing switches atop the gun
grip handles to fire the two weapons. It is the most unenviable position in
a bomber, *any* bomber, and the man most unlikely to escape from a blazing B-17 is that lonely soul in the ball."

The sun was still not up when Dick Nelson's crew took their places and Nelson started the engines. Launching a thousand bombers from two dozen airfields, at minimum intervals, as fast as possible, in the dark is a feat of immense precision. Every pilot had been briefed on his place in the takeoff sequence, his rendezvous point in the sky, and his place in the immense bomber stream. It was a process requiring meticulous choreography with no room for error. Dick Nelson had been assigned a place in the formation that would be number three in the 351st Bombardment Group, or on the right wing of the group leader.

Nelson was taxiing toward the Polebrook runway according to the plan, when suddenly, a jeep appeared out of nowhere. Reacting instinctively, Nelson made a hard right turn, the right main landing gear slid into the mud, and the plane became stuck. Immediate and frantic efforts by a small army of ground crew personnel tried to nudge the bomber from her sticky trap.

By some accounts, they finally freed the stuck airplane, but as Joe Rex recalls in an audio recording in the collection of the Air Force Historical Research Agency, the crew was ordered to transfer their gear to another aircraft named *Ten Horsepower*. By all accounts, *Ten Horsepower* was the aircraft that the crew would fly during Sunday's mission. A Seattle-built Boeing B-17G with the tail number 42-31763, this bomber was one of the hundreds that had arrived since the first of the year, and it had been flown by several different crews on five previous missions since the first of February.

The snafu with the mud cost the crew its coveted position as number three in the group, as anyone who did not make his prescribed takeoff position had to wait for everyone else to go. This put them last in the air, struggling to catch up and flying the position known as "Tail-end Charlie."

As Joe Rex points out, "The day was one of those you feel had to get better right from the start, but which keeps going downhill."

FIFTEEN

SUNDAY, FEBRUARY 20

Thanks to Wally Truemper's excellent navigating, *Ten Horsepower*, the Flying Fortress piloted by Dick Nelson and Ron Bartley, caught up with the rest of the 351st Bombardment Group and took its place in a thousand-plane bomber stream that stretched for 150 miles across the skies over the North Sea.

Some of the elements of the 2nd Division would go nearly as deep as the 1st Division, almost 500 miles from East Anglia, to the city of Gotha, a place that earned its name in the eighth century when Charlemagne wrote that it was a place of "good water." A capital first of the Duchy of Saxe-Gotha, and later of the Duchy of Saxe-Coburg-Gotha, the city was now home to the facilities of Gothaer Waggonfabrik (GWF). The company had originated in the nineteenth century as a builder of railway rolling stock but had branched into aircraft as early as 1914 and was currently manufacturing a variety of its own aircraft for the Luftwaffe, as well as being the largest manufacturer of Messerschmitt's twin-engine fighters.

Other 2nd Division Liberators heading southeast on Sunday were flying toward Braunschweig, the city commonly known in English as Brunswick, about 440 miles from 2nd Division bases. Here, the targets included factories in the city's northern suburbs, as well as at Helmstedt, about a dozen miles to the east, and Oschersleben, 20 miles to the south-east. The Braunschweig area was home to the engine maker Muhlenbau-Industrie AG (MIAG). Though MIAG's stock in trade was power plants for Panther tanks and Jagdpanther armored vehicles, they were also a major manufacturer of engines designed by Daimler-Benz, and they produced components for Messerschmitt Bf 110 fighters.

The 1st and 2nd Divisions would be escorted by a greater number of fighters than had yet been launched by the USAAF on a single mission anywhere. It was a maximum effort, in which every available American fighter plane—18 fighter groups worth—was tapped for service, while the RAF also contributed 16 squadrons of Spitfires and some of its own Mustangs. Drawn from VIII Fighter Command, as well at the Ninth Air Force's IX Fighter Command, there were 73 USAAF P-51 Mustangs, 94 P-38 Lightnings, and 668 P-47 Thunderbolts. The latter, being unable to accompany the bombers all the way to their targets, would, as they usually did on deep penetration missions, go as far as possible, return home to refuel, and pick up the bombers on their way out of *Festung Europe*.

The Flying Fortresses of the 3rd Division, meanwhile, would fly a far northern route which would not cross the paths of the other two divisions after leaving British airspace. Flying across the North Sea and over the northern part of Denmark, they approached northern Germany from over the Baltic Sea.

Their primary targets would be the huge Luftwaffe engineering facility and bomber crew training school at Tutow. The most distant on the 3rd Division target list, the buildings were clustered around the city of Posen. Located 140 miles inland from the Baltic, Posen was a historically Polish city known in Polish as Poznan. It had been part of the Prussian and, later, German empires between 1815 and 1919 and was Polish again for twenty years before Hitler reincorporated it back into Germany in 1939. Here, the primary target was the Luftwaffenfliegerhorst Kreising airfield and factory complex that was located in the suburb of Krzesiny.

The secondary targets for the 3rd Division included the German port cities of Stettin and Rostock, which housed aircraft manufacturing facilities operated by Heinkel Flugzeugwerke.

Part of the plan in sending the 3rd Division so far north was diversionary. Seeing this force on radar or with observers in Denmark, the Luft-waffe would be alerted to counter them by shifting interceptors from central Germany. When it was discovered that the main part of the Sunday mission was coming over central Germany, the fighters that had gone north would have to make a U-turn from a long distance. This would pull them away from the 3rd Division and make them late in intercepting the other divisions—at least in theory.

Following a course that was mainly over the water, the 3rd Division would fly without fighter escort. They would depend for their defense on the other two divisions having lured the Luftwaffe into action over Germany's industrial heartland.

This may have worked to a certain extent, but the ploy could certainly not be proven by the experiences of the 3rd Division crews who were mauled by the Luftwaffe east of Denmark.

The 100th Bombardment Group came south across the North Sea with the 3rd Division bomber stream, crossing the coastline at ten minutes to noon, a little more than three hours after departing British airspace. Contrary to the theory about the Luftwaffe being elsewhere, interceptors were on hand to meet the bombers three minutes after they made landfall. First to attack were Fw 190s, which was perhaps fitting, as the 100th was heading in to attack a Focke-Wulf factory, and these were followed by Bf 109s and rocket-firing Bf 110s and Ju 88s. Several crews reported seeing an Fw 190 carrying a bomb that hung from a cable.

Also known as the "Century Bombers," the 100th Bombardment Group had earned a Distinguished Unit Citation in the Regensburg mission on August 17. The 100th would also be known throughout the Eighth Air Force as the "Bloody Hundredth" for the punishment it had taken from the Luftwaffe and flak batteries in missions going back to the first one to Regensburg.

Unfortunately, the 100th discovered that the clear skies over most of Germany did not extend to the parts of Germany that had recently been Poland. Because the United States still officially recognized Poznan as Polish, the strike force had been briefed to divert to the secondary target if their bombardiers did not have a clear view of their objectives relative to residential areas. Finding cloud cover, they made a "circling climb to the left" and diverted to the port of Stettin, their secondary target.

Here, at four minutes past 2 P.M., a Pathfinder Fortress picked out the target on radar and the other bombers followed its lead. However, any time a diversion is necessary, it is hard to maintain unit cohesion, especially while a formation is under fighter attack, and this axiom was proven that afternoon over northeastern Germany.

"For some reason or other the Group leader was flying slow," John Johnson of the 100th explains in the anthology *Century Bombers* by Richard LeStrange. "On several occasions we were indicating 145 mph and still overrunning the leader. So was everyone else and by the time we reached the target we were not a formation, we were a mob. We bombed but could not be sure if we hit anything."

Edward Huntzinger, in his wartime history of the 388th Bombardment Group, writes that "at the Danish Coast on the route in, in the target area, and on the route out approximately 20 to 25 twin engine aircraft, most Me 210s, and 10 to 15 Fw 190s and Bf 109s were encountered. They used both 20mm cannon and rockets during these attacks." He further notes that two of the group's Flying Fortresses were lost, though most of the crewmen survived to become POWs.

Some of the 3rd Division Flying Fortresses that were hit attempted to make it to neutral Sweden, where they knew internment for the duration would be far more agreeable than imprisonment in a German stalag. They did not all make it. One such aircraft attempting to reach Swedish airspace was *Ain't Mis Behavin*, piloted by Lieutenant Reginald Smith, with copilot Lieutenant Orlin "Mark" Markussen.

"The plane was hit in the number two engine after encountering heavy antiaircraft fire over Stettin," Markussen explains in Richard LeStrange's anthology. "I could not feather the propeller and we dropped out of formation. We called for our Squadron leader to slow down to the airspeed required to keep 'cripples' under the protection of other B-17's. He would not—he panicked and told us to try and make it to the under cast clouds and fly to Sweden for internment. As we broke formation and dived for the clouds we were immediately hit by eight Fw-190s, who, on the first head on pass, shot off our top turret. This was followed by side, quarter and tail attacks which knocked off the left horizontal stabilizer, cut the control cables to the tail section, started a fire in the number two engine and wing tank and broke the glass canopy in the tail gunner's section. . . . Miraculously, not one of the ten of us on the crew was hit. Now we were completely on fire and the wing was about to melt off. We all bailed out over the island of Fyn."

Picked up by the Germans, Markussen was taken for interrogation by the Gestapo at Odense, which was, ironically, his mother's hometown. Everyone else was also captured, except radio operator Ira Evans, who managed to evade the Germans. He was picked up by Danish resistance fighters and he found his way to Sweden two weeks later.

Meanwhile the 3rd Division "diversion" was perceived by the other divisions to have worked to disrupt and limit what the Luftwaffe *might have* done to the 1st and 2nd Divisions. It was a case of contemplating not the mischief the enemy did, but the unquantifiable potential for greater mischief that went unrealized.

In his memoir, *Screaming Eagle*, Colonel (later Major General) Dale O. Smith, the commander of the 384th Bombardment Group during Big Week, explains how the 3rd Division's diversionary tactics seemed to have helped.

"German controllers saw our first force, a diversion of three hundred bound for Poland, swing across the North Sea toward Denmark," he writes. "Believing this a threat to Berlin, the Luftwaffe not only kept their northern fighters in place but dispatched 70 fighters from southern displacements to intercept. Eighty minutes later our main force of 700 bombers thrust at Holland on a direct route to the targets. I led the 41st Combat Wing of almost 60 Forts in this bomber stream. German radar stations soon reported our huge strength and before the 70 enemy fighters sent north could intercept our diversionary force their controllers recalled them. Some 90 local defenders attacked our main force on the penetration to Leipzig, but they had to break off and refuel about target time. The 70 fighters recalled from the north hardly got in the fight before running out of fuel."

That morning, Leipzig lay beneath a blanket of snow, and a deep blue sky. Down there, it was a sunny day—literally, but not figuratively.

"The clouds seemed to open up and there was the target right in the middle of the hole," Lieutenant Richard Crown, the 384th Bombardment Group's lead bombardier recalled. "The hangars stood out plainly against the white snow, and when the bombs hit, those buildings disappeared in one puff. Our bombs swept right through the hangar area of the field. It was one of those days when everything goes right"

"Visibility was perfect and I could see one [target] airfield below with about 25 planes lined up in a row," recalled Staff Sergeant Glen Dick, a radio operator with the 381st Bombardment Group, in a conversation with David Osborne for the book *They Came from Over the Pond*. "You could see big pieces of planes blown into the air when our bombs caught them. I also saw a tremendous explosion down there right after that. There was a big orange sheet of flame in the middle of the airfield."

"Because the weather was uncertain we were provided with a Pathfinder crew especially trained for instrument bombing," recalled Colonel Harold Bowman, commander of the 401st Bombardment Group. "The weather en route was indeed bad and preparations were made for aiming by instrument means but as we approached the target area, the clouds opened up to 'scattered' and a visual sighting was made. The result was, for our group, 100 percent of our bombs were within one thousand feet of the aiming point. Hits were made on the principal assembly shop of the Erla Messerschmitt production factory, and its other large assembly building was observed to be on fire as the bombers left the target area."

"We started out on Pathfinder [using H2X or AN/APS-15 radar]," recalls Tech Sergeant Joseph Purdy, the radio operator in the 384th B-17 named *Mrs. Geezil*. "But the target was clear for miles around. We had very little escort—area cover, and not too good, but the enemy fighters were snowed in and the ground looked pretty. The sky was beautifully empty of everything except B-17s—lots of them."

As the bombers exited the target area over Leipzig, the pilots could see a large number of contrails far to the south and coming toward the American force.

"The distance was too great to see aircraft, but not their telltale contrails," Dale Smith, leading the 384th Group, recalled. "No doubt these contrails were being made by enemy fighters launched late from southern

Germany. I asked the tail gunner if we were generating contrails. 'Affirmative,' he reported, 'heavy ones.' Sometimes a combat wing would make so many contrails that it appeared to be a long cirrus cloud. Oh, oh, I thought. If I could see that Luftwaffe leader's contrails, he could see mine. Yet in the late afternoon we were somewhat up sun from him, and I hoped he hadn't yet spotted us. So I immediately took the wing down into warmer air where we produced no contrails. It worked. The enemy fighters never intercepted."

Not everyone over Leipzig was as lucky as Dale Smith. The "90 local defenders," whom he dismissively describes, had done no small measure of damage. As the 351st Bombardment Group Flying Fortresses headed southwest into Third Reich airspace as part of the Leipzig-bound stream described by Dale Smith, they met some of those "local defenders."

In the "Tail-end Charlie" position, Dick Nelson was pushing *Ten Horsepower* as hard as he could, trying to keep up and not to tempt the Germans to regard the hand-me-down Flying Fortress as a straggler. Meeting the Luftwaffe air defense *geschwaders* in their home skies was an entirely new, and entirely disconcerting, experience. None of the crew had been over Germany before, and with the exception of copilot Ronald Bartley, this was only their second combat mission ever.

As Smith had explained, the local defenders "attacked our main force on the penetration to Leipzig." This was just as the 351st Group's aircraft were entering their bomb run.

Suddenly, all hell broke loose.

Nelson and Bartley barely had time to rest their eyes on the German fighter, emerging out of the fuzzy haze of the streaming contrails of other bombers, closing on them from straight ahead.

The combined speed of the two aircraft rushing toward each other was in the neighborhood of 500 mph, and at that speed you don't have much time to comprehend what is happening, much less to react.

The German pilot squeezed off a burst from his MG 151, sending 20mm shells hurtling toward the Flying Fortress at incomprehensible speed. The white-hot discs racing toward him were the last thing that Ronald Bartley would ever see.

One of them hit the right windshield of *Ten Horsepower*'s flight deck square on, piercing it as though it were not there.

The explosion vaporized the copilot's head, and the shrapnel ripped into the side of Dick Nelson's head and arm.

Across the world in the United States, Bernice Bartley, so recently a new bride, was just then waking up on the first morning of her widowhood.

Crews elsewhere in the formation saw *Ten Horsepower* getting hit just as its bombs dropped. Suddenly more than two tons lighter, the B-17G nosed upward for a moment and then drifted out of formation. With the copilot dead and the pilot unconscious, the Flying Fortress was out of control. It went into a spin and began to fall, dropping from twenty thousand feet to fifteen thousand feet, and still it tumbled downward.

Joe Martin, the bombardier, alone in the nose of the aircraft, looked up into the cockpit and saw the carnage of what he assumed to be two dead men. Being unable to raise anyone on the intercom, he also made an assumption that anyone else who had survived had already bailed out. He popped the hatch and hit the silk as quickly as he could. His assumption was wrong; he would be the only one to jump.

Carl Moore crawled to the flight deck, where he found it drenched from top to bottom with the blood of two men. He grabbed the yoke and strained to fight the centrifugal force that governed the momentum of the out-of-control aircraft.

As Moore battled the controls, *Ten Horsepower* dropped from fifteen thousand feet to ten thousand feet, and still it fell.

Finally, he was able to gain control, and the bomber leveled out at five thousand feet.

The first reaction of most of the crew was to get the hell out of the falling coffin as soon as the centrifugal force no longer pinned them to the nearest bulkhead.

Back topside, Wally Truemper, the navigator, sensed that the aircraft was now in stable flight and ordered everyone to stay put for the time being. Archie Mathies popped out of the frightening confines of the ball turret and made his way to the flight deck, where he and Moore were quickly joined by Truemper.

They took stock of a horrible situation. Blood, brains, and flesh were plastered all over everything, and a nearly 200 mph wind whipped through the shattered windshield.

Bartley was obviously gone, but Dick Nelson, despite horrendous injuries, was still breathing.

As the men looked around, they realized that *Ten Horsepower* was, with the obvious exception of the flight deck, completely intact. All four of her four turbo-supercharged Wright Cyclone engines still thundered as smoothly as they had that morning when she lifted off from Polebrook. As far as anyone could see, the wings and control surfaces were in good working order. The decision was made to remove Bartley and Nelson from the flight deck and attempt to fly the bomber back to England.

They managed to lift what was left of the copilot down into the bombardier's station, but when they attempted to move Dick Nelson, they found him so entangled in the controls that they decided to leave him for fear of exacerbating his injuries.

It has been said that a little knowledge is a bad thing, but on this Sunday, it was good. Between them, Moore, Mathies, and Truemper had enough of a basic understanding of the pilot's trade to keep *Ten Horsepower* level and get the aircraft turned toward home. Truemper, being the navigator, figured out the course, and they headed in that direction.

Archie Mathies, who had watched pilots enough to believe that he could fly the plane, slipped into Bartley's vacant seat and took the controls. Truemper gave him a northwesterly course that they believed would take them home.

However, the Luftwaffe was not finished with *Ten Horsepower*.

From straight above, a Focke-Wulf Fw 190 dived on the airplane, trading streams of tracers with Joe Rex and his .50-caliber machine gun for a few seconds before exploding in a shower of debris. Rex had canceled the Focke-Wulf, but not without being badly wounded in his arm.

Two more Fw 190s came up on the right side, flying parallel with *Ten Horsepower* so close that the crewmen had to do a double take to be sure they weren't escort fighters. As the Germans were studying the damaged Flying Fortress, Russell Robinson, the right waist gunner, fired a burst of .50-caliber lead at them.

The two German planes backed off, then made one firing pass at *Ten Horsepower* before inexplicably disappearing to chase someone else.

Breathing a collective sigh of relief, the crew headed for home.

Tom Sowell, who had crawled into the ball turret abandoned by Archie Mathies, later recalled the surreal view of people just five thousand feet below, standing on the streets of German and Dutch cities and staring up at the American four-engine bomber. Those in the Dutch cities waved.

At that same moment, and in those same skies, another, eerily similar drama was playing out aboard another 1st Bombardment Division Flying Fortress.

Lieutenant William Robert "Bill" Lawley, a twenty-three-year-old pilot from Leeds, Alabama, had taken off from Chelveston that morning in a Flying Fortress on whose nose, the paint proclaiming it as the *Cabin in the Sky*, was still fresh.

Bill Lawley's life had paralleled the lives of so many of the young pilots in the sky that day. He had enlisted for flight training in August 1942, the same month that he had turned twenty-two. He had earned his wings in April 1943, been matched with a crew, trained at Tyndall Field in Florida, and was part of that huge influx of personnel who had flowed into the Replacement Depot Casual Pool in England around the first of the year.

In January, Lawley and his crew received their assignment to the 364th Bombardment Squadron of the 305th "Can Do" Bombardment Group. Like so many of the men amassed for the thousand-bomber maximum effort that Sunday morning, he and his men had yet to fly a mission deep into the Third Reich. However, unlike the crew of *Ten Horsepower*, they had managed to get the experience of multiple shorter missions before that day.

As Dick Nelson and Ronald Bartley had awakened at Polebrook around 3 A.M. to eat breakfast and head over to the 351st Bombardment Group briefing hut, so too had Bill Lawley and his copilot, Lieutenant Paul Murphy, done the same at Chelveston. When the black curtain was pulled back at the 364th Squadron briefing, the string of black yarn stretched, like that on the map at the 510th, from East Anglia to Leipzig. They too saw names such as Heiterblick, Abtnaundorf, and Mockau airfield.

As Wilbur Morrison writes in his book *The Incredible 305th*, Lawley turned to his bombardier, Lieutenant Henry Mason, and said, "Doesn't sound too bad, Henry."

"Who knows?" Mason replied as he stared at the map. "You never can tell about a strike into Germany."

Five hours later, it was not the streets and landmarks on a map or recon photo that bombardier Henry Mason was viewing through his Norden bombsight. It was the streets and landmarks of the *real* Leipzig.

When the time came, he toggled the bomb release, anticipating the sharp jump that a Flying Fortress does when it is abruptly relieved of the groaning weight of around three tons of bombs.

Nothing. There had been a hang-up. The bombs did not release.

However, this problem quickly moved down Mason's list of priorities in the clear skies over the Reich.

As had happened so recently aboard *Ten Horsepower*, and on way too many other Flying Fortresses in the past half hour, all hell broke loose.

A German fighter raced toward *Cabin in the Sky*, making one of those head-on passes that Egon Mayer had helped to turn into Luftwaffe doctrine.

Exactly as had happened aboard *Ten Horsepower*—and probably as the interceptor pilots had been told at *their* morning briefing that Sunday to *make* happen—the Messerschmitt hurled its 20mm shells directly into the flight deck windshield.

As had happened on *Ten Horsepower* less than an hour before, the copilot died instantly. Like Ronald Bartley, the last thing that Paul Murphy saw was those burning hot disks of incoming rounds heading directly at his face.

As Dick Nelson had been seriously injured by the shell that had killed the man in the seat next to his, so too was Bill Lawley.

Unlike Nelson, however, Lawley was still conscious.

In every other respect, though, *Cabin in the Sky* was in much worse shape than *Ten Horsepower*. Unlike Nelson's place, which took a single, deadly hit, Lawley's bomber had been worked over. One engine was on fire, and several of the men had been badly wounded as the fighters raked the Flying Fortress from nose to tail.

To add to their problems, *Cabin in the Sky* was in a steep, almost vertical dive with a full bomb load.

They were going down.

However, Bill Lawley decided *not* to let this happen.

He jerked back on the yoke, but Paul Murphy's lifeless body had fallen forward onto his and was pushing the bomber ever downward.

Though his right hand was badly injured and essentially useless, Bill Lawley managed to maul Murphy's body off the controls and then strain with all he could do with his left hand to get the bomber into level flight at about twelve thousand feet.

As on the flight deck of *Ten Horsepower*, blood was splattered everywhere.

"In the excitement of the moment he had felt sharp pains," Wilbur Morrison writes of Lawley's discovery that he too had been badly wounded. "Only when he wiped his hand across his face and saw the blood was he fully aware that he had been hit by the exploding shell."

While he was pulling out of the dive it had not really mattered, but now that he had managed to level out, Lawley needed to see where he was going, and he would have liked to see his instruments. Accomplishing this necessitated the grisly task of cleaning Murphy's blood and shreds of his flesh—not to mention no small amount of Lawley's own blood—from the windshield and the instrument panel.

As he was doing this, the Luftwaffe hit *Cabin in the Sky* once again.

Lawley instinctively took evasive action, and the fighters broke off their attack. They probably figured that this Flying Fortress was a goner and not worth their attention when the sky was so full of other bombers.

As the engine fire seemed to be getting out of control, Lawley managed deftly to maneuver the plane in such a way that the rush of air provided by the forward momentum knocked the fire back.

Feeling all this evasive action and maneuvering, the crew probably figured that *Cabin in the Sky* was out of control. In fact, the opposite was true. The Flying Fortress was very much in the control of a skilled pilot. One is tempted to say that the plane was in good hands, but given the situation, it was the singular, "hand."

Up to this point, only the flight engineer had bailed out of the aircraft, but the topic was now back on the agenda. Lawley told the crew to go ahead and jump.

"We can't bail out!" Sergeant Thomas Dempsey, the radio operator, replied over the intercom. "Two gunners are so seriously wounded they can't leave the ship."

With this, Lawley made the decision to take *Cabin in the Sky* back to England. He was not about to abandon wounded men. Everyone else who remained aboard decided to stay with him. Nobody wanted to give up the ship.

Henry Mason, the bombardier, who had some flight training, came up out of the nose to help. They were unable to extricate Murphy's body from his seat, so they used his coat to tie him to the seat back, and Mason stood between the seats to help with the controls. They used the bomb release on the flight deck to get rid of the ordnance and lighten the Flying Fortress.

Though he was bleeding heavily from wounds in his face and neck, as well as his hand, Lawley refused first aid. He probably used the phrase "just a scratch."

Cabin in the Sky droned on, with the crew knowing that they would be alone, aboard a vulnerable straggler, for five painfully long hours in skies in which the Luftwaffe might burst upon them at any moment.

Somewhere over France, the shock and blood loss took its toll.

Bill Lawley passed out.

Henry Mason grabbed the yoke from his awkward standing position and jostled the pilot.

"Stay with us!"

Finally, Lawley regained consciousness and wrapped his left hand around the controls once again.

Meanwhile, the 2nd Bombardment Division was sharing an experience more like that of *Ten Horsepower* or *Cabin in the Sky* than like that of 1st Division bombers who had avoided the "90 local defenders."

Over the 2nd Division target area, which spanned a one-hundred-mile swath of German airspace between Braunschweig and Gotha, the Liberators were intercepted by the heavily armed Bf 110 interceptors of Jagdgeschwader 11.

As Wright Lee, a navigator with the 445th Bombardment Group, wrote in his memoirs, the Germans attacked just as the Liberators were approaching Braunschweig.

"Something was wrong," Lee recalls of the approach to the target. "We were almost on the bomb run and no flak or fighters until 1:18 p.m. . . . then the sky seemed to fill immediately with a host of Nazi planes. They came out of nowhere and we were all kept busy calling off enemy fighter positions and firing when the chance came. I had put up my navigation table and was standing by to 'toggle' the bombs, when someone shouted over the interphone, 'Fighter high at 12 o'clock. He's coming in on us.' The nose and upper turrets responded immediately, swinging their guns forward and upward, while the others of us forward—pilot, copilot and navigator— were cringing from the bursting 20mm shells just outside the windows. The German fighter poured them in but we felt no direct hits. Simultaneously our plane shook violently from nose to tail."

What Lee described was the heavy vibration of multiple machine guns hammering away simultaneously.

"The nose and upper turrets were blasting away at the same time at the onrushing fighter," he explains. "Our bullets tore into his right wing and fuselage. Black smoke burst from this Fw 190 as he pulled up and over our plane, seemingly only a few feet from our heads. Within an instant the waist gunner, Eugene Dueben, shouted into the interphone 'Hey, two fighters just ran together behind us.' Later, he told us that while the two turrets were blazing away at the attacking fighter forward, a Bf 109 came up from under the formation for a belly attack, completed an unsuccessful pass, zoomed up and over and collided with the nose attacking Fw 190 right behind us. Both planes went spiraling down in flames and we were credited with two 'kills' that day."

Over the target, Lee was surprised to see that the Luftwaffe interceptors continued to attack, despite the presence of German antiaircraft fire exploding all around them. As the 445th exited the target area, Liberators started dropping one by one.

"Another of our Group's ships, the *Sky Wolfe*, suddenly began dropping with its nose down. He fell right through our formation between [Lieutenant] Winn's plane and ours, nearly taking Winn's wing with him. Our tail gunner watched him continue his helpless spiral downward and he finally blew up. No chutes were observed.

"Meanwhile, the attacks continued with the same fury as when they started and enemy fighters shot down two from the 389th Bomb Group, a part of our [2nd Combat] Wing. In contrast to the air battle's utter horror, it was a picturesque view as we watched the many descending parachutes blend into the terrain's snow covered background. . . . Another Liberator from our Group began falling behind and suddenly the entire tail section fell off. The plane nosed up, went into a spin, burst into flames, then exploded. . . . A half hour after the attack started, the enemy activity ceased, but the toll on us was great. Our Wing of 70 planes had lost seven."

One Luftwaffe pilot in particular became the scourge of the B-24 force. Major Rolf-Günther Hermichen, who had transferred from Jagdgeschwader 26 in October 1943 to become *Gruppenkommandeur* with I Gruppe of Jagdgeschwader 11, shot down four Liberators in the space of eighteen minutes on Sunday.

Beginning at 1:27 P.M., he chased the 2nd Division formations from Holzminden in Lower Saxony toward Gotha, claiming two of the four Liberators in the first three minutes of his relentless spree. Hermichen ended the day with fifty-two aerial victories out of his eventual career total of sixty-four. Of these, twenty-six would be four-engine heavy bombers.

Hermichen's bloody spree notwithstanding, Colonel Dale Smith continued to see Day One in terms of a glass half-full, and to think in terms of the things that the Eighth Air Force had done right, and what damage the Luftwaffe might have done.

"Expecting a reciprocal withdrawal, German controllers marshaled all the refueled fighters, together with many others, along our penetration route, ready to swarm upon us on our way out," Smith says, explaining how at least some of the Eighth Air Force bombers continued to confound the Luftwaffe as the bombers exited the continent on Sunday afternoon. "But we didn't return that way. Instead we turned southwest, detouring in a wide arc south of the Ruhr. By the time German defense commanders discovered our purpose and hastily ordered their assembled fighters south we were well on our way. Only an insignificant number caught the tail of our bomber column as it withdrew to the Channel."

Not everyone had been so lucky, nor would the Luftwaffe be so completely fooled tomorrow.

SIXTEEN

——————

A WING AND A PRAYER

On that cold Sunday afternoon, as the sun began to flirt with the notion of what the poets call "sinking slowly into the west," men began gathering in control towers all across East Anglia, straining their eyes against the bleak winter sky.

It was still too early to expect much. All of the bombers that had aborted for various reasons, mainly mechanical, had long since landed, and it was too early for the others to have completed the round-trips to Braunschweig or Oschersleben, and those who went to Rostock and Leipzig would be even later.

At Polebrook, Sergeant Harold Flint had come on duty at noon as the control tower operator. About three hours later, and about an hour ahead of the expected return of the Leipzig mission, he received a sudden and urgent call over the radio.

"This is Paramount A-Able," the voice said, according to Flint's recollection in a recording in the collection of the Air Force Historical Research Agency. "The pilot has been badly wounded, the copilot is dead. I am the navigator. What shall we do?"

The voice was that of navigator Wally Truemper. Archie Mathies had flown *Ten Horsepower* all the way back to England and was within minutes of coming over the field from which they had departed before dawn. Truemper was communicating with the tower because the radio on the flight deck had been knocked out in the 20mm blast that killed copilot Ronald Bartley. Despite his injuries, radioman Joe Rex had repaired the intercom to the flight deck, so that at least Archie could communicate with Wally.

Colonel Elzia LeDoux of the 351st Bombardment Group's 509th Bombardment Squadron, who was on duty that day as the tower officer, immediately sent word to Colonel Eugene A. Romig, the group commander. Within moments, Romig's operations officer, Colonel Robert W. Burns (who succeeded Romig as group CO eight months later) had arrived in the tower. Romig himself arrived shortly thereafter to watch *Ten Horsepower* make a fast, erratic pass over the field. When the men in the tower learned that one of the gunners was flying the airplane, they were less critical of his technique.

Then it began to sink in that neither Mathies, nor Truemper, the ranking officer on board, had ever flown a B-17—until today—and that *nobody* aboard *Ten Horsepower* had ever landed one.

Romig instructed them to make a pass over the field with sufficient altitude for the other crewmen to safely bail out. He then told Truemper to tell Mathies to point *Ten Horsepower* toward the North Sea coast, which was about forty miles to the east. When they were sure that the Flying Fortress was headed safely out to sea, they were to bail out themselves.

Mathies and Truemper refused.

Truemper said they would make the pass to let everyone else get out, but that Archie Mathies planned to land *Ten Horsepower*.

Why?

They explained that Dick Nelson, despite his severe injuries and his being unconscious, was still alive and still breathing. They refused to abandon him to die in the North Sea.

The officers in the tower were hesitant, but they agreed to try to talk the plane down.

Five parachutes floated down toward Polebrook, and *Ten Horsepower* circled around to make a pass at the runway.

Too fast and too high.

Flint told Mathies to go around.

Too fast and too high, *again*.

When this was repeated, and it became clear that Mathies needed to watch an example of a landing B-17, Romig decided to go up and bring him in. With LeDoux as his copilot, he took off in the Flying Fortress called *My Princess* and rendezvoused with *Ten Horsepower*.

Romig flew as close as he could, close enough to see an exhausted Archie Mathies in the right seat, but not so close that Mathies would collide with him as he tried to control the bomber.

Unfortunately, when Romig tried to speak to Truemper directly, he could not. Yet another communications glitch compelled him to relay his messages for Mathies to Truemper by way of the control tower.

By now, the rest of the 351st Bombardment Group had started to return, but in order to keep Polebrook clear for *Ten Horsepower*, Burns declared an emergency and ordered them to divert to the airfield at Glatton, the home of the 457th Bombardment Group, which was about three miles to the east.

By this time, however, *Ten Horsepower* and *My Princess* had strayed south of Polebrook by about five miles and were closer to the field at Molesworth, home of the 303rd Bombardment Group. Most of the 303rd's aircraft had returned, so Romig and LeDoux briefly considered, then rejected, the idea of trying to bring *Ten Horsepower* down there.

As they approached Polebrook to try again, Truemper and Mathies abruptly made the decision to try putting *Ten Horsepower* down in a large field. Romig tried to instruct them to land on the downslope of this field, but by then, Archie Mathies was already committed, and he proceeded to land uphill.

At first, it looked as though they were going to make it, but this was not to be.

Mathies and Truemper were killed on impact in their valiant, failed effort to save Dick Nelson.

On that day back in 1929, on the trestle outside Library, Pennsylvania, Archie Mathies had embraced danger and looked death in the eye. On that day in 1929, death had blinked.

Today, death exacted its cold, heartless vengeance.

Miraculously, Nelson survived the crash. He was taken from the wreckage of *Ten Horsepower* alive and rushed to a hospital.

He did not make it. He died without regaining consciousness. Some say that he survived through the night, but his headstone in the Rock Island National Cemetery carries Sunday's date.

In Chelveston, about as far south of Molesworth as Molesworth was from Polebrook, the 305th "Can Do" Bombardment Group was recovering its bombers, and eyes were scanning the sky for stragglers. They might have been hoping to see Lieutenant Bill Lawley's *Cabin in the Sky*, but they had already gotten the word from several people who had seen it go down. It was in a nearly vertical dive with an engine on fire. They knew that was one of those things from which you don't often walk away.

There would be, the men in the tower thought sadly, another ten empty bunks at Chelveston that night.

There may have been a glance toward the sky to see if there might be a *Cabin* in it, but there was no *Cabin*. Nor would there be.

Meanwhile, however, contrary to what anyone may have thought they had seen, the *Cabin* was *still* in the sky.

There was no more welcome sight than the line of the French coast looming up ahead of *Cabin*'s crew. They saw the white and sandy crescent where they knew that thousands of young Americans in their age group would be battling their way ashore within a few months to begin the liberation of this continent that had been beneath their wings for the past eight hours or so.

There was no *less* welcome sound than that of one of the Flying Fortress's Wright Cyclone engines starting to choke from lack of fuel.

Bill Lawley, woozy from pain and blood loss, but still in control, feathered the prop on the engine to reduce aerodynamic drag.

Suddenly, he was greeted by another unwelcome turn of events. The engine fire had exploded to life once again. This time, at barely five thousand feet, there would be no diving to use increased air flow to blow back the flames.

They would soon be crossing the English Channel, but Chelveston was still another one hundred miles farther on. Lawley knew they couldn't make it, and most of the crew sensed this as well.

Bill Lawley had dragged *Cabin in the Sky* across hundreds of miles of

Left: General Carl Andrew "Tooey" Spaatz was the first commander of the Eighth Air Force in 1942, and by the time of Big Week in February 1944, he commanded the entire U.S. Strategic Air Forces in Europe. He later served as chief of staff of the U.S. Air Force.

Right: General Frederick Lewis Anderson was probably the most influential planning and operations man for Big Week. Named as the commanding general of the VIII Bomber Command in 1943, he was, by the time of Big Week, the deputy commander for operations of the U.S. Strategic Air Forces in Europe.

General Ira Clarence Eaker took over the Eighth Air Force in December 1942 and commanded it through the period when it began operations, including its first deep penetration missions into the heart of Germany.

All photos courtesy USAAF via author

Top: Boeing B-17G Flying Fortresses of the Eighth Air Force 91st Bombardment Group over Germany in 1944.

Middle: Consolidated B-24 Liberators during the August 1, 1944, Operation Tidal Wave strike against Ploesti Romania, source of most of the Third Reich's refined petroleum.

Right: Boeing Flying Fortresses of the Eighth Air Force 91st Bombardment Group cross the coastline, outbound from their mission over Kiel, Germany, in January 1944, on the eve of Big Week.

Staff Sergeant Archibald "Archie" Mathies was a young Flying Fortress gunner from the coal patch near Finleyville, Pennsylvania. He flew with the Eighth Air Force 351st Bombardment Group and earned the Medal of Honor on the first day of Big Week for his heroism in saving fellow crew members.

Lieutenant William Robert "Bill" Lawley, a pilot with the Eighth Air Force 305th Bombardment Group, earned the Medal of Honor on Big Week's Day One, when he successfully brought his Flying Fortress, *Cabin in the Sky*, home from Leipzig despite having been severely wounded.

Two of Big Week's key operational commanders: General Jimmy Doolittle commanded the Eighth Air Force, while General Curtis LeMay led the 3rd Bombardment Division.

A B-17G Flying Fortress of the Eighth Air Force 3rd Bombardment Division, 452nd Bombardment Group opens its bomb bay to release its ordnance on the Third Reich

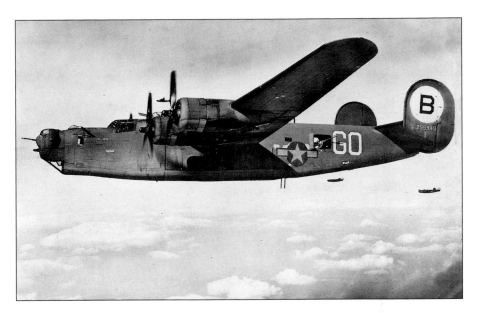

Consolidated B-24J Liberators of the Eighth Air Force 2nd Bombardment Division, 93rd Bombardment Group over Germany in early 1944.

Any landing that you walk away from is a good landing. This B-17G Flying Fortress of the Eighth Air Force 401st Bombardment Group crash landed, presumably at its home base at Deenethorpe, on February 20, 1944, after bombing the Erla Messerschmitt facilities at Leipzig on the first day of Big Week.

Manning their .50-caliber machine guns, waist gunners aboard a B-24 Liberator await an attack from the Luftwaffe.

Waist gunners aboard a B-17 Flying Fortress both eye a suspicious speck in the sky. The heavy, sheepskin-lined leather flying suits worn by gunners can be clearly seen.

A Fifteenth Air Force B-24J Liberator over the Alps. The high mountains presented a challenge for the bomber crews flying into the Reich from their bases in Italy.

Thick contrails flow from the engines of Eighth Air Force 324th Bombardment Squadron Flying Fortresses as they head home from Schweinfurt on February 24, 1944, the penultimate day of Big Week. The Flying Fortress at right center is one of several bombers named *Pist'l Packin' Mama* after the popular song.

Above: With targets in snow-covered Regensburg burning, the B-17 Flying Fortresses of the Eighth Air Force 452nd Bombardment Group turn to begin their long journey back to England on February 25, 1944, the last day of Big Week.

Left: Fifteenth Air Force bombs fall on Regensbrg, home to the largest manufacturing facility for Messerschmitt Bf 109 fighters.

Festung Europa, and he finally nudged the Flying Fortress across the English coastline. They were a sorry mess, all shot up and with an engine fire that was minutes away from burning off a wing.

They had come so far, and had come so close, but they would never reach Chelveston.

"He was looking for an open pasture," waist gunner Ralph Braswell told Richard Goldstein of the *New York Times* fifty-five years later. "All of a sudden, there was a Canadian fighter field. He flashed the emergency signal and we went right in."

It was a terrible landing. The landing gear controls were not functional, so the only choice left to the wounded pilot was a belly landing. *Cabin in the Sky* slammed into grass paralleling the runway at Redhill, a fighter field south of London. It skidded, scraped, and careened.

Now, for the first time since Bill Lawley had pulled it out of that near-vertical dive over Leipzig, the Flying Fortress *was* out of control.

Fortunately the mud slowed the forward momentum and the aircraft would not have long to travel in this condition.

It was a terrible landing, but they always say that any landing from which you can walk away is a good landing.

Some of the men aboard Lawley's plane—including him—were so badly wounded that they did not actually walk away, but everyone who was aboard, except Paul Murphy, who had died over Leipzig, exited the *Cabin in the Sky* alive.

Bill Lawley had told them that he was going to get them back to England safely, and he had.

For their extraordinary heroism on the opening day of Big Week, Archie Mathies, Wally Truemper, and Bill Lawley would all be written up for Medals of Honor.

And then there were heroes less celebrated. At Kimbolton, Lieutenant Paul Breeding landed a 379th Bombardment Group Flying Fortress that had been chewed up by Bf 109s over Bernburg. He too had lost his copilot and had been hit badly himself.

"Rather than stay in his position as lead plane of the second element and chance breaking up the formation, Breeding pulled his plane up 1,000 feet above the others before calling for help," Derwyn Robb writes in his memoir of the unit. Two of the gunners came to the flight deck to help remove the dead man to the bombardier's station, and to take over flying the plane while Breeding received first aid.

"It was not until the dead copilot had been removed that anyone know that Breeding was also badly wounded, as he had continued to fly the plane without a word of his own injuries," Robb continues. "Although the pilot was bleeding profusely and in severe pain he refused to take morphine, maintaining that he would be needed to get the plane down through the undercast at the base."

In the meantime, the crew, facing a dilemma analogous to that which had taken place a short time before aboard *Ten Horsepower*, decided to put the ship on automatic pilot, strap parachutes to Breeding and the dead copilot, and bail out.

"When Breeding heard of this plan, he ordered [waist gunner] Charlie Sans to help him back into the cockpit to take over the controls," Robb explains. "Weak and half conscious from loss of blood and pain, he stayed at the controls to bring his crew down through the clouds and a safe landing. As Breeding taxied his plane off the runway to a stop and reached forward to cut the engine switches, he passed out."

Late that afternoon, at Park House in the London suburbs, where Tooey Spaatz and his staff lived—about sixty-five miles south of Polebrook and Molesworth, and a little less distance from Kimbolton—the teletypes began clattering as soon as the first bombardment group had landed all of its bombers.

As evening approached, the men who had planned Sunday's missions, and the men who commanded the crews who flew the bombers, gathered to view and analyze the results of the day's work. Fred Anderson, Glen Williamson, and Dick Hughes were there, and so too were Jimmy Doolittle and his staff.

"We had been up all night and all day," Williamson later told journalist Charles Murphy. "The reports came in all evening. Group after group reported no losses or only one or two. We couldn't believe it. We were all thinking somebody's going to get wiped out, somebody's going to say he was cut to pieces. When all the reports were in and we added up the totals the figures were unbelievable."

The men who gathered on Sunday night at Park House were expecting to learn of two hundred lost bombers and two thousand lost crewmen. They learned that the Eighth Air Force had lost only twenty-one bombers and four fighters shot down. Losses were losses, but the commanders fixated on those who might have been lost but who were now snoring in their bunks across East Anglia.

The 1st Bombardment Division reported that seven of its Flying Fortresses had gone down, and one had to be written off after it returned. The division had lost seven men killed in action—including Archie Mathies and Wally Truemper—and seventy-two were listed as missing after bailing out over Germany.

For the 2nd Bombardment Division, eight Liberators were lost and three written off. The division reported ten men killed in action and seventy-seven missing. The 3rd Bombardment Division lost six bombers, plus one write-off, three men killed in action, and sixty missing.

Reconnaissance aircraft had been over each of the targets roughly ninety minutes after the bombers had departed.

As soon as they returned to England, the film from their cameras was processed, and the photos were hand delivered to the gathering at Park House. With these and the teletyped reports that were still coming in, Spaatz, Anderson, Doolittle, Hughes, and the others began putting together a picture of what the crews and their bombers had accomplished.

The 1st Bombardment Division reported that of the 417 Flying Fortresses that it sent against the arc of aircraft industry sites around Leipzig, 239 had bombed their primary targets. Another 44 bombed Oschersleben, while 37 attacked Bernburg.

The 2nd Division put 26 Liberators over the primary targets around Braunschweig, and 71 over Helmstedt and Oschersleben, while 87 attacked Gotha. Of the 314 Flying Fortresses of the 3rd Division, 105 reached the Tutow complex, while 76 bombed the Marienehe Heinkel plant near Rostock, and 115 bombed other targets in the area.

The damage at Leipzig was especially extensive. The reconnaissance photos showed, and the Strategic Bombing Survey later confirmed, that the serious destruction that had occurred at all four Allgemeine Transportanlagen Gesellschaft plants included structural damage and impairment to critical machine tools. Erla Maschinenwerke GmbH also took a heavy hit, especially at Heiterblick and the final assembly facility at Mockau.

In the wartime history of the 384th Bombardment Group, Quentin Bland, the group's official historian, working with Linda and Vic Fayers-Hallin, compiled a collection of firsthand accounts. Staff Sergeant Richard Hughes, the ball turret gunner in *Mr. Five by Five*, had an extraordinary view of Leipzig when "the whole place blacked up as soon as the bombs hit. The bomb blasts were like little lights flicking on and off among the buildings down there."

"We had the most perfect bombing conditions I've ever seen," Lieutenant James Miller, the copilot of the 384th Bombardment Group's *Tame Wolf* said as he was debriefed on Sunday night. "There was a big hole in the clouds for a 20-mile radius around the target. The first bomb hit right in between two hangars, and the rest fell in a perfect pattern. If we didn't shake that place today we'll never hit anything."

Meanwhile, the Eighth Air Force bomber gunners claimed to have sixty-five Luftwaffe interceptors. While this is probably an exaggeration because of the usual incidence of double claims, the claims of sixty-one enemy fighters downed by escorting fighters can be considered accurate. Given the loss of just four of the escorts, their results for the day were cause for celebration.

"It was not till late in the evening that the reports came in from the last groups to get back to their fields," Hughes adds of the long vigil at Park House that night. "As the figures came in hourly it became clearer and clearer that we had achieved an astounding victory at minimum cost. Every target had been hit, and hit well, and our casualties had been under five percent of the force engaged. General Spaatz drew his first easy breath and took off for Italy."

As Arthur Ferguson best summarizes Day One of Big Week, "That the first mission was attempted can be attributed to the stubborn refusal of General Anderson to allow an opportunity, even a dubious one [because of the weather], to slip past him. To the intense relief of USSTAF headquarters the gamble paid off."

SEVENTEEN

MONDAY, FEBRUARY 21

Irving Krick promised continued clear weather over Germany on Monday. The high pressure area that Hap Arnold's weather guru had promised would linger had done just that.

As Dick Hughes observed and as Arthur Ferguson reports, "When the weather prospect for the twenty-first indicated continuing favorable conditions over Germany, an operation was enthusiastically undertaken. The feeling was spreading within USSTAF headquarters, and from there to the operational headquarters, that this was the big chance."

It was a big chance that would be seized, although on Monday, instead of the crystal clear weather encountered on Sunday, the high pressure area delivered what should more accurately have been described as "partly cloudy."

Again, as in the wee hours of Sunday, RAF Bomber Command was at work even as Tooey Spaatz, Jimmy Doolittle, and Fred Anderson were still reading the teletypes and congratulating one another at Park House. The Wright R1820 radials on the American Flying Fortresses had barely cooled from Sunday's triumph when Air Chief Marshal Sir Arthur "Bomber" Harris sent his Lancasters and Halifaxes to carpet Germany with bombs. Unlike the previous night's visit to Leipzig, the principal target for the RAF would be a city that was not on the USAAF target list for Monday.

According to the RAF Bomber Command campaign diary for February 1944, there were 826 Bomber Command aircraft that reached their targets that night. Of these, 598 visited the environs of Stuttgart, a penetration mission of around 460 miles. Speaking of aircraft engines, Stuttgart was important to the Operation Argument mission as home to Daimler-Benz, whose ubiquitous DB601 water-cooled V12s were used in Messerschmitt Bf 109, Bf 110, and Me 210 fighters, among others.

The Eighth Air Force, meanwhile, launched 861 bombers before dawn on Monday morning. Whereas Sunday's target list had focused on aircraft manufacturing, today's would see the 1st and 2nd Bombardment Divisions concentrating on the Luftwaffe itself.

The arc of sky across northwestern Germany, generally between Münster and the North Sea, was essentially the gateway to the industrial heartland of Germany. Unless they took a wide detour, all of the RAF and USAAF bomber missions had to pass through this gateway to reach targets—from Hamburg and Berlin to Schweinfurt and Regensburg—deep inside the Reich.

Accordingly, the Luftwaffe had turned this gateway into a corridor of death for the bomber crews, by establishing interceptor bases here. From here, fighters could intercept and maul the bombers on their way in, then land to refuel, and hammer them again on their way home.

On February 21, the Eighth Air Force went after these bases.

Foremost among these, and present on the target list as a primary target for the 1st Division, and as a secondary target for the other two divisions, was the Diepholzer Militär-Flughafen (Fliegerhorst) at Diepholz, about forty miles southwest of Bremen. This large base had an interesting history, having been planned as early as 1934, before Hitler officially abrogated the provision in the Treaty of Versailles that forbade Germany an air force.

Working through the noblewoman Emmy Baroness von Wagner, the city had acquired farmland and sold it to a front company called "Deutsche-Luftfahrts-und-Handels AG (German Aviation Authorities and Trade Inc.)," who had used Reich Labor Service crews to build a massive complex of runways and other facilities that are still in use by both military and civilian traffic in the twenty-first century. The Luftwaffe officially took possession in 1936 and turned Fliegerhorst Diepholz into a major base. There was a certain irony when the Allied bombers appeared overhead, given that in 1940, Diepholz had been home to the He 111 bombers that flattened Rotterdam and brought the Blitz to London.

The 336 Flying Fortresses of the 1st Division, who had had the longest missions on Sunday, drew the shortest for Monday, while 244 Liberators of the 2nd Bombardment Division were sent against Luftwaffe bases slightly deeper. The airfields at Gütersloh, Lippstadt, and Werl, the 1st Division primary targets, were obscured by thick overcast, so 285 of the bombers diverted to secondary Luftwaffe targets at Bramsche, Hopsten, Quakenbrück, and Rheine.

Indeed, the patchy clouds found over so many of the primary targets forced so many diversions to secondaries and targets of opportunity that Lieutenant Colonel William Buck, the commander of the 1st Division's 41st Bombardment Wing, referred to Monday as a "scavenger hunt." Units diverted from their primaries to their own secondaries or the secondaries of other groups, or bombed the next airfield or railroad marshaling yard they could find.

By various accounts, many of the personnel in the air that day recall air commanders urging the units to search for and attack targets of opportunity, and not to return to England without dropping their ordnance on something of importance in Germany.

Meanwhile, the 2nd Division also diverted to their secondary targets at Lingen, Hesepe, and Verden with 214 bombers. Both of the divisions bombed the Luftwaffe fields at Achmer and the notorious Diepholz.

As it turned out, the big base at Diepholz was enjoying clear weather that day. In his book *Might in Flight*, Harry Gobrecht of the 303rd Bombardment Group recalls the Diepholz attack, quoting Major Walter Shayler, commander of the 360th Bombardment Squadron, who said, "We sure hit something at this airdrome. There was a horrible mess of smoke and flames coming up. Somebody was there before us, so we just added a bit to the general damage."

Recollections of two anonymous people who were schoolchildren in

Diepholz on that fateful Monday are contained in the book *100 Jahre Realschule Diepholz* (*100 Years of Secondary School Diepholz*), published in 2000.

"I'll never forget the day that the air base in Diepholz was attacked," writes one. "We were in the basement across from the school, which was still partly on the ground. At first it seemed like forever. The bombers were arranged in their usual formation, then suddenly broke away from a crowd of these associations, turned around and came back. Everyone ran back quickly to the basement. Immediately after the earth shook, I remember that we all stuck our heads in an old sofa, which stood in the old cellar. When the all-clear sounded, we went out to the Bahnhofstrasse, which was downright littered with shrapnel."

Another recalls that "during the bombing, one of our teachers [taking cover with us] in the basement of the Kreissparkasse, said with a worried expression that this war can no longer be won. We never saw him again after the war ended. The Gestapo had picked him up on the same day."

For the 384th Bombardment Group, flying out of Grafton Underwood, the primary target had been the Luftwaffe base at Werl. As historian Quentin Bland reports in the group history, "They found that all the targets in the immediate vicinity were obscured with a solid overcast, and so made a 180 degree turn when they were about fifteen miles northeast of Hamm, before returning along the same route as they had followed in, while looking for a target of opportunity. The lead group noticed quite a number of large openings in the clouds."

The target they chose was Lingen, home to a Luftwaffe base that had been a secondary target assigned to the Liberators of the 2nd Bombardment Division.

"Fortunately the cloud cover was becoming intermittent and one could begin to see more and more of the ground area below," William Kinney, the 384th's lead bombardier, told Quentin Bland in the 1990s. "Suddenly a double or triple tracked railroad hove into view. I gave the pilot directions to turn left and follow the railroad track. The time of day was high noon or thereabouts, and vision was easy as there were no shadows to mislead our aiming. Thus we rode upon and into the town of Lingen.

I opened up the bomb bay doors and everyone else did likewise. As it was a target of opportunity, I could select my very own target, no doubt every bombardier's dream, especially when he has a few hundred planes behind him. As we advanced into the town, I calmly (no fighters, no flak) selected the largest building in the town which was surrounded by a maze of railroad tracks. Everything went SOP [Standard Operating Procedure]. The Colonel was very happy of being relieved of the bomb load."

Staff Sergeant Vernon Kaufman, a 384th ball turret gunner, had a good view and the luxury of being able to take a long, lingering look at what had happened to Lingen that day. As he explained, "I was watching a train puffing along the track. Our bombs smothered some buildings along the tracks and some of them overflowed onto the tracks, right where the train had been."

The 351st Bombardment Group, the unit with which Archie Mathies and Wally Truemper had flown the day before, had been assigned Gütersloh as its primary on Monday. However, cloud cover in the target area compelled a diversion to the Luftwaffe base at Achmer.

Flak knocked out the two inboard engines on the 351st's *Pistol Packin' Mama*, and Lieutenant Al Kogelman had to pilot the aircraft away from the formation. Spotting the straggler, an Fw 190 came by to put a half dozen 20mm shells through the left wing—but Staff Sergeant Gil Dennison, the tail gunner, took out the German fighter.

Almost home over the North Sea, Kogelman lost another engine and could not hold the bomber together any longer. As noted by Peter Harris and Ken Harbour in their book *A Chronicle of the 351st Bombardment Group*, the stricken plane "clipped the top of an 18 to 20 foot swell and bounced back into the air; the second impact was tremendous with the ship coming to an abrupt stop and the tail section snapped off. [*Pistol Packin' Mama*] immediately filled with water and sank within a minute. The crew scrambled out of the top hatch whilst the pilots escaped from their side windows as she went down."

The survivors, including Kogelman and Dennison, were rescued.

Among the 2nd Division units that flew against Achmer that day was the 93rd Bombardment Group, still known as "Ted's Travelling Circus," after Colonel Edward J. "Ted" Timberlake, who first took the group over-seas in 1942. Later commanded by Lieutenant Colonel Addison Baker in August 1943, the 93rd had been part of Operation Tidal Wave, the major assault on the oil refineries at Ploieşti on August 1, 1943, during which Baker had earned a posthumous Medal of Honor.

Today, the B-24s of the 93rd were led by Colonel George Scratchley Brown, who had earned a Distinguished Service Cross for taking com-mand of the 93rd's Tidal Wave contingent when Baker was shot down during the bomb run over Ploieşti. On this Day Two of Big Week, Brown brought the thirty-two Liberators of the 93rd home without a loss.

On Monday, only the 281 Flying Fortresses of the 3rd Bombardment Division had an industrial target on their agenda, a return visit to Muhlen-bau-Industrie AG in Braunschweig.

On previous missions, the Yank bombers had defended themselves in the corridor of death with their own guns. Today they were bringing their little friends, an escorting force of 69 P-51 Mustangs. As usual, the P-47s accompanied the force as far as they could, but there were more than five hundred of them in the air that day.

Despite the fighter escort, the bombers were hammered by the *Reichs-verteidigung* interceptors of Jagdgeschwader 1 and Jagdgeschwader 27, both of which were staffed by a number of aces who had claimed large numbers of four-engine bombers.

At 2:55 P.M., as it made its way home across the Netherlands, one 2nd Division Liberator was claimed over Hengelo by an Fw 190 flown by Jagdgeschwader 1's *Oberleutnant* Rüdiger von Kirchmayr, who is recalled as having been particularly deadly against earlier Eighth Air Force mis-sions. About an hour later, also over the Dutch coast, a 3rd Bombardment Division Flying Fortress became the fifty-fourth aerial victory for *Ober-feldwebel* Adolf "Addi" Glunz, a *Staffelkapitän* with Jagdgeschwader 26.

With the 3rd Division over Braunschweig on Monday was the 96th Bombardment Group, which had earned a Distinguished Unit Citation during the Regensburg mission back on August 17. Today, their 337th Squadron bore the brunt of the Luftwaffe attack. In this squadron, the crew of the Flying Fortress piloted by Lieutenant Alver Smith was on their fourteenth mission when they were targeted in a level attack by a German fighter coming in from five o'clock. As the enemy flashed past, Bernie Monahan, the bombardier, was left dead, the number one engine had exploded into flame, and the bomber began going down.

Dan Kricke and Bill Ford, the two waist gunners, had just managed to strap a parachute on Frank Morales, a fellow crew member, when the bomber nosed over.

"I started crawling up towards the waist door with Morales behind me," Kricke recalls in the history of the group by Robert Doherty and Geoffrey Ward, entitled *Snetterton Falcons*. "I was approximately four feet from the door when I turned for Frank. He was yelling something but I couldn't hear it. As I turned my head back toward the door, I noticed [tail gunner] Bob Means lying face down. His legs were still in the tunnel to the tail compartment. He was not visibly injured. I never saw Bill Ford again. It must have been then that the explosion took place. I lost consciousness. When I came to, I was approximately 8,000 feet off the ground and could see three chutes below me. Pieces of the plane were coming down around me. Some were on fire and I noticed that other fragments had already ripped my chute."

Two days later, as a prisoner of the Germans at Peppenhafen, near Hannover, Kricke learned that five of his friends had gone down with the aircraft. The others survived as POWs.

The plan for February 21 had also called for simultaneous attacks against targets in France and the Netherlands by Ninth Air Force medium bombers, but these areas were blanketed by heavy cloud cover. The partly cloudy conditions that allowed the Eighth Air Force a choice of secondary targets over Germany to which to divert did not extend to the west.

Meanwhile, Spaatz had gone to Italy overnight and had managed to work out a deal to use Fifteenth Air Force heavy bombers for missions in support of Operation Argument. However, on Monday, it was Italy's turn to be fogged in. Indeed, even the area around typically sunny Anzio reported heavy overcast.

It is certainly ironic that on the same day—in February, no less—that southern Italy was covered by clouds, there were clear skies over at least *parts* of northern Germany. Weatherman Irving Krick was either very skilled or very lucky—or both. Tooey Spaatz and Fred Anderson and everyone associated with the Eighth Air Force effort were just lucky.

However, the spotty overcast encountered over northern Germany led to spotty results. Reading the teletypes and examining the reconnaissance photographs that night, Anderson and Doolittle were not nearly as positive about the day's outcome as they had been on Sunday.

There were bright spots, though. As General Fred Anderson reported in a phone call that night to General Orvil Anderson, late of Hap Arnold's staff and now chairman of the ETO Combined Operational Planning Committee, many of the Luftwaffe bases, especially the large complex at Diepholz, were "severely and accurately bombed."

However, he added that the cloud cover over Braunschweig had compelled bombardiers to switch to H2S radar-blind bombing, using Pathfinders, and the bombs did little damage to the intended targets.

Losses were in line with those of Sunday. Including write-offs, the Eighth Air Force lost 19 out of 617 Flying Fortresses launched, and 4 of 244 Liberators, while claiming 19 Luftwaffe fighters shot down.

Among the escorting fighters, two P-47 Thunderbolts and three P-51 Mustangs were shot down, while one P-38 and two P-47s were damaged beyond repair. However, the American fighter pilots took a lopsided toll against the Luftwaffe. Of particular note is the relative effectiveness of the newly arrived Mustangs. The 68 Mustangs that were deployed claimed 14 enemy aircraft, while 542 Thunderbolts claimed 10 German fighters.

EIGHTEEN

TUESDAY, FEBRUARY 22

The results of Day Two of Big Week on Monday paled by those of the previous day, but Tuesday looked more promising, at least as far as the weather was concerned. Indeed, the anomalous stationary high pressure system was still holding in place—as Irving Krick had correctly predicted.

On Tuesday, there were even indications that it was expanding southward, opening up the skies over Regensburg and Schweinfurt, the two targets that planners such as Dick Hughes and commanders such as Fred Anderson most desired to strike.

Overnight, Hughes brought Anderson a target list that included these two cities most coveted, as well as a series of other targets.

By the plan, the Eighth Air Force 1st Division was assigned the Junkers Ju 88 factories and subcontractors at Halberstadt and Bernburg, as well as the nearby Saxon cities of Oschersleben and Aschersleben. At Oschersleben, the specific target was AGO (Apparatebau GmbH Oschersleben) Flugzeugwerke, which had become a major manufacturer of Focke-Wulf Fw 190A fighters. As such, it was a critically important target on the Argument roster.

Most of the crews focused mainly on the location and the defenses of the targets, however, rather than on the reasons for *why* they were targets. They were there just to do their jobs—and survive.

"We were not very interested in high strategy," recalls Jesse Richard Pitts, the copilot of the 379th Bombardment Group Flying Fortress named *Penny Ante*. "We just did our job."

It has long since become axiomatic that the men of the Eighth Air Force, like any similar American organization of that scale in World War II, were a cross-section of American life. There were young men such as Archie Mathies, who had enlisted out of high school. Then too there were men such as Jesse Richard Pitts, who had enlisted after having graduated magna cum laude in sociology from Harvard. You might be tempted to say that Pitts was atypical of the average bomber crewman, but there was no such thing as "typical." At twenty-three, he was a year older than Mathies and a year younger than Bill Lawley, so in that respect, he was as typical as anyone.

While most of the men in the Eighth Air Force had never seen continental Europe until they were looking at it from twenty thousand feet, Jesse had mostly grown up in France. After his veterinarian father from Ohio separated from the woman he had met and married in France during World War I, she went home and took her young son. As a teenager, Pitts became a coffeehouse socialist and dabbled in various causes. He was dogmatically anti-fascist and even flirted with the notion of fighting the fascists in the Spanish Civil War. When the United States entered World War II shortly after he graduated from Harvard, he enlisted to fight the fascists—which brought him to the 524th Bombardment Squadron of the 379th Group.

By 1944, Pitts was a wizened old man of twenty-three, and had put his political theorizing aside. He was, as he recalled in his memoirs, more interested in doing his job than in "high strategy."

On Tuesday morning, when the crack of dawn was still hours away, Jesse Pitts and his pilot, Herschel Streit, were among those who gathered in the briefing hut at Kimbolton to watch the man on the podium reveal "the target for today."

"Finally the screen covering the map did rise, slowly, with all eyes watching intently where the lines of red and blue wool were going to take us that day," Pitts writes in his book *Return to Base*. "Everybody let out a little gasp, a few curses; some half got up."

"The target for today is Halberstadt," Colonel Louis Rohr, the group operations officer, announced.

"We sat down, taking it in," Pitts continues. "Some were still whistling; you'd have figured they were going to Berlin or something, I thought. Self-pity. Those guys would bitch regardless of what the target was. It was not so much worry as exhibitionism. . . . We would think of our wives, of our mothers, of our friends. We would feel ourselves, to see if we were ready to die. Normally we were, in a resigned sort of way, willing to take the chance. Sometimes the visiting general would get up and say a few well-meant words in the heroic tradition, which would go over with the American flyers like a lead balloon, lowering our morale a bit more and making those damned buckwheat cakes heavier still in paralyzed stomachs. For a while we would be completely alone. We would have to get ourselves together, get our bitching, our despair, our anger over with quickly. What was the use; we were going. Remember, we were not eager heroes, just plow boys willing to do a job if we were given a fifty-fifty chance to come back."

Outside, the sky was clear, and stars could still be seen, although by now there was a hint of dawn on the eastern horizon. As the trucks delivered the crews to the bombers, the ground crews were scraping frost off the wings. Takeoff for the 324th Bombardment Squadron was supposed to have been eight o'clock, but the Flying Fortresses didn't begin rolling for almost an hour. Roaring down the runway in thirty-second intervals, the bombers were in the air by nine-fifteen and forming up to head toward the Reich.

Streit and Pitts tucked *Penny Ante* into its slot about three hundred feet below and to the left of the Flying Fortress piloted by the 379th Group's commander, Colonel Maurice "Mo" Preston.

"The Colonel took the whole group formation through a thick cloud bank," Pitts recalls. "For once we were in tight formation, so regardless of the reduced visibility, we could see the ship on whose wing we were flying. The risk of collisions had to be taken; when it came down to it, twenty men were not worth twenty minutes delay. We came out of the cloud bank as tight as we went in."

Those dozen aircraft of the 379th Group were part of a total force of 289 Flying Fortresses that the 1st Bombardment Division managed to get airborne on Tuesday.

If the men of the 379th thought that Halberstadt was going to be bad, infamous Schweinfurt was scheduled to the undivided attention of the Eighth Air Force 3rd Bombardment Division that day.

Meanwhile the 2nd Division was being sent back to their target of Sunday, Gothaer Waggonfabrik in Gotha, the second farthest Eighth Air Force target for Tuesday after Schweinfurt.

Regensburg, the most distant of the major targets, was assigned to the Fifteenth Air Force now that Spaatz had paved the way for their participation in Operation Argument missions. It would have been an understatement to say that Regensburg was an important target for the bombers of the USSTAF. In the archipelago of Messerschmitt locations, the subsidiary known as "Messerschmitt GmbH Regensburg" manufactured the preponderance of Bf 109s at sites all around the city. These included the western suburb of Prüfening, and Obertraubling on the south side.

Unlike the first two days of Big Week, the RAF had flown no maximum effort mission overnight. The only RAF planes over the Reich that night were DeHavilland Mosquitoes on reconnaissance missions to Duisburg and Stuttgart.

Consideration had also been given to a Tuesday Eighth Air Force attack on the Vereinigte Kugellagerfabriken (VKF) ball bearing works at Erkner, about sixteen miles east of downtown Berlin. However, as Fred Anderson decided and as Arthur Ferguson later explained, such a mission "would spread the forces too much and make them too vulnerable to enemy attack. Excellent results had been achieved on the two previous missions by sending the bombers and their fighter escort into enemy territory as a team, only splitting the force when the target areas were neared."

Though bypassed on February 22, the VKF plant at Erkner, a sister factory to the VKF plant in Schweinfurt, would be high on the target lists as the Eighth Air Force began missions against Berlin in the weeks following Big Week.

As it was, Anderson did divide his force, adding a diversionary strike by some elements of the 1st Bombardment Division against the much removed Luftwaffe base at Aalborg in the northern tip of Denmark. A big part of the reason for this attack, like the northern flight of the 3rd Division on Monday, was to draw Luftwaffe assets far to the north in order to keep them away from the main force.

Any fighters that the Luftwaffe sent north from bases within Germany would have to land to refuel on their way back. The theory was that if they were recalled as the bomber force moved into Germany, they would not be able to return and refuel in time to attack the Americans before they were within the protective range of the huge force of P-47s.

Forces beyond Anderson's control soon conspired to divide his armada even further. The 3rd Bombardment Division, tasked with the all-important Schweinfurt mission, ran into trouble as soon as they took off. Despite clear skies over the target, heavy cloud cover over England proved to be the undoing of the division on Tuesday morning. There were 333 Flying Fortresses reported to have been launched, but a series of mistakes led to confusion and vice versa, and then to a series of air-to-air collisions in the poor visibility. Finally, Curtis LeMay, the division commander, ordered the entire Schweinfurt mission to be aborted.

This was merely the harbinger of further difficulties. The 177 Liberators of the 2nd Bombardment Division, bound for Gotha, also ran into trouble forming up over England. Their formations were hopelessly scattered as they began to make their way across the North Sea toward Germany against strong winds. As they crossed over the coastline of *Festung Europa*, the decision was made to abort the mission and release bombs on targets of opportunity inside the Netherlands. These included Arnhem, Deventer, Enschede, and Nijmegen.

After two days, the Luftwaffe had figured out that this was Big Week, and they were scheming ways of confronting this series of maximum efforts. The typical Luftwaffe approach had been to attack the bombers in the target area, when they would tenaciously avoid evasive action in order to stay on their bomb run, or after they exited the target area, a time when stragglers were likely to appear, drifting away from their formations.

On Tuesday, however, the Luftwaffe struck the Eighth Air Force early in the mission, attempting to catch the bombers when they least expected it and before their fighter escorts had formed up with the bombers.

In turn, the Luftwaffe continued to attack the bomber streams in what amounted to a running gun battle across northern Germany. As the primary targets were found to be under cloud cover, the large formations broke up, with aircraft diverting to secondaries and targets of opportunity, and the Luftwaffe seized on the opportunity to attack small clusters and strays.

As the bomber streams passed through the airspace of that narrow gateway to the Reich north of Münster, they were clobbered especially hard by the fighter aces of Jagdgeschwader 26. No man in the Luftwaffe proved himself to be a greater scourge to the bombers of the 1st Bombardment Division on Tuesday than *Oberfeldwebel* Addi Glunz, who had downed a 3rd Division Flying Fortress just the day before.

For three hours in the early part of the afternoon, he single-handedly mauled the bomber force, downing five, and possibly six, B-17s over the Rhineland and Westphalia, as well as a P-47 escort fighter over Geilenkirchen.

It was near Münster, early on Tuesday afternoon, that Jagdgeschwader 26 jumped the 384th Bombardment Group. Major George Harris, commander of the group's 546th Bombardment Squadron said that "they were on us before we knew it. They came at us out of the sun and we couldn't see them until they were right in our formation. The sun was bright and it was as clear as hell. They gave us the works."

"They came at us a dozen at a time, then they would wheel around and attack us from the rear," reported Tech Sergeant Jack Shattuck, a navigator aboard a 384th Bombardment Group Flying Fortress, of an encounter near Münster. "Suddenly four P-51s jumped in and the result was amazing. Their mere presence seemed to carry a terrifying effect for the German pilots because they just turned tail and ran—about 40 or 50 of them. I doubt if a shot was fired by those Mustangs because the Jerries cleared out in such a hurry."

However, the "rescue" was short-lived. Harris later had occasion to complain about the sloppiness of the fighter escort that day. The P-47s had been with his squadron for less than half an hour, and the four Mustangs that showed up had abandoned the Flying Fortresses as they entered the target area.

The crews headed to Halberstadt also felt the wrath of the Focke-Wulfs of Jagdgeschwader 26. The fighters came in, firing rockets from the five o'clock position. In *Penny Ante*, Herschel Streit and Jesse Pitts watched a rocket explode about twenty yards ahead of the bomber next to theirs. For a moment, nothing seemed to be amiss, but then Pitts started seeing "plumes of gasoline set afire by exhaust fumes starting to eat the trailing edge of his right wing. . . . Streit and I decided to get out of his way in case he should explode. I felt cowardly to leave my friend like that. Here his wing was burning and I was leaving him as if he had leprosy. Our leaving him could only mean that he was condemned, and I was ashamed. Later he might reproach me for it, but what could I do? If he exploded in our faces we were done for."

They passed through a wall of flak over Münster, and saw another Flying Fortress in trouble, this time above them. As Pitts explains, there were "small tongues of fire flitting through the closed bomb-bay doors; fire in the bomb bay with all the gas lines interconnecting there—that was bad! All those hose connections were not as tight as they should have been; there were small leaks, and the fire attached itself to these leaks like a bloodsucker."

As they watched, they could see the bomb bay doors open, and crewmen climb into the bomb bay to try to extinguish the conflagration, "emptying fire extinguishers on the fire and trying to beat down the flames with empty B-4 bags, while trying to keep their hands from getting burned. One of them must have been on the narrow catwalk, with no parachute and the ground 21,000 feet below. For a minute, it seemed that the fire was losing out to the efforts of the crew. But it was only for a minute. Bombs kept falling one by one. The fire grew, though still limited to the bomb bay. Time went by; how long before the final explosion?"

The question was answered shortly after the stricken plane left the formation, and as the crew was preparing to bail out.

Below them, Streit and Pitts watched as people near whom they had been seated at the briefing that morning were thrown from the exploding wreckage. Pitts saw the mangled body of his friend Tex Robins tumbling through the air and hoped that he was already dead.

As the formation reached its Initial Point at a few minutes before 2 P.M., and turned into its bomb run, it came over a blanket of cloud cover that completely obscured the section of Halberstadt where the factories were.

Passing over Halberstadt with a tailwind pushing their speed to 300 mph, the bomber crews could see a break in the clouds, and through that break they could see the Holtemme River and, on the nearby slopes of the Harz Mountains, the snow-covered tile roofs of the picturesque hill town of Wernigerode, their "target of opportunity."

The aircrews of the 1st Bombardment Division found both Oschersleben and Halberstadt under overcast, and most, like the 379th, diverted to secondary targets or targets of opportunity. Thinking they could see something under the fringes of the cloud bank, eighteen bombers dropped on Halberstadt, while forty-seven bombed the targets at Bernberg and thirty-four attacked Aschersleben. The remainder diverted to targets of opportunity, but of the nearly three hundred bombers that launched with the 1st Division Tuesday morning, only three in five were able to attack any target.

Tech Sergeant Jack Shattuck, the navigator who reported on his impressions of the effect Mustangs had on the Luftwaffe, spoke glowingly of the success of the 84th Bombardment Group at Aschersleben. After the mission, he said simply that the Junkers facility in the city "doesn't exist any more. Our bombs made a beautiful bull's eye smack on that plant, smoke reached upward in terrific amounts and I could still see it mounting when we were miles away, as we had excellent visibility. We had a clear shot at target and the bombardiers certainly made the most of it."

In the south, 118 Fifteenth Air Force bombers were able to attack the Messerschmitt facilities at Regensburg, but the city was heavily defended by antiaircraft batteries. The 376th Bombardment Group, the "Liberandos," who had earned a Distinguished Unit Citation during the Operation Tidal Wave assault on Ploeşti in August 1943, took a hard hit from the flak over Regensburg. Indeed, two flak-damaged Liberando Liberators collided over the city.

"About two or three minutes off the target I saw ship No. 99 ram No. 53 (*KO Katy*) from above and between the waist windows, breaking the ship in two," Staff Sergeant John A. Masiewics recalled at his debriefing that night. "One man fell out of the tail section of the plane and his chute opened. Three men fell out from the main body of the tail and it appeared to me that they didn't have chutes on. I followed the two crashed ships down. I didn't see any more chutes. Ship No. 99 slowly started to break up and disintegrate in mid-air. Ship No. 53 finally blew up and it seemed that the man with the open chute went limp about that time and that's the last look I took because there were fighter planes amongst us. The weather over the target was clear. Our altitude at the time of the accident was 20,000 feet and the ships that crashed were at about 20,500 feet."

Meanwhile, Sergeant Horace "Hort" Quinn was the radio operator aboard *KO Katy*, which was piloted by Lieutenant Alfred Folck.

"Our last flight was going quite well for us," Quinn reported in James Walker's anthology entitled *The Liberandos*. "However, we watched several of our planes fall out of formation and head home with engine trouble, etc. Also saw several of them go down. Then just as I heard bombs-away from the bombardier, I felt an awful shudder and heard a loud noise. When I awoke I was in a piece of the plane aft of the bomb bay. After digging free of the debris I was tangled up in, I bailed just before hitting the ground. Eyewitnesses told us that a plane of the 515th Squadron came down on top of us and only Frank Fox and myself lived from the 20 boys aboard the two planes."

Quinn was captured, but survived incarceration in a prisoner of war camp to tell his story.

The Luftwaffe also took a heavy toll on the Fifteenth Air Force mission to Regensburg, given that it was the only one to reach southern Germany on Tuesday. Just as they had back on August 17, 1943, Hughes and Anderson envisioned simultaneous attacks on Schweinfurt and Regensburg to compel the Luftwaffe to divide their interceptors between two large forces. However, on that mission, the best laid plans went awry, and the Luftwaffe was able to gang up on a single force.

Now, half a year later, Fifteenth Air Force crews flying both to and *from* Regensburg, had to fight their way through the *Reichsverteidigung* net thrown up by Jagdgeschwader 53, based at Vienna-Seyring in Austria. One of the aces from this unit who proved himself to be especially lethal to heavy bombers was *Oberfeldwebel* Herbert Rollwage. Sometimes credited with 102 victories, including 44 four-engine bombers, Rollwage scored his fiftieth victory, over one of the Fifteenth Air Force Liberators, on Tuesday between Altötting and Straubing in southeast Bavaria near the Austrian border.

"I remember the 15th Air Force raid on Regensburg. We lost our second echelon of eighteen airplanes in about half an hour, once past the Alps," wrote John T. Upton, a bombardier with the 301st Bombardment Group who faced Rollwage and his *geschwader*-mates that day. Upton's recollections came in a letter to the 301st Group's veteran's association that was penned almost four decades after Big Week, in May 1983.

"The fighters then moved upon our lead formation so we speeded up and formed in with the 97th [Bombardment Group] for protection," he recalls. "We got some trouble there but it looked and felt good to be among a Group we knew and trusted and fought back like demons. The formation was so tight that it seemed that anyone could walk from one plane wingtip to another—or the waist gunner could jump out of his opening and land on the wing of the plane next to him. I'll never forget coming back from Regensburg and seeing all those funeral pyres on the ground marking where the shot down planes hit. My plane was the only survivor of my squadron."

In his memoir of the 301st Bombardment Group entitled *Who Fears?* Kenneth Werrell quotes a gunner who recalled that "on the return to base, I could see fires all over the Alps. The place was covered with wrecked, burning planes."

In Glen Williamson's characterization, the Luftwaffe was like a high wall around the vulnerable points of the German economy. On Tuesday, February 22, thanks in no small part to Addi Glunz, that wall was at its highest and most insurmountable, and it exacted a heavy toll from those who attempted to surmount it.

One of the 1st Division bombers that went down over the Netherlands was a Flying Fortress piloted by Lieutenant Charles Crook, with the 360th Bombardment Squadron of the 303rd Bombardment Group.

"We were in the open and an Fw 190 had spotted us," recalls Crook's fight engineer, Tech Sergeant Louis Breitenbach. "He came from below and at the rear. The rear guns were out and he was too low for the other gunners to shoot at. He gave us a burst of machine gun fire and the shells ripped through the ship. Our pilot was doing some beautiful flying, but we were defenseless and the German came in from the left and to the rear again. We could see his whole wing light up with orange flame from his machine gun and cannon fire. We fired the best we could, but it only took a split second for him to get us in his sights and fire away. His bullets came crashing into the plane, knocking out two more engines. A cannon shell passed between the two waist gunners, missing them by inches, and blew a machine gun off its position and out into the air."

Crook and his crew were lucky. He managed to crash-land the aircraft near Wijk Bij Duurstede, about twenty miles southeast of Utrecht.

"We were going down and we were too low for all of us to jump in safety," Breitenbach continues, writing in his story "The Last Flight of a Flying Fortress," which is excerpted in Harry Gobrecht's anthology *Might in Flight*, "Things happened so fast, it is hard to say what really happened. We were all crouched down and waiting for the first bounce. It came and plenty hard. We bounced up into the air, came down again with a loud crash, and were sliding along the ground, taking fences and everything along with us. Things were flying all around inside the ship: ammunition, radio sets, flares, and boxes of all kinds. A thousand thoughts passed before me. Will the plane catch fire and blow up? Will we crash into a house? The feelings of terror and suspense that gripped us can't be put on paper."

The fact that only one Eighth Air Force division was over northern Germany on Tuesday, as opposed to three on Sunday and Monday, gave the Luftwaffe a much higher attacker-to-defender ratio, thus increasing their effectiveness. Indeed, it was a good day for the Luftwaffe and Big Week's worst day of losses for the Eighth Air Force.

Of the 430 bombers credited with bombing a target, 41 were shot down—mostly from among the 1st Bombardment Division—for a loss rate of nearly 10 percent. Over Regensburg, meanwhile, the Fifteenth Air Force lost 14 of its aircraft, a loss rate of 12 percent. The escort force, meanwhile, lost three Mustangs and eight Thunderbolts, while claiming approximately 60 Luftwaffe aircraft.

As Anderson, Williamson, and Hughes studied Tuesday's results that night, the reconnaissance photos brought further disappointment. The Junkers Flugzeug-und-Motorenwerke facilities at Aschersleben were seen as having been 50 percent destroyed, while the facilities of the Junkers suppliers at Bernburg were perceived as having been more than 70 percent destroyed. However, elsewhere, the Eighth Air Force had little to show for Tuesday's efforts, nor had the Fifteenth Air Force made a serious impact at Regensburg.

The men of the 379th Bombardment Group, who had dropped 110 tons of bombs on Wernigerode, which looked a bit like a storybook village as they flew over, felt a little queasy.

"Later, back at the base, they would tell us that the town of Wernigerode was a [rest and recuperation] home for the Luftwaffe, so we might have taken out some experienced German pilots in what appeared to some of us as a senseless killing of civilians," Jesse Pitts recalls. "We suspected, though, that this was a story put out by our PR officers to alleviate our guilt. On our last few missions, many of us had lost our sensitivity about targets. As I had experienced on my last pass, when the Germans bombed London, they made no pretense of going for strategic targets, so why should we?"

His group had lost four aircraft that day, leaving forty empty bunks in Kimbolton. Colonel Mo Preston's aircraft had been hit and he was wounded badly enough to be bunking in a hospital at Diddington that night.

The Eighth Air Force lost more than 400 men on Tuesday. There were 35 who were known to have been killed in action and 397 who were missing and presumed dead or captured. Charles Crook would make it out alive and get home, but he was one of a handful.

There was a lot of gnashing of teeth that night at Park House.

"After the third day of successive operations, General Doolittle, from the Eighth Air Force, began to protest violently," Hughes recalls. "His crews were getting more and more tired, and subsisting primarily on an alternate diet of Benzedrine and sleeping pills. Still Fred Anderson drove them on. Whenever Jimmy Doolittle's phone calls came through, I'd stand near Fred Anderson's shoulder as he answered the telephone, and, morally supported by me, he would daily tell Jimmy to 'shut up' and carry out his orders."

NINETEEN

WEDNESDAY, FEBRUARY 23

On Tuesday night, all across East Anglia, as the crews who had survived the day ate their dinners and staggered back to their quarters, the operation people were on the horn to the engineering people tasked with processing the damaged aircraft.

"How many can you get ready to fly tomorrow?" the operations staff asked the engineers in a conversation paraphrased by Derwyn Robb of the 379th Bombardment Group in his memoirs.

"Tomorrow!" replied the engineering supervisor, standing in a cold and drafty open hangar staring at Flying Fortresses with holes chopped in them. He had just put out three days of maximum efforts and his airplanes were getting badly beaten up. "What the hell, you kiddin'?"

"No," replied the operations man from the comfort of a heated, soundproof building. "How many can you get ready to fly?"

"Let's see—nine engine changes, five wings, tires . . ."

"I don't give a damn what's wrong with them, all I want to know is how many will fly tomorrow."

"Well, that's what I'm trying to tell you if you'll just hold your fire."

"OK but hurry up, I don't have all night," the operations man replied impatiently. He had generals at High Wycombe breathing down his neck for this information, and *they* had generals at Bushy Park breathing down their necks. "Well look, let's leave it this way. We need 42 planes [from your group alone] to go out. . . ."

"Forty-two planes. You're crazy in the head. We couldn't get that many kites in the air tomorrow, let alone planes. Who do you think we have working out here—supermen? Forty-two planes. Of all the crazy ideas. Why, we've got more planes to patch up than . . ."

"Look, Mac, don't tell me your troubles, I've got plenty of my own. Give me a call back in a little while and let me know the score, will ya'?"

"OK, But 42 planes. Of all the . . . ideas."

"Let 'em chew on that awhile," the operations man said to his colleague, who was sitting nearby.

"You shouldn't be so rough on those guys," he replied.

"Well, somebody has to keep those guys on the ball or they'd forget there's a war on."

The obvious irony in this yarn was that everyone in those hangars, like everyone who had spent ten of the longest hours of his life in the bombers that day, *knew* that there was a war on. They had seen it and felt it, or they had seen and felt the effects of flak and fighter.

The exhausted men whom Jimmy Doolittle colorfully described as "subsisting primarily on an alternate diet of Benzedrine and sleeping pills" knew very well that there was a war on. They could close their eyes and see it just as vividly as they had seen it over Hitler's *Festung Europa* for the past three days.

On Wednesday, though, Jimmy Doolittle got his wish.

There would be a day of rest for his exhausted crews. The high pressure area that had prevailed for a rare three straight days was gone, and Anderson ordered the Eighth Air Force to stand down. Dr. Irving Krick promised that good weather would return on Thursday, but for the moment, most of the bombers stood silently in their hardstands. As on the previous night, the RAF also stood down its great bomber fleet, sending out only a handful of Mosquito flights over the Reich.

For the Fifteenth Air Force, and its commander, General Nathan Twining, however, Wednesday was not to be a day of rest. For them, Wednesday brought 102 of their bombers to the Steyr Walzlagerwerke, the anti-friction bearing works in the industrial city of Steyr—which had been in central Austria until the 1938 Anschluss had merged Austria into greater Germany.

As noted in the postwar report on anti-friction bearings issued by the Strategic Bombing Survey, the site was then gearing up to produce up to 15 percent of the bearings needed by German industry. The location was one of the beneficiaries of the dispersal of the bearing industry that took place after the October 14 Schweinfurt attack.

"Well before we reached the target it became apparent that this was not to be a milk run," Tech Sergeant Max Rasmussen, the top turret gunner on the Liberator *Harry the Horse*, piloted by Lieutenant Marvin Grice, recalls in James Walker's 376th Bombardment Group anthology. "Bombers that had preceded us to the target were returning and they approached us head on at lower altitudes. Their condition was noticeably critical. Formations were almost nonexistent and many planes were on fire. As we approached the target, German fighters, mainly Bf 109s, began attacking the formations. The entire formations in front and to the right of us disappeared within a short time and it was then that we were attacked.

"Gunners Hermann and Root called in to report fighters climbing and coming up fast at three o'clock. I watched them as they hit the eleven planes in the high flight formation. They were attacking with about seven to ten fighters in succession and in their first pass downed Tail-end Charlie. In about ten minutes they had wiped out the high element, attacking from every hour of the clock. Then they hit our element and we fought them into the target. That battle into the target probably lasted 30 minutes."

The Luftwaffe was up in force against the Fifteenth that day. Lieutenant Ben Konsynski, a section leader with the 376th "Liberandos" Bombardment Group remembers that "the mission seemed routine except that it was very cold and two of the 513th [Bombardment Squadron] planes turned back because of perceived mechanical difficulties, leaving six planes from the 513th and an unknown number from the [515th] squadron flying with us in our section. About 20 minutes from the target our formations were attacked by 75 to 100 German aircraft, there were Bf 109s, Bf 110s and Fw 190s. We lacked air cover at this point. When we saw the enemy planes attacking the high boxes it took a few minutes to tighten up our section and to move in close to the 'A' and 'B' sections of our formation.

"When I next looked up I saw three B-24s coming down out of control from the 'B' section. The Germans were shooting rockets and 20 mm cannon with telling effect. The attack continued from that point up to the target. In the low section we were not getting the brunt of the attack until inexplicably the formation leader of the lead group decided to turn off course, without notice, and head back. We had not reached the IP so we continued on alone and that is when we were hit by rocket and cannon fire from attacking planes."

"As we had no fighter escort, all crews were very alert for signs of enemy aircraft," Major Harry Gillett, commander of the Liberandos' 512th Bombardment Squadron, recalls in James Walker's anthology. He was flying right seat with Lieutenant Gerald Brown, 512th operations officer. "After passing Klagenfurt the first Bf 110s, with their rockets, started attacking the [other] formations. Although intelligence information indicated they carried only two rockets, I saw four fired by a Bf 110 into the 98th Bomb Group on our right from about 1,000 yards. Several aircraft were hit and blew up. On some of their attacks they were not too accurate, as the rockets exploded ahead or behind the formation. None attacked our formation but you had the feeling you would be next. Time went by and we survived the attacks."

Lieutenant Harry Hanson, a 376th Bombardment Group navigator, recalled in Walker's anthology the terror of the Steyr mission. He wrote that "it was about enough to discourage a guy. Our flight of five aircraft lost three. Bf 109s were coming right through our formation and split us all over the sky. Just before the IP one B-24 parallel with us, was all afire, and several guys jumped out the waist window without chutes. None of our crew was injured. I figured I wouldn't last a month. Sunday I went for a long walk alone and thought about my Dad mostly, and realized I had to finish the job. I never had a problem with missions after that, however they never got that tough again."

Meanwhile, tail gunner Staff Sergeant Glynn Hendrix agrees that the missions never again got as tough as Steyr, adding that "never before or since did I see the enemy so wildly aggressive, pressing their attacks in very close. I could actually see debris fly from the nose and cowl of a Bf l09 as I fired point blank. Thought he might collide.

"I recall thinking, 'If I don't get this b****d he's gonna kill me.' His fire was just above my head right up the fuselage and I think he hit the top turret. The enemy this day attacked, almost to a man, from the rear and not too high and they just lined up on you and bored on in. We were in a good position, formation-wise, but three or four planes behind us were shot down so we [became] 'Tail-end Charlie' and getting a drubbing when the attack broke off."

As Ben Konsynski led his section into their bomb run over Steyr, the Luftwaffe fighters backed off, leaving the Liberators at the mercy of the flak batteries, who could fire at will, knowing that the Americans would not take evasive action until they had dropped their bombs. However, Konsynski noticed a single Bf 109 flying level and parallel to his B-24D, just out of the range of the .50-caliber guns aboard the bomber. Suddenly, he accelerated far ahead of Konsynski's aircraft.

"He then made a 180-degree turn and came straight at us," Konsynski continues. "We could see his guns blinking as he approached, Lieutenant Ferber, copilot, slid to the floor, Sergeant Glove, engineer, got behind the armor plate in back of the pilot's seat, and I scootched down as low as I could and still see to fly the plane. As if the instrument panel would protect us if the enemy aircraft would have hit us!

"Lieutenant John Konecny, navigator, took the .50-caliber gun in the nose of the B-24D we were flying and started firing; it was point-blank shooting. I thought the enemy aircraft was going to ram us, but he flipped to his right, our left, exposing his bottom and Konecny kept on firing. The Bf 109 blew up. It is difficult to understand the German pilot's actions, except that we were flying the only 'pink' [desert-camouflage color] B-24 left in the [Mediterranean] Theater and it was in the lead position of the formation. He may have thought that there was some significance to the combination."

"It appeared that we were slowly falling behind our formation," recalls John Pizzello, the nose gunner aboard *Harry the Horse*. "Before getting into the nose turret I asked John Byrne [the bombardier] to be sure to check the doors of the turret if we had trouble and I was not out. I made sure to put my chute where it would be out of the way and I could get to it if I had to. I then entered the turret.

"We went over the target, dropped our bombs and were on our way back. We were falling behind more now and I had lost contact as the intercom system in my turret was not working, I tried to call anybody but no luck. I tried for some time to get my doors open but couldn't. I now started to pray. I just sat back and relaxed while praying. I was at ease, I can't understand that at all, but my doors suddenly opened. Thanks, John."

Exiting their bomb runs, the Liberators were once again pounced upon with full fury by the Luftwaffe. Aboard *Harry the Horse*, Max Rasmussen observed that "everything happened at once. A fighter passing from nine to three o'clock blew off our left elevator and rudder and instantly killed [fellow gunners] Hermann and Root. John Pizzello came out . . . and manned both waist guns. I was firing at some fighters coming in at nine bells when from out of nowhere a 20mm hit our number two engine and wing. You could have driven a tank through the hole in the wing. [This] engine ran away and the propeller tore off the shaft. The prop cut into the fuselage behind Grice and cut the control cables.

"Just then a shell came in past my head and exploded in my turret, knocking off my dome and finishing my guns. This numbed me completely although I felt a sharp twinge in my left shoulder. I felt like the whole right side of my face was blown away, but I wiped my hand over my face and there wasn't any blood. The plane dropped out of formation and Grice tapped my foot as I looked down and saw him go out the bomb bay and hit the silk. I got down from my turret, helped the skipper and hit the silk also, not knowing the fate of the crew in the waist until we joined up with Pizzello after we landed."

Pizzello, Rasmussen, and the other survivors of *Harry the Horse*'s crew spent the remainder of the war in German stalags.

"I remember the February 23, 1944, Steyr mission better than most," writes Max Simpson, a waist gunner in Lieutenant L. V. Lockhart's 376th Bombardment Group Liberator. "After a few minutes off the target, Bf 109s picked us up. They had yellow noses [and] wing tips, and pilots wore yellow helmets. We called them Göring's flying circus. In a few minutes we had lost our wing planes on both sides. [It] seemed like we were by ourselves. Tail turret malfunctioned and [probably tail gunner] Raymond [Dickey] called out each attack and the gunners would switch to the rear and try to keep them away. Bf 109s came in from every direction. After what seemed like an hour P-38s showed up and enemy took off. A B-24 trying to fly formation with us almost stuck his wing tip in waist window. I called the front and told the copilot to watch him. He was all shot up, top turret plastic was gone and he was in bad shape. With P-38s at our side we returned to home base."

Eight of the 376th Bombardment Group Liberators were not so lucky, although the group claimed nineteen German fighters shot down, plus four probables. The Liberandos also lost a total of 84 crew members, either killed in action or missing and presumed captured on Wednesday's hard fought mission.

Adolf Hitler's war machine had also paid a price at Steyr on Wednesday, though by comparison to other places and other days during Big Week, the price had been less than exorbitant.

The Fifteenth Air Force knocked out 20 percent of the Steyr Walzlagerwerke, which could be extrapolated as about 3 percent of the antifriction bearing needs of German industry.

TWENTY

THURSDAY, FEBRUARY 24

Looking ahead to Thursday, Dr. Irving Krick asserted that good weather was sure to be in store again, and Fred Anderson sent orders to Doolittle to prepare accordingly.

"For us, this was the 'make or break' of the whole air war," Dick Hughes said enthusiastically, "and we were determined not to let a single Eighth Air Force bomber sit around as long as this fantastic freak of weather lasted."

As Krick promised, the "fantastic freak" was back, and it was time to resume the maximum effort program.

For five combat wings of the Eighth Air Force 1st Bombardment Division, Thursday would be an opportunity to make up for its aborted maximum effort against Schweinfurt on Tuesday. When the curtain over the operations map came up, lines of red and blue yarn come together deep in the heart of Hitler's Reich. It was like a metaphor for the pit of your stomach, which is where the crews took it, and took it hard.

For most of the men in the 1st Division, the idea of "making up" for the aborted Schweinfurt mission did not sit well. They would have been happy to have seen the mission scrubbed permanently. Even if they had not been in England in October, they all had heard of Black Thursday.

The mere mention of the word "Schweinfurt" conjured up a dark sense of foreboding.

The idea of two coordinated attacks in the southern part of the Reich, which had been planned but failed to materialize, on Tuesday was back on the agenda for Thursday. This time, as the Eighth Air Force 1st Division would attack Schweinfurt, the Fifteenth Air Force would return to Steyr, their objective of the previous day.

George Webster of the 92nd Bombardment Group wrote in his memoir, *Savage Sky*, that when the intelligence captain at Podington pulled back the curtain covering a map of Europe, the crowd of flyers gasped and groaned.

"I see faces go pale," Webster recalls. "A nearby flight engineer bows his head and begins to pray. The red line goes deep into central Germany to the city of Schweinfurt, a name that strikes fear in the flyers of the Eighth Air Force. The target is crucial because factories at Schweinfurt manufacture ball bearings that are vital to German military production. If we knock out ball bearings, we deal a big blow to production of planes, tanks, trucks, and machinery. The Germans know it and are ready to defend the city furiously.

"The Eighth Air Force fought its way to Schweinfurt twice before. In August of 1943, our bombers smashed the ball bearing plants, but the Germans shot down 36 of our bombers. Germany rebuilt the plants in record time, requiring a mission in October of 1943. Our bombers again destroyed the ball bearing factories, but at a cost of an astounding 60 of our bombers destroyed. That is equal to three bomb groups. Six B-17s from the 92nd Group were lost in that raid, so combat veterans fear a Schweinfurt mission. It's a death sentence for some of us. Everyone looks grim. Some are obviously frightened. A fellow next to me covers his face and mumbles that he wishes he'd written to his wife last night."

While most of the 1st Division aircrews had never seen Schweinfurt, Major George Shackley of the 381st Bombardment Group had been to Schweinfurt on the Black Thursday October 14 mission—*and* on the August 17 mission.

Today, he would be making his *third* trip to the capital of ball bearings and suffering. He would be leading 32 Flying Fortresses of the 381st out of their base at Ridgewell, one of five groups tasked with the Schweinfurt mission.

Shackley was flying right seat to Lieutenant George Sandman, the pilot of *Rotherhithe's Revenge*. A brand-new B-17G christened just ten days earlier, its namesake was an illustration of the hellishness of the war and why the Allies—especially the British—were so single-minded in pursuing the Combined Bomber Offensive.

Rotherhithe was a community in the London borough of Southwark, located on a promontory on the south bank of the River Thames, near the Surrey Commercial Docks. In September 1940, during the London Blitz, the fire that swept through the area was described by Peter Stansky in his book *The First Day of the Blitz* as the most intense single fire ever seen in Britain. Rotherhithe was bombed repeatedly by the Luftwaffe throughout the Blitz and the remainder of the war, losing its old town hall in the process. The commemorative bomber was christened by city fathers, using a bottle of locally brewed ale.

As the 1st Division bombers passed over the Netherlands, there were a higher than usual number of aircraft dropping out of the formation for mechanical reasons. Maybe it was nerves, or maybe they were hearing sounds inside those Wright Cyclones that made them worry about something other than the Luftwaffe emptying the bunks tonight.

Jesse Pitts called it "the point of no return. For those in our wing and in our division who had discovered deficiencies in their ships that made the mission a losing gamble, this was the time to turn back home."

A couple of the gunners aboard *Penny Ante* told Pitts and the pilot, Herschel Streit, that they thought they heard something in the engines. The pilots listened but could not hear anything wrong. *Penny Ante* pressed on.

As they reached the Initial Point, five hours out of Kimbolton, the number three engine sputtered to a stop. It had prematurely run out of fuel. Pitts cranked up the other three so that *Penny Ante* could keep pace with the rest of the formation, as Streit started transferring fuel and scolding Pitts for not paying attention.

Penny Ante would bring her crew home that day as she always had. The aircraft had gotten its name from a ritual that had been started by the ground crew chief, in which he loaned the pilot a penny at the start of the mission, which was repaid upon the aircraft's safe return. As long as the pilot carried the penny, *and* the responsibility of repaying the debt, the aircraft would always return. This gave the plane an aura within the squadron of being a "lucky ship."

For three combat wings of the 2nd Bombardment Division, Thursday would involve a return to Gothaer Waggonfabrik in Gotha. The 3rd Bombardment Division, meanwhile, would send five combat wings to the Focke-Wulf complexes located in the northeast corner of the Reich.

The clear weather that materialized in Thursday's predawn hours allowed the Eighth Air Force to coordinate the activities of its three divisions with almost textbook precision. The 1st Bombardment Division successfully launched 231 Flying Fortresses, which headed south and east. With them for most of their penetration of the Third Reich were 238 2nd Division Liberators.

Leading the 2nd Division bomber stream to Gotha on Thursday was 14th Combat Wing, in turn spearheaded by the 579th Squadron of the 392nd Bombardment Group. The green flare shot from the tower was seen at 8:30 A.M. and the Liberator pilots, led by the crew pilot, Lieutenant Jim McGregor, began their takeoff roll. The thirty-one aircraft of the 392nd took off at thirty-second intervals and formed up at twelve thousand feet.

"Turning to the southeast towards Gotha, the white snow-covered landscape four miles below looked cold and lifeless; only large communities, rail lines and an autobahn stood out in relief," wrote Lieutenant Myron Keilman, also of the 392nd Group's 579th Squadron, in the 392nd Bombardment Group oral history anthology *20th Century Crusaders*, compiled by Ian Hawkins. That day, he was flying deputy lead on Jim McGregor's wing. At their altitude, the ambient temperature was forty degrees below zero, but there was hardly a cloud in the sky.

"The gray and white landscape 21,000 feet below looks cold and wintry," George Webster writes, echoing Keilman's description of the landscape that they saw so clearly from far above. "It seems quiet down there, but I know that air raid sirens blare in towns, and people hurry to hide in underground shelters. I see a countryside of dark forests and white fields dotted with cities and villages, all connected by roads and rail lines. While

I fill my log with everything that I see, I gaze at the Rhine River, spanned by dozens of bridges, and lined with cities pouring smoke into the air from factories. The sky is brilliant blue, but it is filled with myriad white trails high overhead. They twist and circle as our fighters battle what looks like an immense number of German attackers. I tremble from cold and fright. My headache is back, and it's killing me."

To again cite Glen Williamson's metaphor, the Luftwaffe erected a substantial wall to protect Gotha and Schweinfurt from the other divisions, hammering the Eighth Air Force bombers almost continuously to and from the targets, and giving their fighter escorts a serious run for their money. Over Schweinfurt, the escorts lost ten of their own while downing thirty-seven Luftwaffe interceptors. The 1st Division lost eleven Flying Fortresses, but the 2nd Division paid a steeper price on the Gotha mission, losing thirty-three Liberators.

"The fighters' wings blink as their many guns fire," George Webster remembers. "Orange streams shoot toward the bombers like fire from hoses and smash into a B-17. Pieces of the unlucky bomber fly off in a cloud of smoke. Gunfire hits the Plexiglas dome of a bomber's top turret, and it explodes in a white cloud that turns red with blood from the gunner's head. The first bomber catches fire, then the second, each trailing a long stream of orange flame. Both B-17s wobble as blazes engulf them in seconds. No one gets out. The men are burning alive in there. In thirty seconds, the bombers are flaming torches, totally enveloped in fire. The blazing planes tip over and fall, trailing long tails of flame. Fighters wheel around and race back from the rear toward the hapless formation of bombers. Red tracers from bombers stray out toward the fighters. Orange fire spews from the fighters' wings. It hammers a B-17, hitting wings and engines. Smoke and fragments erupt from the bomber. Fire spurts from its engines, and the big plane dissolves in a mass of flames."

Meanwhile, over Osnabrück, on the approach to Gotha, the Liberators of the 2nd Division were also under attack, and flying without fighter support because they were ahead of schedule.

"My log records the first continuous opposition in the Osnabrück area at 1200 hours, noon," Wright Lee of the 445th Bombardment Group reports. "Here we turned south, deeper into Germany. We were eleven minutes ahead of schedule now and still had no fighter assistance. As we looked out of the windows, we saw enemy fighters coming up in droves. Bf 109s, Fw 190s, Ju 88s, and Bf 110s came zooming into our area and the individual attacks began. A B-24 blew up behind us and I logged it for the record. This was the first of five bombers which our 445th Group lost around noon within six minutes. It was later estimated that we had been attacked by 150 German fighters. It was impossible to individually log all of this activity but I did my best."

As the 445th Bombardment Group was passing northeast of Osnabrück, Lee could watch the fighters taking off from their bases far below.

"Outside of the greater Osnabrück fighter defense sector, I looked down and it almost made me sick to see what more was in store for us," he continues. "The fighters were taking off in pairs, one twosome after the other, and all circled and climbed to get into the fight. They were all around us and still we had no help, all because we were ahead of schedule."

Another 2nd Division, 14th Combat Wing Liberator outfit, the 392nd Bombardment Group, reported that the fighter escort caught up with the bombers as they neared the target, and as Luftwaffe activity increased.

"Fighter attacks became more persistent," Myron Keilman writes of the 392nd's approach to Gotha. "By the time we reached our Initial Point to begin our bomb run, the sky around our three squadrons was full of busy P-38s and P-51s fending off the enemy fighters. Our little friends dived down past our lead ship, chasing the Bf 109s and Fw 190s which were making head-on attacks. Our gunners got in a lot of shooting, too. The staccato of the turrets' twin .50s vibrated throughout the airplane. It was really frightening."

As the 392nd Bombardment Group made a gradual left turn over the IP, red flares from McGregor's Liberator were the indicator that it was time for the bombardiers to open their bomb bays. In the noses of the Liberators, the Norden bombsights were uncovered, gyroscopes were stabilized, and bombing switches turned to the "on" position.

"I've got the target!" Keilman recalls of the lead bombardier's words. In the crystal clear air, this came as no surprise. How could he not?

"Lieutenant Good's target folder didn't contain a snow-covered, wintry view of the Messerschmitt Aircraft Plants," Keilman writes in Hawkins's anthology. "He had to use his keen judgment and trained skills in locating the briefed aiming point. Only his one eye, peering through the bombsight optics, could determine where to place the cross-hair. He gave a running commentary to the command pilot and crew of what he saw and what he was doing in steering the lead B-24, and the following formation of bombers, to the bomb release point. But only he, the lead bombardier, knew for sure what was viewed through the bombsight."

"On airspeed, on altitude," lead pilot McGregor replied, handing control of the Liberator to the bombardier at 160 mph and eighteen thousand feet. "You've got the airplane."

"The bombs were smack 'on target,' but the battle wasn't over," Keilman continues. "No sooner had the 14th Wing left the target's flak than we were again attacked by enemy fighters. . . . The interphone was alive with excited calls of enemy action. Head-on and tail attacks, in singles and 'gaggles.' Rockets, 20mm cannon shells, and machine gun fire were all encountered as the battle progressed. Seven of our B-24s were shot down and many of us were shot up."

Meanwhile, the 2nd Combat Wing suffered a snafu over the target when the lead bombardier passed out from an oxygen system failure and accidentally began dropping bombs on the wrong target. The Liberators following him proceeded to do the same, but the 445th Group lead bombardier noticed the error and led his group to the correct target.

"The upcoming target was clear and easily identified," Wright Lee remembers. "The Bf 110 factory buildings were snow covered but stood out clearly. The interphone suddenly crackled and over came, 'Bombs Away' from the pilot. I hit the salvo handle and away they went at 1:19 P.M. from 20,000 feet. I leaned down over the glass bottom of the nose and watched as our bombs fell toward the target, both of us moving forward at about the same speed. Then they hit the buildings which seemed to disintegrate and fly into the air. Black smoke and flames accompanied the explosions. For a second I thought that what I was seeing was flak bursting and jumped back. Then I realized that it was the target 'exploding.' Lieutenant Cassani, bombardier in our lead plane, had done a great job."

The 445th Bombardment Group would receive a Distinguished Unit

Citation for this mission because of its having deviated from the erroneous target to the correct one.

Exiting the target area, however, the 445th once again was piled on by the Luftwaffe.

"We passed over the town of Gotha and made a sharp right turn," Wright Lee remembers. "Fighters resumed their attacks with a vengeance. As I looked out of the window at our lead plane not more than 100 feet from us, I saw its nose suddenly light up with a blinding flash . . . then nothing, no explosion. The plane's bomb bay doors opened and the landing gear was lowered as they continued in formation. After a few seconds the plane's wing wagged, the signal for the deputy lead to take over. The injured ship gently moved to the left and our ship moved with it. . . . A tense drama was unfolding in the lead ship, [which was] now aborting. . . . The blinding flash which I saw was a 20 mm shell exploding in the cockpit, injuring Major Evans, the pilot and our Squadron Commander, but missing Captain Bussing, the copilot. With all of this confusion, Major Evans gave the order to 'lower the wheels . . . we're going down.' The lowering of the wheels was an International Code that the plane was surrendering in the air and would fight no further and would make a landing. Opening the bomb bay was a precaution in case of an explosion and to allow any man to leave the plane via parachute."

As Lee watched, the 389th Bombardment Group, flying forward and right of the 445th and leading the 2nd Combat Wing, took the brunt of the Luftwaffe attack. "Men were bailing out randomly from all positions in these planes, nose to bomb bay to tail," he writes. "Some chutes opened right away but other men fell free, arms and legs dangling as they dropped in the sky. Some came very close to our planes, perhaps one hundred feet, but I didn't see any hit. The sky was a mass of parachutes and I estimated that twenty-five were all around us. . . . Out in front at 'twelve o'clock high' I watched as ten Bf 109s lined up ready to attack. Down they zoomed, heading straight for us, and I could almost feel the bullets hit me, but by some miracle they missed and [the German fighters] sped by to our side and under us, so near that I could see the black crosses clearly and the pilots' faces looking out of the cockpits."

Among the faces of the Luftwaffe fighter pilots bedeviling the 1st and 2nd Divisions on Thursday were those of several aces whose toll of Eighth Air Force bombers was already in double digits, such as Hermann Staiger of Jagdgeschwader 26, whose eventual score of sixty-three victories would include twenty-six four-engine bombers. On Thursday, he downed a 1st Division Flying Fortress south of Quakenbrück-Rheine near Münster.

The *Gruppenkommandeur* of Jagdgeschwader 11's III Gruppe, Anton "Toni" Hackl, credited with thirty-four heavy bombers during his career, took out a B-17 straggler late in the afternoon, fourteen thousand feet over Glückstadt in Schleswig-Holstein.

"The sky around us filled with fighters slashing through bomber formations, and bomber gunfire spurting toward fighters," George Webster writes, painting a hellish portrait of a hellish bomb run. "Bombers catch fire, and fighters trail smoke as they fall toward the earth. A fighter pilot jumps from his stricken fighter and opens his parachute. A bomber's tail gunner fires a long burst at him. The pilot's body jerks and hangs limply from his parachute. Fighter pilots must have seen the killing, because two Fw 190s attack the tail gunner's bomber. Their guns smash the tail gunner's position to shreds and hit the engines until the B-17 explodes in another ball of fire."

Another Luftwaffe ace, who had been with Jagdgeschwader 26 for about a year, *Oberleutnant* Waldemar "Waldi" Radener caught the Schweinfurt mission both coming and going, downing one bomber on the way south plus another bomber and an escort fighter over Wetzlar in Hesse about two hours later.

Oberleutnant Rüdiger von Kirchmayr of Jagdgeschwader 1, who had destroyed a 2nd Division Liberator over the Dutch coast on Monday, claimed another over Westphalia on Thursday. These were two of an eventual ten heavy bombers that he claimed. The total of twenty-six heavy bombers credited to *Oberfeldwebel* Anton-Rudolf "Toni" Piffer of Jagdgeschwader 1 would include a 2nd Division Liberator that he shot down on Thursday over Diepholz.

The man who did the most damage to the Eighth Air Force on Thursday was Walter Dahl, flying a Bf 109G-6, armed with a 30mm MK 108 cannon. He was the *Gruppenkommandeur* of Jagdgeschwader 3's III Gruppe, which was reassigned to *Reichsverteidigung* duties from Kursk on the eastern front during the summer of 1943. Dahl had shown an aptitude for battling bombers and had led the III Gruppe to intercept the USAAF offensive against Schweinfurt and Regensburg on August 17.

Dahl claimed four on February 23, plus one of the escorting P-38s. As Luftwaffe records show, he shot down two B-17s in the space of four minutes around noon and two more in the space of eight minutes about an hour later—while chasing down the P-38 in between. He was eventually credited with costing the Americans as many as three dozen four-engine bombers.

As they had done on Sunday, the 3rd Division sent 236 Flying Fortresses across the North Sea, to pass over Denmark and drive south toward the Baltic coast.

The 3rd Division targets, beginning with Tutow, were all related to the production of Focke-Wulf Fw 190s. The most distant of these was the Luftwaffenfliegerhorst Kreising complex at Krzesiny, just outside the city of Posen. Known as Poznan before the war, when it was part of Poland, it would become and remain Poznan, Poland, again after the war.

As had occurred on Monday, clouds over the target prevented the bombers from dropping their bombs. Despite Hitler's impression of the scope of dominions, the United States still considered this to be Poland, and there would be no bombing unless the Luftwaffe complex was visually identifiable.

With Tutow also under cloud cover, the entire force diverted to strike nearby Rostock, home to Heinkel Flugzeugwerke facilities.

As had also been the case Monday, the unescorted 3rd Division strike force met spirited but limited Luftwaffe resistance and was able to withdraw over open water—first the Baltic, then the North Sea—rather than having to battle its way across the German landmass for hours, as did the other divisions.

The Fifteenth Air Force would attack Steyr as they had on Wednesday, though their specific "target for today" would be different. Today it would be the factory complex of the big industrial corporation Steyr-Daimler-Puch. Formed in 1934 through a merger of carmaker and gunmaker Steyr-Werke AG and Austro-Daimler, a former subsidiary of the German

Daimler company, Steyr-Daimler-Puch had been a major manufacturer of high-end automobiles before World War II and was now manufacturing weapons, military vehicles, and aircraft components. The latter earned it a place on the Operation Argument target list.

The Fifteenth launched 114 bombers, of which only 87 continued all the way to Steyr, because of the weather. The others, becoming separated from the main formation, diverted to secondary oil refinery targets in the Italian Adriatic port city of Fiume (now Rijeka in Croatia).

As had occurred the day before, the bombers that reached Steyr were subjected to merciless and effective mauling by the Luftwaffe. Not only were they attacked at close range by Bf 109s and FW 190s, they were targeted by twin-engine fighters firing rockets at longer range and even air-to-air bombing attacks, which had become rare over northern Germany since 1943.

The Luftwaffe went after the 2nd Bombardment Group, which flew last in the formation, with particular ferocity. The total losses for the Fifteenth Air Force that day totaled seventeen aircraft, or 20 percent of those that had reached Steyr. Ten of the seventeen losses represented the *entire* complement of the 2nd Group. Every last one.

Despite relentless Luftwaffe interference, Friday's major Eighth Air Force attacks on Gotha and Schweinfurt took place under ideal visual conditions and yielded the kinds of results that men from Tooey Spaatz to Fred Anderson to Dick Hughes had craved.

At Schweinfurt, clear skies prevailed, and bombardiers were confident in their work. George Shackley, leading the 381st Group that day aboard *Rotherhithe's Revenge*, observed that he could see for miles. At his later debriefing he colorfully reported that "bombs were slamming down on factories and other targets in the city for at least half an hour. Our own bombing was one of the best. This was one hell of a lot different from my first two Schweinfurt missions."

Patting the group leader on the back, Lieutenant Thomas Sellers, the pilot of *Little Duchess*, wrote in his own after-action report that the Schweinfurt mission was "the best coordinated mission of any of the 20 I have flown. It showed careful, detailed planning. Major Shackley did a perfect job of leading the wing. Bombing was perfect. The town and target were plastered both by us and the wings ahead."

Also aboard *Rotherhithe's Revenge*, the 381st's lead bombardier, Captain Lawrence Potenza, confirmed that "the bomb run was beautiful. I could see hits from our bombs right in the factory area. Heavy smoke was over the town from bombs dropped by the group ahead of us and fires were everywhere."

Potenza had even more to be pleased about. Thursday marked his twenty-fifth and *last* mission with the Eighth Air Force.

While the Schweinfurt attack effectively hit and destroyed many of its intended targets, the Strategic Bombing Survey would later rank the October 14, 1943, mission to the ball bearing capital as having done more damage to the overall bearing industry, simply because it took place before major efforts were made to decentralize the industry. For example, in the four intervening months, Vereinigte Kugellagerfabriken had moved 549 machines, or 27 percent of its manufacturing equipment, out of Schweinfurt.

"Nevertheless the bearing plants suffered heavy damage in the raids," Arthur Ferguson writes, "especially in the departments processing rings; and the ball department, already half-dispersed, lost another ten percent of its machines."

The weather was so crystal clear over central Germany that day that the 1st Division Flying Fortresses over Schweinfurt could see the 2nd Division Liberators over Gotha in the distance. The lead navigator with the 384th Bombardment Group, Captain James Martin-Vegue, later recalled at his debriefing that he could see the B-24s, and "the smoke was piled up to 10,000 feet. We could see [the Gothaer Waggonfabrik factory complex] far off to our right, burning to beat hell. It must have been 50 miles away, but that's how good the visibility was. It was a beautiful mission. Our target was covered by smoke from a preceding formation when we got there, and the smoke was right where the buildings were supposed to be. When we left, the whole area was on fire."

Citing the postwar Strategic Bombing Survey, Arthur Ferguson writes that the bombing at Gotha "was especially accurate, and probably more important strategically than at Schweinfurt. Over 400 bombs, both high explosive and incendiary, fell in the target area, 93 of which hit buildings; this does not count the large number of fragmentation bombs (180 tons out of a total of 424) dropped also. Almost every building in the very compact factory area was damaged. The eastern half of the plant, where the aircraft manufacture was centered, was generally destroyed, although machine tools, the vital part of the production system, received surprisingly slight damage, considering the amount of damage to buildings. Most of the loss of machine tools resulted from fires. . . . Much time and labor had to be expended clearing heavy girders from the machines caught under them."

The Strategic Bombing Survey went on to estimate that as a result of the February 24 attack, Gothaer Waggonfabrik lost about six to seven weeks' production and compelled a dispersal of operations that placed a "heavy drain" on other factories in the Messerschmitt production network.

The damage *to* the Eighth Air Force in the February 24 Schweinfurt mission was nothing like the horrendous toll exacted by the Luftwaffe in October, but still, the mood was somber that night as airmen in the mess hall pondered the empty chairs of those who would never come back.

While the 1st Division had emerged from Schweinfurt with a loss rate of less than 5 percent, the Liberators of the 2nd Division had taken a hit of nearly 20 percent of their effective force.

Late Thursday afternoon, on the observation deck of the control tower at Tibenham, the home base of the 2nd Division's 445th Bombardment Group, Colonel Robert Terrill watched and waited for his B-24s to return. Of twenty-five planes that his group had sent out, three had aborted early in the mission.

"Well, I guess this is the early bunch," Wright Lee quotes him as having said when he had watched nine of the twenty-two Liberators land. "The others should be right behind."

Lee reports that when Terrill was told that nine were *all* that remained of his group, "he almost died of shock."

For the 1st Division, it may have seemed easy to look at the bright side and say that "it could have been much worse," which Schweinfurt certainly could have been—but it is hard to look at the bright side when you are looking at empty bunks.

"I think they better pay us more," 92nd Bombardment Group bombardier Ralph Ballmer said to George Webster at dinner that night, trying gallows humor to bring some lightness to a gathering of shaken flyers.

"How you doing?" fellow airman Ken Tasker asked Webster.

"I've never been so scared," came the reply. They had just heard that the 92nd had lost three bombers.

The crews of the 379th Bombardment Group, meanwhile, had gone off on Thursday morning expecting the worst, but for them, at least, this failed to materialize. The group lost only one man, a gunner who had been struck and killed by a flak fragment over the target. It was like a freak accident.

"Much to the surprise of nearly everyone on the base (to say nothing of the delight of the aircrews) the Forts [B-17 Flying Fortesses] roared in late that afternoon and landed," Derwyn Robb recalls. "Most of the planes weren't expected back, but they all came back. None lost! At [the debriefing] crews related 'lots of flak, and our own fighter pilots took care of most of the Jerries.' The P-38s and P-51s picked up the formations after the P-47s left and fighter attacks against our group were meager. With the comforting closeness of the 'little friends' and perfect bombing weather, not a cloud within miles of the target, the lead bombardiers Joe Brown and Ed Millson took full advantage of the situation and dropped the bombs 'with the highest degree of accuracy.' "

Robb interprets the phrase as meaning that the bombers "plastered hell out of the target."

Late that same night, 734 RAF bombers, using as their beacon the fires still burning from the American attacks, came over Schweinfurt and continued the rain of terror on the erstwhile capital of the German antifriction bearing industry.

Said General Fred Anderson, "We did a job that day."

TWENTY-ONE

FRIDAY, FEBRUARY 25

When the sun came out on Friday, and it *did* come out all across northern Europe, the bombers were already in the air. That phenomenon, which Dick Hughes had described as "one of the strangest freaks in February European weather," had now delivered the fifth of five clear days in six.

Buoyed by Thursday's successes—albeit *costly* successes—the USSTAF planners planned big, and they planned bold. With weather and visibility no obstacle, they had the luxury of picking any targets they wished, and the decision was made to go deep, deeper even than Schweinfurt, and to go deep with the *entire* Eighth Air Force.

As the crews learned at their "targets for today" briefings in the pre-dawn darkness on Friday morning, the 1st Bombardment Division was tasked with Stuttgart and Augsburg, 460 and 550 miles from East Anglia, respectively—and more than ten hours, round-trip. The 2nd Bombardment Division would send its Liberators 500 miles to Fürth, and the 3rd Division would be making the 570-mile trek to Regensburg.

More than 750 bombers moved south from England in a single stream, with all three bombardment divisions traveling together for mutual protection, with a coordinated fighter force of 73 P-38s, 687 Eighth and Ninth Air Force P-47s, and 139 Eighth and Ninth Air Force P-51s. They would

fly together almost as far as Schweinfurt before peeling off in four directions. The 1st Bombardment Division would send 196 Flying Fortresses
to Augsburg and 50 to Stuttgart. Of the 2nd Bombardment Division Liberators, 173 would head to Fürth.

At the targets in and around Regensburg, 267 of the 290 Flying Fortresses launched by the Eighth Air Force 3rd Bombardment Division would
be met by 176 bombers from Nathan Twining's Fifteenth Air Force. They
would be making the nearly 600-mile journey from their fields around
Foggia, across the Alps, to strike Regensburg from the opposite direction.

Friday was to mark the first time that the Eighth and the Fifteenth
coordinated respective maximum effort attacks on the same city on the
same day.

As missions went, those planned for Friday promised to be as chal-
lenging and dangerous as those on any day of maximum effort that the
Eighth Air Force had ever flown. The weather and the growing availability of P-51s as escorts were the only things that the Eighth Air Force had
on its side. Because of the extremely deep penetration, the bombers would
be at the mercy of the Luftwaffe hours longer than on missions to northern Germany, and in those hours, anything could happen.

The major objective of the day was Messerschmitt AG, the originator
of the Bf 109, the backbone fighter of the Luftwaffe. More than thirty-five
thousand of these aircraft would be built, compared to around twenty
thousand Focke-Wulf Fw 190s, making the Bf 109 the most widely produced fighter plane in history. Messerschmitt AG, Germany's leading
planemaker during World War II, originated in 1926 in Augsburg as Bay-
rische Flugzeugwerke AG (Bavarian Aircraft Works), but was renamed in
1938 after its founder and chief designer, Willy Messerschmitt, who was
still at the helm of the company.

As Dick Hughes, Fred Anderson, and Glen Williamson spread out the
map of northern Bavaria and began picking Messerschmitt targets, they
naturally noted Augsburg, the firm's home city, but their eyes also fell
upon Fürth. Here, the firm of Flugzeugwerke Bachmann von Blumenthal
assembled Messerschmitt's twin-engine Bf 110, the Luftwaffe night fighter
that was often pressed into service against the Eighth Air Force by day.
However, when they thought of Messerschmitt, their greatest attention

turned to Regensburg, where the factories of the Messerschmitt GmbH Regensburg subsidiary built most of the Luftwaffe's Bf 109s.

Stuttgart, the fourth city in the crosshairs of the USSTAF on that sunny Friday, was an industrial city well known as home to Daimler-Benz, but also one of the locations where Vereinigte Kugellagerfabriken manufactured anti-friction bearings.

"Bombing was very good," Lieutenant Happy Hendryx, the lead bombardier of the 381st Bombardment Group, reported of his group's mission to Augsburg. "We knocked out at least three-quarters of the factory. We had a good formation and made an ideal bomb run, laying our bombs in a tight pattern. All we could see was smoke when we turned to head back."

One of the 1st Division Flying Fortresses that almost didn't make it was *General Ike* of the 91st Bombardment Group, piloted by Lieutenant John Davis. Going into Augsburg, the 91st's bombers entered their bomb run at twenty-eight thousand feet. Bomb bay doors came open, and the aircraft began dumping chaff to bamboozle the German radar. An unopened package of chaff about the size and shape of a carton of cigarettes impacted the number two engine of *General Ike*, rupturing an oil line and causing a fire.

"The pilot took evasive action," Tech Sergeant George Parrish told Marion Havelaar for his history of the 91st, entitled *The Ragged Irregulars*. "One of the lower bombs in the rack didn't release and others fell on it."

With the bombs piled up inside the bomb bay, the crew debated whether to abandon ship or try to limp home. Deciding on the latter, they did what they could to try to lighten the aircraft in order to keep up with the other B-17s, which had been able to drop their loads.

"As we went over the water with the coast about twenty to twenty-five miles away, we continued to lose altitude," Parrish recalls. "The No. 2 engine's propeller could not be feathered and because of that, it was windmilling and beginning to fall apart. Lieutenant Frank Varva, the navigator, was giving the pilot instructions, saying the airfield was straight ahead. As we approached we were actually lower than the height of the cliff. With a lot of prayer that propeller froze, eliminating the drag, and allowed us to lift high enough to go over the cliff."

Davis managed to get the plane down safely at the 91st's home base at Bassingbourn.

Meanwhile, some of the 3rd Division Flying Fortresses did not even make it to Regensburg. As had been the case often during Big Week, the Luftwaffe began hammering the aircraft as soon as they entered German airspace, and kept at it. The deeper into the Reich a plane was headed, the longer the hammering went on.

Waiting for the Americans north of Fürth and Stuttgart were the aces of Jagdgeschwader 26 with their Messerschmitt Bf 109G-6s. Hermann Staiger, who had cost the Eighth Air Force a Flying Fortress over Münster on Thursday, downed another over Birkweiler, about forty miles northwest of Stuttgart, on Friday.

Waldi Radener, who had downed two bombers the day before, claimed two more, although one was a *herausschuss*, a bomber merely knocked out of formation. Klaus Mietusch, the *Gruppenkommandeur* of Jagdgeschwader 26's III Gruppe claimed two heavy bombers, although one of his claims was a *herausschuss*.

"Near the German town of Saarbrücken, on the French-German border, suddenly there were three bursts of flak, right at our altitude," recalls pilot Merlin Chardi in the history of the 447th Bombardment Group compiled by Doyle Shields. "With this I started evasive action, a slow right turn. The next group of flak bursts were on target with one right in our number three engine setting it on fire and disconnecting the propeller from the engine drive. This increased the noise level considerably. With some panic we tried without success to put the fire out. Within seconds, the wing panel right behind the engine began to buckle up and melt down.

"One more look out the window and I quickly gave the order to abandon the good old ship. . . . With the plane still in a dive and steep right bank, I looked back only to find the radio compartment door closed so I had no idea if the crew was out."

Chardi bailed out at ten thousand feet, worrying that Sergeant Magruder, the ball turret gunner, would not have had enough time to get the turret rotated up so that he could escape.

"I started counting chutes and got to nine knowing we had a crew of ten," Chardi continues. "I said, cursing, 'he didn't get out of the ball turret.' I had failed to count myself. . . . No one was seriously hurt except for bad backs due to hard parachute landings and small flak wounds. . . . We spent the next fifteen months as guests of the German Government."

Several of the units flying with the 3rd Division on Friday had been bloodied in the first Eighth Air Force mission against Regensburg back on August 17 and were going back for a return visit. These included the 96th and "Bloody Hundredth" 100th Bombardment Groups.

"As we began our bomb run on Regensburg at about 26,000 feet, the German fighters pulled back and the flak became very heavy," recalled Sergeant Bill Cook, the tail gunner aboard the 100th Bombardment Group Flying Fortress *Mismalovin*. "Just after we had dropped our bombs we received a hit in the left inboard engine and lost oil pressure immediately. The propeller began to run away and vibration became very severe; to the point that we thought we might have the engine fall off. We finally were able to feather the prop and stabilize the plane. As you would expect, we lost altitude rapidly; the rest of the Group formation had left us, and we were faced with returning to base alone. As you know, Regensburg is deep into Germany, and the crew debated on whether or not to fly to Switzerland or try to make it back to England alone. Obviously we made the decision to try for England."

Unable to gain altitude, *Mismalovin* flew very low and came under frequent fighter attack as the pilot, Lieutenant Stewart McClain, pushed the B-17 toward the home of the Bloody Hundredth at Thorpe Abbotts. Though the Luftwaffe failed to bring the plane down, several men were shot and killed during these sporadic attacks.

"I was wounded on four separate occasions," Bill Cook recalls. "In spite of the licking we were taking, we still managed to give a pretty good account of ourselves. The engineer shot down two fighters, the bombardier had one possible, and I shot down two of which I am sure. As we approached the English Channel, we flew over Calais, France, and as we passed the coast we again picked up heavy fighter attack. At one point we were close enough to England that we could see the cliffs of Dover, and still were being attacked by fighters."

When the bomber began a gradual left turn, and Cook could no longer raise the pilot on the intercom, he headed toward the flight deck, hoping to take control of the aircraft, much as Archie Mathies had done on Sunday with *Ten Horsepower*.

"I knew we were going to crash if something was not done to prevent it," Cook recalls in Richard LeStrange's anthology. "Since I had flown the plane on many occasions, I left the tail gunner's position and headed for the cockpit. As I reached the main entrance to the plane, I saw Staff Sergeant George Knudsen, a waist gunner, jump from the aircraft. At this point we were only about 100–150 feet from the English Channel and I knew we did not have sufficient altitude for a chute to open. Our ball turret gunner, Staff Sergeant Lawrence Bennett, was standing in the door ready to jump. I reached for him, pulled him back into the plane, and told him to take off his chute because we were about to crash. He was having some difficulty removing his chute, and I was assisting him when the plane crashed into the Channel.

"I was knocked unconscious in the crash and woke up floating in the water. When I regained consciousness, I saw one other person (a spare gunner flying with us that day—he replaced Staff Sergeant John Walters, and I don't remember his name) who had survived. We were picked up by some German Marines, taken to hospital in Calais, France, where we stayed for about three or four days, and I was then moved to an interrogation center in Frankfurt. I spent about twenty days in Frankfurt (in solitary) and was then sent to a prisoner of war camp."

Of the crew of *Mismalovin*, only Cook and the "spare gunner," whose name was Claude Zukowski, survived to see Saturday's dawn.

Meanwhile, an hour from the target, one of the 96th Bombardment Group Flying Fortresses, *The Saint*, piloted by Lieutenant Bob Arstingstall, had been attacked by a German fighter head-on, killing copilot Curt Mosier.

"Out of that late winter sun, came a silver arrow with guns blazing," recalls navigator Stan Peterson in his account in *Snetterton Falcons* by Robert E. Doherty and Geoffrey Ward. "There was a thickening thud. Then silence followed by the scent of cordite. . . . Bob Arstingstall, our pilot, asked me to come up to the cockpit where I saw that copilot Curt Mosier was dead, the main oxygen line was severed and the 30mm shell which had done the damage was still smoking on the flight deck floor behind Arstingstall's seat. . . . I remember hustling all over the bomber in an effort to find spare oxygen bottles to keep my pilot supplied for another four hours."

For getting *The Saint* back to the 96th Bombardment Group base at Snetterton, Lieutenant Arstingstall was awarded a Silver Star.

The Eighth Air Force 1st Division lost thirteen bombers on the Augsburg-Stuttgart mission, while the 2nd Division lost a half dozen Liberators shot down and two later written off. More than three hundred Eighth Air Force airmen bailed out, most of them disappearing into the hellish world of the Stalag Luft system, the prisoner of war camps that were specifically established for captured Allied airmen.

As Arthur Ferguson writes of the Fifteenth Air Force effort at Regensburg that day, the Fifteenth "lacked escort of sufficiently long range to provide protection during the most distant phase of the penetration. It suffered also from the handicap of a relatively small force. Only bombers equipped for long-range flying could be sent as far as Regensburg, and, although the Fifteenth dispatched that day almost 400 bombers, only 176 were airborne on the main mission. The remainder hit yards and port installations at Fiume, the harbor at Zara, warehouses and sheds at Pola [on the eastern side of the Adriatic Sea], rail lines [in Austria] at Zell-am-See, and the airfield at Graz-Thalerhof [also in Austria]."

As the 3rd Division and the Fifteenth Air Force rendezvoused over Regensburg that day, they, in turn, were met by Jagdgeschwader 3, whose III Gruppe leader, Walter Dahl, had claimed four bombers the day before. On Friday, two more Flying Fortresses would fall to his guns in the space of twenty-one minutes.

Attacking the Fifteenth Air Force contingent as they were between the Alps and their targets was Jagdgeschwader 27, based at Wiesbaden, which had taken a heavy toll of forty-five Eighth Air Force bombers during the deep penetration mission to Stuttgart on September 6, 1943.

Werner Schroer, who led the *geschwader*'s II Gruppe, and who had personally downed four American aircraft during the September debacle, now claimed two more toward his eventual total of twenty-six four-engine bombers. One of these was near Altötting in southeastern Bavaria, and the second was over the Chiemsee, the lake that lies on the Austro-German border between Rosenheim and Salzburg.

The 3rd Division lost a dozen Flying Fortresses getting in and out of the target area at Regensburg, a loss of just 5 percent. However, before it was over, the unescorted Fifteenth Air Force contingent took the worst punishment of the day, losing thirty-nine bombers, or nearly a quarter of the force that it sent to Regensburg. In Arthur Ferguson's words, "It was another proof of the fact, long since conceded by American strategic bombing experts, that a daylight bomber force without full fighter cover could not hope to get through an aggressive enemy without excessive losses, especially when, as in this instance, the enemy chose to concentrate on the weaker and more poorly protected force."

The men flying the missions did not need "another proof."

Unlike previous days during Big Week, every bombardment group from the Eighth Air Force was able to bomb its primary target, and the clarity of the weather meant a higher degree of accuracy than had been the case on other missions.

As Ferguson writes, "The main Messerschmitt plant at Augsburg underwent drastic treatment. Blast and fire from over 500 tons of bombs destroyed approximately thirty buildings. Production capacity was reduced by about 35 percent. Almost one-third of all machine tools were damaged, and 70 percent of stored material destroyed."

"Our bombs made a hell of a hole in the place and black smoke shot up thousands of feet," recalled Staff Sergeant James Fisher of the attack on Augsburg. He was a waist gunner aboard the 384th Bombardment Group Flying Fortress known as *Loose Goose*. "Visibility was excellent. I saw a B-24 [of the force that attacked Fürth, sixty miles to the north] knock down two of three enemy fighters attacking it and then one of our fighters came in and shot down [the third]. On the ground we could see the Focke-Wulfs taking off to come up at us. We passed by Stuttgart before our other planes got there and fires were still burning from the RAF raid of a couple of nights ago."

At Regensburg, which had now been bombed twice by the Fifteenth Air Force and once by the Eighth Air Force during Big Week, every building in the target areas had been damaged and many were destroyed. By Messerschmitt's own reckoning, monthly output fell from 435 aircraft delivered to the Luftwaffe in January to just 135 in March.

Despite the frightful losses suffered by the Fifteenth Air Force, Friday's Regensburg mission was regarded as having been their most successful mission across the Alps to date.

On Saturday, General Ira Eaker, commanding the Mediterranean Allied Air Force, cabled General Twining his congratulations on the success enjoyed by the Fifteenth. He noted that the photoreconnaissance images "for the second successive day have given us an example of precision bombing at its very best. Being engaged in one of the greatest air battles in history yesterday your force fought through the heaviest opposition it has encountered. The Air Force's record of reaching the objective and accomplishing the assigned task was maintained with distinction. Aircraft factory destroyed by you in this attack is estimated to produce at the rate of 250 per month. When considering the losses sustained, this fact should be borne in mind."

General Spaatz, now back at Bushy Park in England, sent his own telegram, writing that "Strike photographs of the Regensburg attack [have been] examined and I consider that superior results were obtained. The Fifteenth Air Force accomplished a superior job of bombing and vital destruction to enemy installations in the face of heavy air attack, without fighter support and with heavy losses. Even without consideration of the 93 enemy fighters shot down by our bombers, the results far outweigh the losses."

The same might have been said about the entirety of the results of the six days that came to be known as Big Week.

Walt Rostow wrote half a century later, "Looking back, I can see again the faces of Hughes, Anderson, and Spaatz, as well as the key figures in British intelligence, on whom the American effort was based—as able, imaginative, and dedicated a group of men and women as was ever assembled. . . . The German single-engined fighter force never recovered from its unlikely defeat by the American long-range bombers. [Big Week] was the week that, in effect, a mature US Air Force emerged."

TWENTY-TWO

ALL ROADS LED TO OVERLORD

"On February 23, 1944, [Erhard] Milch visited me in my sickroom," wrote Albert Speer, Hitler's all-powerful armaments minister. Milch, meanwhile, held the post of state secretary in the Reich Aviation Ministry. "He informed me that the American Eighth and Fifteenth Air Forces were concentrating their bombing on the German aircraft industry, with the result that our aircraft production would be reduced to a third of what it had been, at least for the month to come."

When Milch came to him as the bearer of bad news—from Schweinfurt, from Regensburg, from Gotha, from Fürth, and from all those other places—Speer had been hospitalized for more than a month for exhaustion. As he wrote in his memoirs, "The nearly two years of continuous tension had been taking their toll. Physically, I was nearly worn out at the age of 38. The pain in my knee hardly ever left me. I had no reserves of strength. Or were all these symptoms merely an escape?"

Big Week brought plenty of bad news that Speer would yearn to escape, but from which he could not.

Saturday, February 26, marked the "morning after" of Big Week. A low pressure area had moved into Europe on the seventh day, and the curtain fell. It was the metaphorical curtain, brought down on an epochal operation made possible only by the "strangest freak" of a window in the weather *and* by the men who were in a position to exploit it.

It was also a literal curtain, brought down by a bleak weather system that would cloak the continent in clouds for the better part of a month. The maximum effort officially designated as Operation Argument had come to an end.

In the American media of February 1944, Big Week was overshadowed by great land battles—the Battle of Anzio and the marine landing on the Pacific atoll of Eniwetok were ongoing simultaneously, and Overlord was on everyone's mind. In the coming months, though, Big Week would come to be recognized as a significant crossroads on the highway to victory in World War II. Albert Speer and Erhard Milch were already seeing the handwriting on the wall of Speer's sickroom.

Big Week did not destroy the Luftwaffe, nor the German aircraft industry, but it did destroy the complacency that had come to Speer and Milch from possessing air superiority and assuming that certain targets in certain regions were essentially untouchable by Allied strategic airpower.

Big Week, like Gettysburg eight decades earlier, did not herald a conclusion to a bloody war so much as it marked, in retrospect, a high water mark. Never again after Gettysburg would Robert E. Lee threaten to take the Civil War onto northern soil. Never again after Big Week could the Luftwaffe truly claim to possess and exercise air superiority over German soil.

With postwar access to German data, the Strategic Bombing Survey later concluded that Big Week had "damaged or destroyed 75 percent of the buildings in plants that at the time accounted for 90 percent of the total German production of aircraft." Production recovered, and faster than Allied analysts realized at the time, but it did so under the hardship of the time and expense of dispersal, and under the cloud of knowing that wherever it was dispersed, it was now potentially vulnerable.

As Arthur Ferguson writes in the official history of the USAAF in World War II, "The German authorities, whose plans had hitherto rested on unduly optimistic foundations, now apparently for the first time showed signs of desperation. . . . The February bombings did deny many hundreds of aircraft to the enemy at a time when they were badly needed and could probably have been brought into effective use against the Allied invasion of Europe. The fact that the Germans suffered only a temporary setback in their overall program of aircraft production is less important than that they lost a significant number of planes at a critical point in the air war and that, at the same critical juncture, they were forced to reorganize and disperse the entire industry.

"According to the US Strategic Bombing Survey, the February campaign would have paid off even if its only effect had been to force the enemy into an intensive program of dispersal. For that program not only accounted indirectly for much wasted effort and production loss; it also left the industry vulnerable to any serious disruption in transportation. The dispersal policy did, in fact, defeat itself when Allied bombers subsequently turned to an intensive strategic attack on transportation."

After the tipping point, the tide had not simply turned, it was running out.

It has often been asked how *big* the week had really been. It was, indeed, the largest sustained maximum effort by the Combined Bomber Offensive to date. The Eighth Air Force flew more than 3,300 sorties, and the Fifteenth Air Force flew more than 500, while RAF Bomber Command contributed more than 2,350. The ten thousand tons of bombs dropped by the Americans were roughly the equivalent of what the Eighth Air Force had dropped in its entire first year of operations.

Big Week had been as successful as it was big. Based on the experiences of the earlier Schweinfurt and Regensburg missions, the USSTAF planners and leadership had braced themselves for the probability of losing 200 bombers each day. In fact, the Eighth Air Force lost just 137 for the week, the Fifteenth lost 89, and the week cost the RAF 157 heavy bombers.

The force of USAAF escort fighters lost around 30 of their own, but total claims of Luftwaffe interceptors, both by the fighters and by the bomber gunners, was more than 500. The Oberkommando Luftwaffe (Luftwaffe High Command) itself recorded a loss of 456 fighters in February, including 65 night fighters. Assuming the majority of the daytime losses for the month occurred during Big Week, the ratio was in the vicinity of ten to one in favor of the Americans.

Not all the damage done to the Luftwaffe during Big Week was done by the bombs. As Glen Williamson mused, "The wall [of Luftwaffe fighters] which had been so difficult and dangerous, shrank each day [following Big Week]. It was wonderful how fast we got along after we broke down that wall."

Or, as Ferguson puts it, "There is reason to believe that the large and fiercely fought air battles of those six February days had more effect in establishing the air superiority on which Allied plans so largely depended than did the bombing of industrial plants."

Big Week had also marked the turning point in terms of one critical component of Luftwaffe doctrine—pilots. The supply of this vital element of earlier Luftwaffe successes was now seen to be precariously finite. As John Fagg of New York University writes in the official USAAF history, the problem of a continuous flow of top quality replacement pilots "calls attention to the importance of the air fighting during the spring of 1944. It was as a result of the air battles, especially those of the Big Week, that the Luftwaffe was for the first time forced to admit defeat. . . . By March the ability of the Luftwaffe to defend the Reich and engage in combat on anything like equal terms with Allied bombers and fighter forces had passed its marginal point and was steadily deteriorating whereas the capabilities of the Allies were improving."

Adolf Galland, the Luftwaffe's own inspector general of fighters, was driven to comment that Big Week had cost "our best Squadron, Gruppe and Geschwader commanders. Each incursion of the enemy is costing us some fifty aircrewmen. The time has come when our weapon (the Luftwaffe) is in sight of collapse."

The erosion of German air superiority was due to a number of factors, including the burgeoning size of the Eighth Air Force and the substantial damage done to the Luftwaffe and the German aircraft industry during Big Week.

If any specific American weapon were to be singled out as critical to the success of Operation Argument, it would be the P-51 Mustang escort fighter, which had made its debut in significant numbers in January and had proven itself indispensable during Big Week. With 108-gallon external fuel tanks, the P-47 Thunderbolt, which had long been the mainstay for Eighth Air Force bomber escort duty, had the combat radius to accompany bombers about 475 miles from British airspace. The Mustang could do this without external tanks.

Equip a Mustang with two 75-gallon wing tanks, and its radius was extended to 650 miles. With 108-gallon tanks, the P-51 could function as a "little friend" to bombers flying 850 miles from their bases. This meant that the Mustangs could fly to distant targets such as Schweinfurt and Regensburg—or *Berlin*—and be prepared to do battle. The number of Luftwaffe fighters shot down, for the much smaller number of Mustangs lost, is indicative of how well the new American fighter was able to function in those battles—*and* in the air battles over Germany from Big Week to the war's *final* week.

By the end of March 1944, the Eighth Air Force had its 4th, 355th, and 357th Fighter Groups fully operational with the Mustang, and in addition the Ninth Air Force's 354th Fighter Group. The veteran 4th Fighter Group, commanded by Colonel Don Blakeslee, had entered Big Week with around 150 total aerial victories, and by the middle of March, the number had topped 400.

With its range, plus its speed and high altitude maneuverability, the P-51 had not only quickly dominated the aerial battlefield, it gave the Eighth Air Force leadership the confidence to plan missions to even the most heavily defended targets in Germany.

On March 4, 1944, the Eighth Air Force for the first time bombed Berlin. Weather forced the diversion of all but 31 of the Flying Fortresses, but two days later, 658 heavy bombers reached the German capital, followed by 460 on March 8 and around 300 on March 9.

The targets included the Vereinigte Kugellagerfabriken ball bearing works at Erkner, which had long been eyed by Dick Hughes and the other American planners and considered as a target on Day Three of Big Week. Also on the target list were the facilities of Robert Bosch AG in the suburb of Klein Machnow. Now known as Robert Bosch GmbH, the company is today a world leader in engineering and electronics, but during World War II it was a prominent supplier of electrical components for aircraft and military vehicles, and therefore worthy of a place on the Pointblank target list.

Aside from the damage done to the targets—the VKF plant at Erkner suffered mightily from seventy-five direct hits on March 8—the effect that the Berlin missions had on morale was significant. With the American public, a first USAAF attack on an Axis capital was cause for celebration. For the British, an American attack on the capital of the country whose bombers had devastated London in 1940 was seen as a gesture of solidarity. The *London Evening Standard*'s editorial page called the attacks "a sign of the unshakable comradeship" and ran a headline that read ALLIES OVER BERLIN, rather than just AMERICANS OVER BERLIN.

For Berliners, who had been bombed before—but by the RAF at night—the sight of rows of gleaming Flying Fortresses over their city in tight formation, *and* with fighter escorts, spoke volumes about the loss of air superiority in the Reich.

For the German propaganda machine, it was a challenge to spin this new reality. Indeed, the best reaction seemed to be to just say that things were not as they seemed. The *Voelkischer Beobachter*, the official Nazi Party daily, explained to its readers on March 13 that "if occasionally they fly in a clear sky without at the moment being pursued by the dreaded German fighters, only the layman is fooled, and then only for a few minutes. . . . In their case the closed drill formation is not a sign of strength."

With Big Week behind them, Allied planners were able to turn to the future of the strategic air offensive against the Reich. As Dick Hughes writes, "Now, for the first time, I was able seriously to think of the destruction of the entire Axis oil industry—the decisive target system which I had mentally selected, as far back as the summer of 1941, as being the one the destruction of which would most nearly accomplish our purpose. . . . By the early spring of 1944, both the Eighth and Fifteenth Air Forces had large numbers of heavy bomber groups at their disposal, together with the necessary long-range escort fighters. The German fighter defenses, while still containing many a sting, were no longer deadly. . . . At last the time was ripe to destroy the German oil industry."

Walt Rostow writes in his OSS *War Diary* that Hughes formally presented his "Oil Plan" to General Spaatz on the evening of March 5 at Park House. Rostow added that Fred Anderson "had already read the plan and was an advocate of it."

Rostow, who was apparently present at the meeting, explains that "discussion began before dinner and ran into the early hours of the morning around the Park House conference table. Despite the effort to emphasize, within the plan, the will to complete the attacks on the Pointblank [target] systems, General Spaatz quickly appreciated that it was to all intents and purposes an oil plan. [Spaatz] explored at length the issues at stake, and especially the capabilities of the Eighth and Fifteenth Air Forces with respect to the number of targets involved, and ordered the plan completed for prompt presentation to Air Marshal Portal and General Eisenhower."

Hughes interpreted this as the plan having met with Spaatz's approval.

However, the Oil Plan was developing even as there was about to be a major reshuffling of the Allied command structure in anticipation of Operation Overlord, which was now imminent.

As of April 1, operational control of Spaatz's USSTAF was to pass from the Combined Chiefs of Staff to the Supreme Headquarters, Allied Expeditionary Force (SHAEF), in anticipation of Operation Overlord. The idea was that control would revert back once Allied ground forces had established themselves ashore on the continent, but for the time being, the fate of the USSTAF was not in its own hands. Suddenly, as Hughes puts it, "for the first time in a long while, we were no longer free to operate as we ourselves wished."

At the head of SHAEF was Eisenhower, the supreme commander, with whom Spaatz had excellent relations. However, directly beneath Eisenhower was his deputy supreme commander, and the overlord of Overlord air operations, RAF Air Marshal Arthur Tedder.

Counterintuitively, Tedder's point of view on the use of strategic airpower in support of Operation Overlord came not from professional airmen, but from a civilian consultant who had attached himself to Tedder's headquarters while he was in his earlier post as the commander of the joint Mediterranean Air Command. The man came to Tedder's staff, not from the staff of an Allied air force, or any military or economic organization whatsoever. Solomon "Solly" Zuckerman came to this post of great influence and responsibility within the RAF from the London Zoo!

Zuckerman was a South African–born zoologist who had graduated from University College Hospital Medical School in London and whose prewar career had been at the London Zoological Society. When the war began, Zuckerman consulted for the British government on several projects and wound up in North Africa working with the RAF. Given an honorary officer's commission, he eventually became the "scientific director" of the British Bombing Survey Unit (BBSU). In this role, he gradually became indispensable to Tedder.

When Tedder came to London ahead of Overlord, Zuckerman came along and was assigned as the advisor to Air Marshal Trafford Leigh-Mallory, Tedder's subordinate. Leigh-Mallory commanded the Allied Expeditionary Air Force (AEAF), an amalgam of the British and American tactical air forces that would support Overlord.

It had long been understood that the Eighth Air Force would participate in the preparations for Operation Overlord. They would join the AEAF effort to attack the rail transportation network, specifically railroad marshaling yards, in order to "isolate the battlefield" across northern France. It had not originally been intended that the Eighth Air Force should be under the AEAF *command*, but Tedder now insisted that it should be. Zuckerman had convinced both Tedder and Leigh-Mallory that this was the best use of strategic bombers.

Zuckerman's abrupt arrival on the scene, and his ideas, which were at odds with existing USSTAF doctrine, put him in direct conflict with the Eighth Air Force and the EOU.

Walt Rostow recalled many years later, that "at the intellectual level, EOU was squared off against Tedder's one-man brain trust, Solly Zuckerman, a scholar of the sexual and social life of apes; under the curious but not untypical imperatives of war, he became an expert on the physical effects of bombing which he applied in the Mediterranean, and then he became a bombing strategist. There are Americans (and some British) who to the end of their days regarded (or will regard) the last year of the struggle in Europe as a war against Solly Zuckerman rather than Adolf Hitler."

As Dick Hughes explains, Zuckerman "had been taken into the Royal Air Force to conduct a series of experiments on monkeys, in an endeavor to determine the effects of bomb blasts on human beings. From this, being very astute and ambitious, he had gradually worked his way up to [being] an expert on the effects of bombing of all kinds, and from thence it had been fairly easy to insert himself into the realms of target selection and operational planning. He had assisted Air Marshal Tedder in planning the raids against the transportation systems in Italy, and had sold himself to Tedder as an individual who would be of value in planning the air operations in support of the [Operation Overlord] invasion—during which it would be of utmost importance to interrupt and delay the movement of German reinforcements towards our bridgeheads."

Zuckerman's reputation had preceded him. Hughes went on to say that the staff of the Eighth Air Force and the EOU had "received word by the grapevine from Italy of his failings, and were more than alarmed when Sir Trafford Leigh-Mallory placed complete confidence in him and gave him a free hand to prepare the invasion plan. This led to the bitterest argument over air planning that I was ever to experience."

Essentially, it was the Oil Plan formulated by Dick Hughes facing off against the Rail Plan of Solly Zuckerman.

The battle lines were drawn, not between the British and Americans, but between the Anglo-American command staff at SHAEF on one side and the upper levels of command at USSTAF on the other. Apparently there was also a division of opinion within RAF Bomber Command. Some within that service were displeased with being assigned to fly essentially tactical missions, but their chief, Arthur Harris, sided with Zuckerman and Tedder, referring to the EOU staff and their allies as "the Oily Boys."

As Rostow points out, "Spaatz took the view that attacks on marshalling yards would have diffuse, generalized effects but would not interdict military supplies because the minimum essential lines could be repaired overnight and because the Germans would not engage their beleaguered fighter force to defend marshalling yards. Thus, his primary and overriding responsibility of Allied air supremacy on D-Day would be at risk."

Regarding the specific targets picked by Zuckerman, Hughes writes that the USSTAF was "convinced, from information received from [the Fifteenth Air Force in] Italy, that a rail transportation system could be much more effectively and economically interrupted by the destruction of railroad bridges [which are difficult to repair or replace] rather than by bombing marshaling yards. The latter belief contained a bonus in that if the railway system were economically paralyzed by the destruction of bridges, then there would be enough surplus effort remaining available to destroy the oil industry—with the long term benefit of seriously hampering the operations of the German army and air force, and of German industry, for the whole of the rest of the war."

Zuckerman countered by insisting that aircraft could not destroy targets as precise as bridges, despite the fact that he had just come from the Mediterranean Theater, where bombers *had* successfully destroyed most of the key rail bridges in Italy. During the coming weeks preceding Overlord, both Ninth Air Force medium bombers and Eighth Air Force heavy bombers proved, and on numerous occasions, that airplanes could, in fact, accurately hit and destroy railroad bridges.

Eventually, the argument went all the way to the upper levels of command, with both Prime Minister Churchill and General Eisenhower weighing in. Ultimately, at what Rostow calls "an historic meeting" on March 25, Eisenhower "decided in favor of Tedder and marshalling yards on the grounds that the latter would provide some immediate help in the landings and their aftermath, whereas the military effects of the oil attacks might be delayed."

However, Eisenhower did compromise to a certain degree, allowing that the Eighth Air Force would be released from the rail campaign whenever weather conditions over Germany promised good visibility for precision attacks against the petrochemical industry targets favored by the Oily Boys, in concurrence with Spaatz and Anderson.

"I am convinced," Hughes writes, "that General Spaatz did not want to argue the point with any force. His prime concern was that in case Overlord should fail, no one should be able to point a finger at him and his air forces and blame them for not cooperating with General Eisenhower's requests in every way."

As has been written in numerous accounts of the weeks leading up to Operation Overlord, it was a time of serious anxiety and nail-biting. Spaatz, and indeed Eisenhower himself, knew that the success of the Normandy invasion was not a foregone conclusion and that should it fail, it would be a major catastrophe that would seriously delay the end of the war.

Nevertheless, contrary to Hughes's interpretation that Spaatz did not want to rock the boat, Rostow writes that at one point Spaatz went so far as to threaten to resign over the diversion of his assets to support the Rail Plan.

In any case, the Oil Plan advocates were vindicated after a large number of petrochemical facilities across central Germany were attacked in one of the "compromise" missions by a force of around eight hundred Eighth Air Force heavy bombers on May 12. Rostow told an OSS symposium half a century later that decryptions done by the codebreakers of the British "ultra" project of German messages transmitted in the wake of the May 12 missions "promptly and unambiguously provided evidence of the Germans' panic as they elevated the defense of their oil production to top priority, even ranking above factories producing single-engined fighters. The evidence was sufficient to convince Tedder that the oil attacks should be immediately pursued."

Rostow reports that Tedder's actual words were "I guess we'll have to give the customer what he wants."

By this he meant that Eisenhower was now convinced of the value of the mission for the strategic bombers.

Even with more than half a century of 20/20 hindsight, we know Spaatz was right to acknowledge that in the two months preceding June 6, 1944, there was no more important Allied strategic goal in the European Theater than ensuring the success of Operation Overlord. All roads did, indeed and rightly so, lead to that single purpose.

With the same clarity of retrospection, especially with the knowledge of the Ultra decryptions—which were known to Hughes when he wrote his memoir but which were still secret—we understand that Hughes was also right to see the "big picture" significance of the petrochemical industry as a follow-on to the Operation Pointblank campaign against the German aircraft industry. Without oil, the war machine could not run.

It is also clear that the USSTAF had handed SHAEF the *luxury* of concentrating on the rail transportation network by virtue of what had been done to the Luftwaffe during Big Week.

Overlord's D-Day, originally penciled into the Allied offensive calendar during May, was postponed to June 5, and finally to June 6. On that D-Day, which Cornelius Ryan famously dubbed the "Longest Day," as 156,000 Allied troops crossed the beaches of Normandy against heavy

German ground fire, the skies above were clear of the Luftwaffe. Thanks to the hard work and sacrifice of American bomber crews during Big Week, Eisenhower was able to say to the troops, "If you see fighting aircraft over you, they will be ours."

Indeed, General Werner Junck, the Luftwaffe's fighter commander in Normandy, admitted during a postwar debriefing that he had only 160 aircraft available, and just half of these were operational. Within a short time, his complement increased to 600, but counting all the aircraft assigned to it, Leigh-Mallory's AEAF had around 12,000 aircraft available for Overlord.

In the afternoon of the Longest Day, one of those Allied aircraft was a Flying Fortress piloted by General Fred Anderson—and crewed by five generals and two colonels. Standing at one of the waist gun positions, Richard D'Oyly Hughes stood ready to man the .50-caliber Browning if a Luftwaffe fighter should appear. As had been the case earlier that day as General Laurence Kuter made his own observation flight in this same airspace, the only aircraft Hughes saw, and he saw hundreds, were friendly.

"There was cloud [cover] over England to an altitude of some 10,000 feet, and we spiraled up through this until we finally broke into the clear to find ourselves near a group of Eighth Air Force B-17s on their way to bomb Caen [a city near the invasion beaches]. We quickly joined this formation and halfway across the English Channel the clouds dispersed and the whole invasion coast lay spread out before us. . . . Our bomb run to Caen was uneventful, with no antiaircraft fire and not a sign of a single German fighter plane in the sky."

While Big Week had not crushed the Luftwaffe out of existence—that final struggle was yet to come—what Big Week *had* accomplished was tellingly demonstrated in the skies over Normandy on that Longest Day in June.

TWENTY-THREE

AGAINST THE WALL

A great weight was lifted from the shoulders of those Allied leaders—from Eisenhower down through the chain of command—who had sweated through the planning process for months. Difficult battles lay ahead—indeed, it would not be until July 25 that the Allies finally broke *out* of their Normandy beachhead—but the great invasion that had been the all-consuming object of the war against Germany since the beginning, had succeeded.

With the success of the Normandy invasion and the establishment of a solid Allied beachhead in northern France, the USSTAF could once again return to the strategic mission for which it had been created. On June 8, two days after the invasion, Spaatz issued an order to Jimmy Doolittle at the Eighth Air Force and Nathan Twining at the Fifteenth to give their top priority to the "Oil Campaign" that had been drafted by Hughes, Rostow, and the Oily Boys of the EOU.

The Eighth Air Force and the RAF would focus on synthetic fuel plants in the Ruhr, as well as crude oil refineries around Hamburg, Bremen, and Hannover. Meanwhile, the Fifteenth, now based in Italy several hundred miles closer to Ploieşti than it had been at the time of Tidal Wave a year earlier, would make itself a frequent visitor to that sprawling complex that still accounted for a significant proportion of the Reich's petroleum needs. This renewed campaign began with an average of around four hundred heavy bombers hitting the Romanian oil country on two consecutive days in late June.

On August 25, exactly one month after the breakout from Normandy—which had been facilitated by massive Eighth Air Force attacks on German ground forces—the Allies had liberated Paris. General George Patton's fast moving Third Army had almost single-handedly swept the Germans from the northwest corner of France, moving faster and capturing more territory than any American army in history. By September, both Eisenhower's and Spaatz's headquarters had been relocated there from England.

Ironically, all of the rail bridges, marshaling yards, and infrastructure across northern France that had been destroyed a few months earlier by the Tedder-Zuckerman Rail Plan were now in Allied hands and being repaired to serve the armies of those who had destroyed them.

A month later, the Anglo-American Allies were pressing close to the borders of Germany itself. So much optimism was flowing that some overly optimistic commentators dared suggest that the war might be over by Christmas.

However, the German war machine that had seemed to crumple before Allied might in August and September was not yet through. Though the Allies would not know the full extent until after the war, the German aircraft industry had actually resumed its expansion two months after Big Week while the USSTAF was isolating the Normandy battlefield.

"Illogically, it seems, German aircraft production had continued to rise during the months immediately following the great Pointblank successes of early 1944," writes John Fagg in the official history of the USAAF in World War II.

As had been the case since the earliest days of the Combined Bomber Offensive, Allied strategic airpower was not arrayed against a static German economy, but one that was more resilient than the Allies had imagined. Indeed, it was presided over by a clever and innovative administrator. Thanks to the management genius of Albert Speer, who had risen from his sickbed to consolidate aircraft production under the control of his Armaments Ministry in the aftermath of Big Week, the German aircraft industry was actually expanding, even at the moment that the Allies were ready to count it out.

"Most baffling of all at first glance is the fact that the German aircraft industry continued to expand throughout 1943 and most of 1944 despite the severe and accurate pounding given it by daylight bombing forces," observes Arthur Ferguson in his chapter on Big Week in the official USAAF history. "To be sure, it suffered two serious setbacks. The raids of the summer and fall of 1943 are estimated to have caused as much as three months' loss of production; those of February 1944, a total of two months.

"To the Allied strategists, accurately informed about damage to plant buildings if not to the inner workings of the factories, it seemed at the time that the Luftwaffe must certainly be on the decline from sheer inability to replace its losses. After the February 1944 attacks, their ability to oppose daylight bombing missions tended rapidly to deteriorate, and this fitted Allied expectations, but there was to be a surprise after the termination of hostilities. Investigation of German production records revealed the astonishing fact that, despite the staggering blows delivered by the Allies in February, aircraft acceptance figures for single engine aircraft rose rapidly until September 1944."

In their detailed postwar analysis, economist John Kenneth Galbraith and his Strategic Bombing Survey team discovered that monthly production of fighter aircraft actually increased from 1,104 in February to 2,449 in June, which was on par with production in the United States. By comparison the average of monthly factory acceptances of fighter aircraft by the USAAF in 1944 was 2,015, and of heavy bombers, the average was 1,241.

However, the USAAF inventory of heavy bombers stood at 9,278 at the time of Big Week, and 12,526 in September. As the numbers pouring out of American factories were increasing every month, the German aircraft industry was about to nose over like a damaged Messerschmitt and spiral downward.

Back in 1940, when the Air Corps possessed fewer than 3,000 combat aircraft, President Roosevelt had proposed that they should have 36,500, which seemed at the time to be an unapproachable number. By the autumn of 1944, the USAAF inventory exceeded 69,000.

The Strategic Bombing Survey goes on to say that the German aircraft industry's increase in output during the middle of 1944 is explained only "by the adoption of energetic rationalization measures, by drawing on the pipeline of components, and by the fact that a large scale expansion of the industry had been planned previously. To what extent bombing prevented the realization of these plans is difficult to decide. It is possible that production would have been 15–20 percent higher in the absence of bombing."

Ferguson adds that the survival defied the odds. He writes that "when Speer brought aircraft production under the control of his ministry [after Big Week], he began to disperse the entire industry and to accelerate the repair of bombed plants. Dispersal may have proved ultimately to have been wasteful, but until late 1944 it was highly successful. The factories were so small, concealed, and scattered that Allied intelligence found it exceedingly difficult to locate them and bombers often failed to hit their vital parts. Allied air leaders failed to assess the German effort with complete accuracy."

Conversely, in his own analysis of the results of the aircraft industry dispersal, John Fagg writes that Big Week's "February bombings deprived the Luftwaffe of a substantial number of fighter planes at a time when they were badly needed and that in forcing the German aircraft industry to expedite dispersal of its factories they caused considerable indirect loss of production and, what is even more important, left the industry extremely vulnerable to any dislocation of transport facilities. When that dislocation finally came about as a result of the concentrated attack on transportation, it contributed more than anything else to the complete breakdown of the aircraft industry."

Indeed, it was an industry that was pressed to its limits. It was an industry that was now compelled to cut corners, to get by with less, and to respond to the inefficiencies of dispersal by pressing workers to the limit and ultimately by the use of slave labor.

Meanwhile, the industries that supplied the all-important aircraft industry were struggling, and this would have an effect on the decline of aircraft production after September. The Strategic Bombing Survey notes that "the production of ball bearings in the second quarter of 1944 fell to 66 percent of the preraid average. An energetic dispersal policy, however, made it possible for production to reach almost the preraid average in the third quarter of the year. In the meantime, careful use of stocks, substitution of plain bearings for anti-friction bearings, and redesign of equipment to eliminate the previously luxurious use of bearings, enabled the Germans to prevent the fall in bearing production from affecting the output of finished munitions."

The Oil Campaign also played an important role in preventing the increase in aircraft production from turning into a resurgence of Luftwaffe aggressiveness. The Strategic Bombing Survey points out that synthetic fuel production fell from an average of 359,000 tons prior to the beginning of the campaign to 134,000 tons in June and 24,000 tons in September, adding that "the aviation gasoline output of these plants fell from 175,000 tons in April to 5,000 tons in September.

"In the same period stocks of motor and aviation gasoline fell by two thirds, and only drastic curtailments in consumption kept them from falling still further," states the Survey. "As in the case of ball bearings and aircraft, the Germans took the most energetic steps to repair and reconstruct oil plants. As many as 350,000 men were engaged in reconstruction projects and the building of underground plants, but these measures proved of little value. Reconstructed plants were soon reattacked, while underground plants even at the end of the war produced but a fraction of Germany's then minute oil supply."

The shortfall in available fuel not only impacted Luftwaffe mission availability rates, but forced strict limits on training at a time when the loss of experienced pilots demanded that replacements be trained and pressed into service. Training, rather than availability of aircraft, turned out to be an Achilles' heel for the Luftwaffe's intrepid attempts to pick up the pieces after Big Week.

As noted in the postwar USSTAF report *The Contribution of Air Power to the Defeat of Germany*, by mid-1944, "training in tank warfare became for the Germans a luxury beyond reach, and even the Luftwaffe reduced its training period to a few insufficient weeks because aviation gasoline could not be spared."

John Fagg goes on to say that by the second half of 1944, "no matter how many aircraft were produced they were of no possible use unless men were available to fly them. This appears to have been the weakest point in the entire German air situation. The bottleneck within this bottleneck was the training program.

"They could, therefore, follow two alternative courses: either fall short of the required replacements or cut hours of training so that fuel allocations would be sufficient to produce the required number of pilots. They chose the latter policy, with the result that pilots entered combat increasingly ill-trained. Faced with thoroughly trained American and British pilots, these replacements fought at a disadvantage, which helps explain the increasing rate of attrition imposed on the Luftwaffe. The consequent rise in the demand for replacements simply completed the vicious cycle."

Within the context of petrochemical production, the Strategic Bombing Survey reports that "by the end of the year synthetic nitrogen output was reduced from a preraid level of over 75,000 tons to 20,000 tons monthly. The Germans were forced to curtail the use of nitrogen in agriculture, and then to cut supplies used for the production of explosives. Methanol production also necessary for explosives manufacture was similarly cut. These shortages were largely responsible for the 20 percent loss of ammunition production in the last half of 1944."

Also noted by the Strategic Bombing Survey is that in the last quarter of 1944, steel production fell by 80 percent, and "attacks on panzer production set back an ambitious expansion program and caused a 20 percent loss of output in the latter half of 1944."

After September, as the Eighth Air Force was routinely launching strategic missions comprised of nearly a thousand bombers, other industries were starting to implode. By now, Doolittle had 2,100 heavy bombers at his disposal, and Twining had nearly 1,200, while Arthur Harris's RAF Bomber Command had more than 1,100. Beginning in October, the three entities coordinated their efforts through a Combined Strategic Targets Committee.

Meanwhile, as the numbers of bombers steadily increased, bombing accuracy was also improving. The Fifteenth Air Force reported that the percentage of bombs falling within one thousand feet of the target grew from 18 in April to 32 in June and 50 in August, compared to a progression of 29 to 40 and 45 for the Eighth Air Force.

In April and May, the Eighth Air Force had resisted its being diverted away from the strategic mission in order to join with the Ninth Air Force in the tactical campaign of attacks against the transportation network in France. Four months later, the transportation network in France was in Allied hands, and the attention was turned to the transportation network inside Germany.

This was not done to isolate the battlefield, but to disconnect the interconnectedness of the German economy. German industry, having been dispersed, was more dependent than ever on being able to move components and subassemblies to the myriad of dispersed assembly locations. Without rail transportation, this all began to fall apart.

The effects of this stage of the air campaign were what the Strategic Bombing Survey later called "the most important single cause of Germany's ultimate economic collapse."

As the survey notes, between August and December freight car loadings fell by about half, and "the progressive traffic tie-up was found to have first affected commodities normally shipped in less than full trainload lots—finished and semifinished manufactured goods, components and perishables. The effects of the attack are best seen, however, in the figures of coal transport, which normally constituted 40 percent of rail traffic. Shipments by rail and water fell from 7.4 million tons in August to 2.7 million tons in December.

"The index of total munitions output reached its peak in July 1944 and fell thereafter," the Strategic Bombing Survey reports. "By December it had declined to 80 percent of the July peak, and even this level was attained only by using up stocks of components and raw materials. Air raids were the main factor in reducing output, which in their absence would probably have risen. A loss of armaments output somewhat above 15 percent can be credited to bombing in the last half of 1944. This compares with a five percent loss for the last half of 1943 and a ten percent loss for the first half of 1944.

"By the third quarter of 1944 bombing had succeeded in tying down a substantial portion of the labor force. This diversion amounted to an estimated 4.5 million workers, or nearly 20 percent of the nonagricultural labor force. This estimate includes 2.2 million workers engaged in debris clearance, reconstruction and dispersal projects and in other types of activity necessitated by bombing, a million workers engaged in replacing civilian goods lost through air raids, and slightly less than a million workers in the production and manning of antiaircraft weapons. Air raid casualties were not numerous. . . . Late in 1944 the diversion of laborers due to bombing began to lose importance because the disintegration of the economy had reached a point at which the full utilization of the total labor force was no longer possible."

By December, contagious optimism reigned in Allied headquarters all across the western front. Since the liberation of Paris in August, the only thing that had slowed the surging onrush of Allied land armies had been their outrunning their own supply columns as they chased the Germans toward their border.

The war would not be over by Christmas, but it was seen as just a matter of time. The 21st Army Group, comprised of the British Second Army and the First Canadian Army, had pushed its way to Germany's border with the Netherlands. The 12th Army Group, incorporating the United States First, Third, and Ninth Armies, was lined up against the German border in Belgium, Luxembourg, and eastern France.

As the winter weather slowed the Allied advance, planners sat down to consider operations that would take their forces into Germany itself. For the final push, there was naturally a great desire for the immense firepower of the Eighth Air Force. During the second week of December, General Courtney Hodges of the First Army and General William Hood Simpson of the Ninth Army were each on the threshold of marching his army into Germany, and each requested that Spaatz support his offensive.

On December 15, Spaatz ordered Dick Hughes and Fred Anderson to fly to First Army headquarters to sort out the details with the two three-star generals. Along with General Hoyt Vandenberg, commanding the Ninth Air Force, and General Pete Quesada, commander of the IX Tactical Air Command of the Ninth Air Force, Hughes and Anderson met Hodges and Simpson at Hodges's headquarters early on the morning of December 16.

"We persuaded Generals Simpson and Hodges to sit side by side on a sofa, facing operational maps pinned to the wall," Hughes recalls. "Over these maps, I fastened the acetate overlays portraying our air support plan. General Anderson commenced to explain it in detail to the two generals. Suddenly, the telephone rang. General Hodges took the call, turned to us in great excitement, and told us that the Germans had launched a surprise attack in force and had broken through his southern flank in the Ardennes. So began the Battle of the Bulge."

Hughes took down the acetate overlays and, observing that "confusion, bordering on panic, arose in First Army headquarters," suggested to Anderson that they move along and let Hodges "fight his own war for himself."

TWENTY-FOUR

TOTAL COLLAPSE

It was a surreal situation. The day before, General Fred Anderson and Richard D'Oyly Hughes had been calmly discussing operations against a foe that had been presumed to be on the ropes. Now they found themselves *personally* stranded in the very path of a major German offensive that had taken the Allies completely by surprise—and one which, at least on the morning of December 16, appeared unstoppable.

The German Ardennes Offensive, code-named Wacht am Rhein (Operation Watch on the Rhine, named for a German patriotic song of the same name) had been intended to divide the 12th and 21st Army Groups from each other, while capturing the great Belgian port city of Antwerp, now a key supply hub for the Allies, and encircling as many as four Allied armies. The idea was to force a negotiated armistice before the Allies crossed into Germany, which would then allow the Germans to concentrate all of their forces against the Soviet armies on the eastern front.

The information coming in concerning the German breakthrough was not good. In fact, it was downright demoralizing. Four German armies, comprising more than a dozen divisions and around two hundred thousand troops, had crashed their way across American lines in a lightly defended part of the front in the Ardennes highlands of southern Belgium. Hundreds, perhaps thousands, of Americans were reported to have been killed or captured.

The Sixth Panzer Army was headed for Antwerp, and the Fifth Panzer Army was racing to recapture recently liberated Brussels, while the German Seventh Army, backed by the Fifteenth, was pushing south into Luxembourg. Hughes and Anderson learned that a German armored column was headed their way, with nothing in between but a military police company.

"The only sensible thing would have been to get out in a hurry," Hughes observed. "But General Hodges refused to evacuate his headquarters, so Pete Quesada could not move, and we were just plain ashamed to leave them all in the lurch."

Since the weather had turned bad, with heavy snow falling, Hughes and Anderson could not fly out, so Quesada invited them to spend the night at the house he had requisitioned in the town of Spa.

"Early next morning we woke up fully expecting to see German tanks patrolling the streets, but all was quiet and we soon learned that the German armored column had taken a fork in the road some four miles short of Spa and passed by to the south of us."

When Anderson and Hughes got in touch with Spaatz to request orders, Spaatz told Anderson to drive back to rejoin him in Paris, while Hughes was ordered to remain at the headquarters in Liege with Vandenberg.

On December 19, with the Germans still on the move, Vandenberg decided to return to his own headquarters in Luxembourg. Because of the weather, he could not fly there, and because of the Germans having created such a "bulge" in the line, the only way to get to Luxembourg from Liege was to drive there by way of Paris.

Dick Hughes was anxious to get out as well. He writes that "as I no longer seemed to be serving a useful purpose in Liege I telephoned General Spaatz and asked for permission to drive back in General Vandenberg's car."

He adds that another man who asked to hitch a ride with them was William Randolph Hearst Jr., who was in Europe serving as a correspondent for his father's chain of newspapers.

"The three of us, together with a welcome bottle of brandy, took off for Paris together through the fog, driving at an average speed of fifteen miles per hour, [and] arrived at General Spaatz's house many hours later."

Vandenberg's first remark to Spaatz was that his assistant chief of staff for intelligence had just been sent back to the States for medical reasons, and he wondered whether Spaatz knew where he could get someone to take his place.

"What about Dick?" Spaatz replied, looking at Hughes.

"All right, sir," Hughes replied.

After all of his years planning strategic operations for heavy bombers, Hughes abruptly transferred to tactical operations with the Ninth Air Force.

"I was not sorry to go," Hughes recalls. "Except for minor day to day details, our strategic plans for ending the war had all been made and as an ex–infantry man I had an intense desire to see something of the ground war at first hand."

Vandenberg was also pleased. As Hughes soon learned, Vandenberg was anxious to have someone on his staff who was in the confidence of General Spaatz, who was the senior USAAF officer in the European Theater.

Meanwhile, as Hughes was changing jobs, the Battle of the Bulge was unfolding as the largest single land battle fought by the Americans in World War II, costing eighty-nine thousand American casualties. The German advance was not halted until December 26, and the German armies were not pushed back to the pre-offensive lines until the third week of January 1945.

To add insult to the injured Allies—not to mention additional injury—on New Year's Day, in the midst of the ground battle, the Luftwaffe launched its own surprise offensive, called Operation Bodenplatte (Base Plate). At a time when most Allied planners assumed that the Luftwaffe was finished, the Germans managed to muster more than a thousand aircraft, mostly Fw 190s and Bf 109s, for a massive coordinated attack. These were sent against Allied airfields across France and Belgium, in the biggest German air offensive since well before Operation Overlord.

The Allies lost around three hundred aircraft destroyed, mostly on the ground, and around two hundred damaged, while the Germans lost slightly fewer than three hundred aircraft shot down.

Wacht am Rhein and Bodenplatte were large, well-planned, and generally well-executed attacks. However, they represented an enormous and desperate gamble that cost much and returned little other than to give the Soviet armies a monthlong lead in the final and inevitable battle inside Germany. The Battle of the Bulge was the last offensive hurrah of the German armies on the western front.

Beginning in January 1945, the enemy in the ground war, as viewed at firsthand by Dick Hughes, was a defender of his homeland. As such, he was a determined foe, gradually becoming more exhausted and more desperate.

Although their Ardennes offensive had failed, and they had lost a great deal of valuable personnel and materiel, the Germans had succeeded in striking, if not fear, at least a case of the jitters into the Anglo-American Allies. The mood among Allied leaders and planners in January 1945 was suddenly one of cautiousness bordering on the pessimistic. In retrospect, this was born out of a nervousness that the optimism of the autumn had been groundless to the point of absurdity.

"We have a superiority of at least five to one now against Germany and yet, in spite of all our hopes, anticipations, dreams and plans, we have as yet not been able to capitalize to the extent which we should," Hap Arnold himself wrote nervously to Spaatz on January 14. "We may not be able to force capitulation of the Germans by air attacks, but on the other hand, with this tremendous striking power, it would seem to me that we should get much better and much more decisive results than we are getting now. I am not criticizing, because frankly I don't know the answer and what I am now doing is letting my thoughts run wild with the hope that out of this you may get a glimmer, a light, a new thought, or something which will help us to bring this war to a close sooner."

Those who had seen, just a few weeks earlier, a glass half-full with the tap turned on, now saw a glass half-empty and being drained by the fear that previous assumptions had been *totally* wrong.

Where they had once been seduced by a phantom that spoke of the war being over by Christmas 1944, Allied leaders now heard the phantom who whispered of a resilient Reich supplied by impregnable underground factories, untouchable by Allied strategic airpower, and who predicted that the skies over Germany would soon be filled with Messerschmitt Me 262 jet fighters in numbers that matched those of the Bf 109s and Fw 190s of a year earlier.

It was in January that the jet fighter became the very emblem of a Luftwaffe perceived to have been "reborn." It was as though planners—on both sides—suddenly woke up to the promise of reinvigorating, and indeed *reinventing*, the Luftwaffe with a fabulous new technological wonder weapon.

As the Allies saw the great potential danger, Adolf Hitler now saw "his" jet fighter as the ticket to the Reich's salvation. The Messerschmitt Me 262 twin-jet fighter possessed such a potential. It was the fastest fighter in the world, and superior even to the great P-51 Mustang. It could have been the pivotal secret weapon that stopped the Allied Combined Bomber Offensive in its tracks.

Hitler was right about his jets, but he was at least a year too late.

However, the frightening thing about this "might have been" is that there had been no technical reason why the Me 262 *could not* have been available in large numbers one year earlier than January 1945. Admittedly, the Me 262 had been slow to evolve—but the project dated to 1939, so there had been plenty of time. Its development program, and that of its Jumo 004 turbojet engine, had been long and complicated, as engineers faced the challenges always encountered when the boundaries of technology are pushed to their limits.

However, the biggest stumbling block in the development of the aircraft that would have answered Hitler's fondest desire for an eleventh-hour, war-winning secret weapon was resolute sabotage from within the heart of the Third Reich. The saboteur was Adolf Hitler himself.

Had it not been for Hitler's conscious efforts to hinder the jet fighter's development back in 1942 and 1943, added to Göring's own initial ambivalence, the Luftwaffe would have been able to deploy significant numbers of Me 262s during Big Week.

As Albert Speer and others have written, Hitler had deliberately halted large-scale production of the aircraft in 1943, and as late as the summer of 1944, against the protests of Adolf Galland and the since-converted Göring, the Führer had ordered the jet fighter deployed only as an attack bomber against ground forces, a task for which it was ill-suited. It was only at the end of 1944 that Hitler woke up to an appreciation of the weapon that he had denied himself. As Speer writes in retrospect, "With such last-ditch efforts, hopes arose, which could [only] be construed as signs of increasing confusion."

The jet fighter now existed only as a symbol. For Hitler, it was symbolic of an unreasonable optimism that he could still win the war.

For the Allied strategic planners, it was symbolic of unrealistic pessimism, and the unfounded fear that all of the work that had been done would *not* win the war any time soon.

In the Allied camp, January's phantom of doom was even wider off the mark than had been November's phantom of sanguinity. The German economy and the German military machine were teetering on the edge of utter collapse. Even as Anderson, Spaatz, and Arnold furrowed their brows, Albert Speer spoke of the "catastrophic situation in armaments production" in Germany. Indeed, he went on to say in his memoirs that this industry, which fell under the supervision of his ministry, "began to disintegrate by late autumn" 1944.

Contrary to what the Allies feared, the strategic air campaign against the German petrochemical industry and infrastructure *had* paid off. The economy and war machine were running on empty. Far from being on the verge of rebirth, the Luftwaffe was dangling by a thread. Not only were fuel supplies running short, most of its best pilots were dead or exhausted by overwork and stress.

The first Combined Bomber Offensive plan drawn up after the departure of Dick Hughes from the EOU and the Eighth Air Force appeared in January 1944. Known as the "Interim Plan," it was drafted by the Combined Strategic Targets Committee and it targeted railways west of the Rhine that could contribute to supporting German armies facing the Anglo-American Allies.

Meanwhile, USAAF commanders remained adamant that strikes on the German rail network be concentrated on large, industrial-scale marshaling yards and not on targets such as small-town railway stations. In an "eyes only" memo to Spaatz on the first of January, Ira Eaker had pointed out that this would only serve to convince the German people that the Americans were indeed the "barbarians" that Hitler described. As Eaker insisted, "You and [assistant secretary of war for air] Bob Lovett are right and we should never allow the history of this war to convict us of throwing the strategic bomber at the man in the street."

As John Fagg writes, "Eighth Air Force mission reports for most of January show enormous numbers of heavy bombers, sometimes as many as 1,500, going out day after day to bomb targets whose neutralization would benefit Allied ground forces but would not directly accelerate the dislocation of Germany's industries. The preponderant weight of such air effort went on what was officially a secondary objective, enemy communications. Some 147 rail and road targets, rail centers, marshalling yards, repair shops, junctions, bridges, and traffic bottlenecks received USSTAF raids during the month."

Nevertheless, as Fagg points out, citing the postwar Strategic Bombing Survey, "German economic traffic in the west had already been choked off from the rest of the Reich to a dangerous degree."

February 1945, the one year anniversary of Big Week, was marked by an increase in the strategic efforts against Germany that finally precipitated the total collapse of the economy of the Third Reich. Indeed, on February 22, the anniversary of Day Three, the weather across all of Germany cleared as though offering up a reminder of the weather that week, and the Eighth Air Force launched a maximum effort involving 1,359 heavy bombers. While this mission involved double the average number of bombers that the Eighth put out during Big Week, it was a sign of the times that by now, it was becoming common for the Eighth to launch missions with 1,200 bombers.

The Fifteenth Air Force, meanwhile, restricted to sending fewer than 200 bombers over the Reich a year earlier, was now capable of launching 600.

The 1,359 bombers launched by the Eighth on February 22 were supported by a fighter force that flew 822 effective sorties. In was also a sign of the times that the Luftwaffe countered this vast effort with only around 70 interceptors, and they flew mainly ineffective sorties. Only seven bombers were lost to flak or fighters that day, and the jets were still rarely seen. Indeed, by February, Luftwaffe interceptors of any kind were becoming a rarity. Some missions were even going unchallenged by fighters, although the flak was as ferocious as ever.

As Fagg writes, it was during February that "the strategic air forces destroyed any serious possibility that Germany might unduly protract the war. The heavy bombers expended their greatest efforts since June 1944. Although flying conditions in the first half of the month were the worst ever experienced and 80 percent of the missions were blind attacks, the Eighth and Fifteenth Air Forces each carried out large-scale operations on twenty days during the month. The results were impressive in every respect. The oil campaign, into which USSTAF and Bomber Command poured 24,800 tons during the month, remained well under control with complete victory coming into view. The Germans failed utterly to make anything out of the program for underground plants, largely because of the breakdown in transportation."

RAF Bomber Command, meanwhile, was routinely launching in excess of a thousand four-engine bombers on each mission. On March 17 and March 18, Bomber Command put out two consecutive missions against industrial and petrochemical targets in the Ruhr that averaged 1,094 heavy bombers dropping an average of more than 4,800 tons of bombs, record numbers for the RAF. Because of the general absence of Luftwaffe opposition, the RAF was now frequently flying daytime raids.

The Strategic Bombing Survey notes that in February 1945, coal deliveries, partly through the loss of Silesia and the Saar, fell to 25 percent of normal. In March they fell to 16 percent and, by the end of the month, to only 4 percent of normal. Indeed, coal shipments were scarcely adequate even for the needs of the railroads themselves. The survey goes on to remind us that Germany's raw material industries, her manufacturing industries, and her power supply were all dependent on coal.

German boys a generation younger than Archie Mathies were on the threshold of experiencing rounds of bleak seasons with fewer, if any, trestles and coal trains than there had been a few years earlier.

However, in the coming dark, cold winter, there would no longer be skies filled with bombers, and cities no longer would be gutted with fire.

Those boys would grow to manhood with neither war nor Hitler and with a determination that their nation would be never again benighted by his kind.

It was in March, while steam locomotives were running out of coal, that the large scale jet fighter menace finally—and so very belatedly—revealed its full potential. The world's first all–jet fighter wing, Jagdgeschwader 7, had been formed in January under *Oberst* Johannes Steinhoff, a veteran Luftwaffe ace with more than 150 aerial victories when he took command. However, lack of fuel and materiel delayed its entry into combat until February, and into large scale operations until March 3, when the wing flew twenty-nine missions and claimed eight bombers.

On March 18, after two weeks of relatively light Luftwaffe opposition, Hitler's dream—and Spaatz's nightmare—was in full swing. Had the events of that day been routinely repeatable, or if they had occurred a year earlier, the story of the strategic air campaign against the Third Reich would have been much different.

Jagdgeschwader 7 attacked Eighth Air Force aircraft over Berlin with 37 Me 262s, shooting down a dozen bombers and a fighter, while losing three of their own. It was a four-to-one victory for the Luftwaffe. Had this occurred during Big Week, it really would have been worthy of the kind of serious reappraisal that Fred Anderson had feared was necessary in January.

However, the Eighth had launched 1,251 four-engine bombers that day, so the losses amounted to just 1 percent, and Jagdgeschwader 7 was in no position to put up the numbers of jets that had any hope of slowing, much less turning, the tide.

By March 18, the United States Ninth Army had been across the Rhine for more than a week, other American and British units were following suit, and the Soviet armies were closing in on Berlin from the east.

On April 7 and April 10, the Luftwaffe managed to muster nearly sixty jets, but on the latter date, the nineteen bombers and eight fighters lost by the USAAF cost the Luftwaffe twenty-seven Me 262s and sixty Bf 109s.

It will be remembered that in the wake of the debacle of Black Thursday over Schweinfurt in October 1943, Ira Eaker had wired Hap Arnold with the absurd characterization that the Luftwaffe was done for, when in fact it was at the very apogee of its prowess. In his words, Black Thursday had been the "last final struggle of a monster in his death throes."

Now, eighteen months later, the men of the USSTAF really *were* watching the almost theatrically spectacular, and jet-propelled, "last struggle of a monster in his death throes."

Had Eaker held his colorful characterization, he would have been right on the mark. Of course, by April 1945, even the most pessimistic of Allied leaders could see that the end had come.

In the meantime, the Luftwaffe had been collapsing from the inside. A growing number of experienced pilots, fed up with Göring's erratic leadership, were speaking out. Among them was Adolf Galland, who was fired from his post as inspector general of fighter aviation for his impertinence. He promptly returned to flying status and organized an all–jet fighter squadron known as Jagdverband 44. To staff his new organization, Galland recruited most of the top scoring aces in the Luftwaffe. It was a dramatic gesture, but it was too little too late by a wide margin. As with Jagdgeschwader 7, Galland's dream team might have impacted the air war significantly if it had appeared a year—or even half a year— sooner.

"The fate of Germany was sealed," Galland wrote in his postwar memoir *The First and the Last*. "On April 25 the American and the Soviet soldiers shook hands at Torgau on the Elbe. The last defensive ring of Berlin was soon penetrated. The Red flag was flying over the Ballhausplatz in Vienna. The German front in Italy collapsed. On Pilsen fell the last bomb of the 2,755,000 tons which the Western Allies had dropped on Europe during five years of war. At that moment I called my pilots together and said to them, 'Militarily speaking the war is lost. Even our action here cannot change anything. . . . I shall continue to fight, because operating with the Me 262 has got hold of me, because I am proud to belong to the last fighter pilots of the German Luftwaffe. . . . Only those who feel the same are to go on flying with me.'"

Galland flew his last mission the next day—against American medium bombers.

Four days later, in his bunker deep below a Berlin that had been bombed almost beyond recognition, Adolf Hitler killed his dog and entered into a suicide pact with Eva Braun, his wife of less than forty hours.

By now, the strategic air war had come to an end, and the Luftwaffe was a defeated relic. The Luftwaffe was ridiculously outnumbered at every turn and could essentially do nothing. As John Fagg writes, "Lavish fighter escort flew with the [Allied] bombers even when operations were a matter of roaming over the prostrate Reich looking for targets. This escort was available to a high degree now that Doolittle had taken his fighters off strafing tasks lest friendly troops or prisoners be killed. Most of Germany was not enemy territory any longer."

On April 7, RAF chief Peter Portal had suspended large scale bombing operations, expressing concern that "further destruction of German cities would magnify the problems of the occupying forces."

About a week later, on April 16, from his headquarters in Reims, Spaatz sent a personal memo to Jimmy Doolittle at the Eighth Air Force and Nathan Twining at the Fifteenth, which read: "The advances of our ground forces have brought to a close the strategic air war waged by the United States Strategic Air Forces and the Royal Air Force Bomber Command.

"It has been won with a decisiveness becoming increasingly evident as our armies overrun Germany. From now onward our Strategic Air Forces must operate with our Tactical Air Forces in close cooperation with our armies.

"All units of the US Strategic Air Forces are commended for their part in winning the Strategic Air War and are enjoined to continue with undiminished effort and precision the final tactical phase of air action to secure the ultimate objective—complete defeat of Germany."

In its conclusion, the Strategic Bombing Survey summarized the climax of the Allied strategic air campaign by stating that "as in most other cases in the history of wars—the collapse occurred before the time when the lack of means would have rendered further resistance physically impossible."

By the time that collapse came, Germany's once invincible war machine had little in the way of means, and virtually nothing in the way of a will, to continue fighting.

"The German economy," Albert Speer had written in his March 15 report, "is heading for an inevitable collapse within four to eight weeks."

Seven weeks later, it was all over.

The end came on VE-Day, which was actually a period of about forty-eight hours, beginning on May 7, when Field Marshal William Keitel, the chief of Oberkommando der Wehrmacht, the German high command, traveled to Eisenhower's headquarters in Reims to sign the unconditional surrender. The following day, a similar formal surrender ceremony took place in Berlin, now in Soviet hands.

Billy Mitchell had written two decades earlier, "Air power holds out the hope to the nations that, in the future, air battles taking place miles away from the frontiers will be so decisive and of such far-reaching effect that the nation losing them will be willing to capitulate without resorting to a further contest on land or water on account of the degree of destruction which would be sustained by the country subjected to unrestricted air attack."

The strategic air campaign that defeated the Third Reich had begun with little more than the idea promulgated by Mitchell that a major industrial power could be defeated in war from the air.

The campaign began in 1942 with a handful of aircraft, a handful of crews, and only a general idea of how to proceed. Over the course of its first year, the shape and form of the strategic air campaign gradually gained clarity. At Berkeley Square, a strategy took shape. In East Anglia, a bomber force moved toward critical mass. The dogged determination of the men in USAAF to stick with the doctrine of precision daylight attacks was questioned, ridiculed, and finally proven correct.

Big Week, as its planners had hoped, did constitute the beginning of the end. After that week, nothing was ever again the same. Albert Speer knew it and so did Hitler.

Big Week, as its planners had hoped, constituted a vindication of the strategic air campaign. Though there would be bumps in the road on the downhill slide that began that week, it was clear that Germany's war economy had begun unraveling from that point.

Just as the Allies had found the skies over Normandy devoid of the Luftwaffe on the Longest Day, the Allies who pondered a defeated Germany saw a nation without an infrastructure.

Thanks in no small part to the men of the EOU, the complex interrelationship of the components of Germany's war economy, such as ball bearings to aircraft manufacturing, and petrochemicals to the entire economy, had been examined, understood, and articulated as targets.

Thanks to the tenacity of the bomber crews—and the fighter pilots and *all* the ground crews—these targets were systematically struck, then struck again, and then again, until the very foundation of the German war economy had been destroyed. The promise of which Mitchell had spoken was fulfilled.

Thanks to the heroism and the vision of all of these people, the Third Reich and the dark curtain that it had drawn across Europe and the world, like the dark curtain in an Eighth Air Force briefing room, had been torn down forever.

As had happened on the final, climactic day of Big Week, the sun had come out across Europe.

EPILOGUE

At the 4th Fighter Group field at Debden, David Mathies had known that February 20, 1944, was going to be a big day. There were sixty Thunderbolts on the flight line, with the mechanics running up the engines for a maximum effort. Overhead came the thunder of dozens of bombers, wave after wave of 91st Bombardment Group Flying Fortresses, taking off from nearby Bassingbourn.

"I understand you have a brother who's a gunner with the B-17 outfit over there," an armorer, who was one of David's friends, casually remarked as they went to work that morning. He nodded to the northwest, in the general direction of Polebrook and a half dozen other Eighth Air Force bomber fields.

"Yes, that's right," David replied. "And I don't mind telling you that I'm very apprehensive about it too. You can tell from all the activity that's going on around here that this is going to be a big mission."

In the middle of 1943, David had gotten a letter from their mother reporting that brother Archie had volunteered as an aerial gunner and was training down at Tyndall Field in Florida.

"As soon as I received that letter, I knew that Archie was on a collision course with his destiny," David later recalled. "One of the words that he was continually kicking around was 'predestiny.' It means that from the moment you're conceived, your date and time of death is written down somewhere. I didn't believe too much in that, and I always figured there is no sense in rushing things either . . . but Archie believed in it with all his heart."

A couple of days later, near the crescendo of the Big Week activity, David Mathies went over to the Red Cross tent for his usual cup of tea and casually picked up a copy of the *News Chronicle*, then one of London's numerous daily newspapers. On page one, there was a small picture of Archie and a recounting of his remarkable heroism on February 20.

"I was just absolutely shattered," David recalled grimly. He'd had no idea that this had happened. "I don't think I slept a wink that night, but the next day, I got an emergency Red Cross leave and I went up to Pole-brook."

When David was ushered in to meet Colonel Eugene Romig, the commander of Archie's 351st Bombardment Group, the first thing the colonel said was that he was recommending Archie for the Medal of Honor.

David next visited the base dispensary, where he was introduced to three of the men who had broken their legs bailing out of *Ten Horsepower* over Polebrook.

"When it was my time to go," Tom Sowell told him, "I looked forward. Archie was in the seat flying, and for some reason or another, he turned around to me and he gave me Winston Churchill's famous 'V for Victory' sign. He thought he could make it, but I'm afraid the odds were stacked against him."

David was then taken down to the barracks where they kept the personal effects of the men who would never come back. Archie's billfold was there, as was his gold US Army Air Forces ring with the single-bladed propeller across the top.

"I kept that ring for 27 years until my son Archie came of age," David recalled a half century later, with a lump in his throat. "I gave him that ring. There's never a day goes by in that fellow's life that he hasn't got that ring on his finger."

Back at his own barracks in Debden, David wrote home to their mother, explaining what had happened. He figured that the letter would reach her sometime after the official War Department telegram—*that* telegram, the one like the ones that were received by four hundred thousand other American mothers during World War II—but his letter arrived first. As he put it, "Maybe it was apropos that my mother learned of her oldest son's death from her youngest son."

On July 23, four months after Archie's death, his posthumous Medal of Honor was presented to Mary Mathies. Wally Truemper's mother received his Medal of Honor on the Fourth of July.

Rather than traveling to Washington, DC, Mary Mathies elected to receive Archie's medal at the Presbyterian church in Finleyville, the same church that Archie had attended, often under protest—because Sunday morning followed too closely on the coattails of Saturday night—and always at his mother's insistence.

Fredericka Truemper received Wally's medal while seated in a rocking chair on her font lawn in Aurora, Illinois. Wally's father, his sister, and his two brothers were also present that evening.

In 1976, at the age of eighty-four, having outlived her oldest son by more than three decades, Mary Mathies was on hand for the dedication of one of the Pittsburgh Coal Company mines, renamed in Archie's honor. In 1987, the noncommissioned officers school at RAF Upwood, an installation operated by the US Air Force in Cambridgeshire, near Molesworth, not far from the field in which Archie Mathies died, was formally rededicated as the Archibald Mathies NCO Academy.

Bill Lawley, the only man to earn the Medal of Honor during Big Week and survive, received his medal from General Spaatz personally on August 8, two weeks after Mary was given Archie's. He had gone on to fly fourteen additional combat missions after Big Week, with his last coming in June, as Operation Overlord was in full swing. He remained in the US Air Force after World War II, served in a number of locations, including the Pentagon, the US Air Attaché's office in Brazil, and at the Air University at Maxwell AFB in his home state of Alabama. He retired as a colonel in 1972.

Ralph Braswell was one of the gunners aboard *Cabin in the Sky*, the heavily mauled Flying Fortress that Bill Lawley had brought home against all odds on the first day of Big Week. He went to see his pilot shortly before

Lawley's death in 1999. Lawley apologized to Braswell as they greeted each other, because his battle-scarred hands were crippled with arthritis.

"After I shook his hands," the former gunner recalls, "I said 'They're beautiful. They saved my life.'"

Joe Rex, the radio operator who repaired the intercom wiring aboard *Ten Horsepower* so that Archie could communicate with Wally as Wally communicated with the Polebrook tower, remained in the radio business. He went on to a long career—made possible by his life having been saved by Wally and Archie—during which he enriched the lives of generations as a popular newscaster on radio station WMBD in Peoria, Illinois.

Jesse Richard Pitts, the man who had graduated magna cum laude from Harvard before flying as copilot aboard the 376th Bombardment Group Flying Fortress called *Penny Ante*, returned to academia, having formed an export business in Morocco to finance his further education. He married the daughter of French Resistance hero Claude Bonnier, received his PhD from Harvard, and became a prominent sociologist. He published numerous sociology textbooks and founded the *Tocqueville Review*, a bilingual journal studying social change.

Penny Ante herself, the "lucky" Flying Fortress protected by the ritual of the crew chief loaning the pilot a penny before each mission, which was repaid at the mission's successful completion, "protected" Pitts, Streit, and the original crew, who all made it through their tours safely. As Pitts writes in his memoir, the ritual was abandoned by later crews. *Penny Ante* was shot down on May 24, 1944, over Berlin.

Of the household name officers who oversaw the USSTAF and the Eighth Air Force before and during Big Week, Tooey Spaatz continued to command the USSTAF as it burgeoned into a force with more than three thousand heavy, four-engine bombers later in 1944. Spaatz received his fourth star in March 1945, and when the Third Reich was defeated, he was reassigned in July to do to Japan what he had done to Germany, as commander of the US Strategic Air Forces in the Pacific. He never had the chance. The war against Japan ended within a few weeks of his arrival.

Spaatz is recalled as having been the only general who was present at the surrender of Japan on September 2, 1945, as well as at the surrender of Germany to the Anglo-American Allies on May 7, and of Germany to

the Soviet armies on May 8 in Berlin. After the war, he succeeded his boss
and mentor, Hap Arnold, as the commanding general of the USAAF, and
in 1947, he became the first chief of staff of the newly created US Air Force.

Jimmy Doolittle continued to command the Eighth Air Force through
the defeat of Germany and was in the process of relocating the Eighth to
the Pacific Theater when Japan surrendered. After the war, Doolittle
reverted to inactive reserve status as a three-star general, but undertook
a number of special projects for the US Air Force through his retirement
in 1955. Though he commanded the USAAF's largest numbered air force
through its greatest triumph, he will forever be best remembered for that
April 1942 mission when he led sixteen bombers to Japan for a daring feat
of short duration that is summarized in the title of the 1944 Hollywood
movie about it, entitled *Thirty Seconds Over Tokyo.*

Curtis LeMay would go on to greater glory, even as many of his fellow
commanders were in the twilight of their careers. In August 1944, he was
reassigned to the Far East to command the first strategic bombing missions against the Japanese home islands since Doolittle's "thirty seconds."
The weapon was the Boeing B-29 Superfortress, the largest strategic
bomber of the war. Half again larger than a Flying Fortress or a Liberator,
it could carry triple the bomb load and fly twice as far.

When the B-29 entered service in 1944, Hap Arnold decided to use it
only against Japan, and to make sure that the aircraft was used only as a
strategic weapon, he retained command of the new Twentieth Air Force
himself. LeMay was originally assigned to command the Twentieth's XX
Bomber Command, but he later acted as the de facto field commander of
the entire Twentieth Air Force offensive against Japan.

It was after World War II that LeMay became a household word. After
planning the Berlin Airlift in 1948, he was named to head the US Air
Force's Strategic Air Command (SAC). Under LeMay's unprecedented
nine years of uncompromising leadership, SAC evolved into a well-oiled
war machine, operating a vast, globe-spanning fleet of B-47 and B-52 jet
bombers, as well as the first generation of intercontinental ballistic missiles. LeMay eventually served as chief of staff of the US Air Force.

Haywood "Possum" Hansell, the veteran of the Air War Plans Division who served as one of the Eighth Air Force's principal early leaders,

went on to a career marked by controversy. He missed Big Week, having been recalled to Washington after the Operation Tidal Wave mission against Ploeşti in August 1943. Here, he was back at Hap Arnold's side as the USAAF planner on the Combined and Joint Staff as plans were being laid for the strategic air campaign against Japan. He helped to develop and deploy the Superfortresses, and he was Arnold's original choice to be his field commander for the strategic campaign against Japan.

In the Pacific, Hansell commanded the Twentieth's XXI Bomber Command, based in the Mariana Islands in the Pacific, while LeMay commanded the XX Bomber Command in China. When the results achieved by Hansell using daylight precision bombing were not considered effective, he was replaced by Arnold with LeMay, who was seen as a more aggressive commander who could accomplish the job of destroying the Japanese economy.

Ironically, LeMay would adopt the RAF Bomber Command tactic of nighttime area raids against Japanese cities, rather than staying exclusively with the precision tactics that the Americans had so vociferously advocated in Europe.

Hansell was reassigned, first to a training wing, and later to a transport wing, both based in the United States, and took early retirement in 1946. As this author knows from firsthand conversations with both, Hansell and LeMay continued to insist, until the end of their lives, that strategic air-power could have ultimately brought about the defeat of Japan without the use of nuclear weapons.

Ira Eaker, who left his command role at the Eighth Air Force just as the Eighth was coming into its own, served as commander of the Mediter-ranean Allied Air Forces (MAAF) until April 1945, the eve of the defeat of Germany. Recalled to Washington by Arnold, over his objections, Eaker served on the Air Staff of the USAAF until it became the US Air Force. After his retirement in 1947, he served as a vice president at Hughes Air-craft and later at Douglas Aircraft.

Larry Kuter, the veteran of the Air War Plans Division who helped build the Eighth Air Force, went back to Washington to a staff job that returned him overseas to be present at some of the pivotal turning points in World War II. Having been Hap Arnold's personal observer in the sky over the beaches of Normandy, Kuter substituted for Arnold at the Yalta Conference in February 1945 after the chief suffered his fourth wartime heart attack. Like LeMay, Kuter went on to a long career with the postwar US Air Force. He was the architect and the first commander of the Military Air Transport Service (MATS) and commanded the Far East Air Forces (FEAF) command as it became the Pacific Air Forces (PACAF) in 1957.

Of the British officers who served at the top ranks of the RAF during the war, both Arthur "Bomber" Harris and Charles "Peter" Portal retired within a year of VE-Day. Arthur Tedder succeeded Portal as chief of the RAF, serving until 1950, when he retired to become the chancellor of the University of Cambridge. Portal went on to a business career, serving as chairman of British Aluminium and later of the British Aircraft Corporation.

Harris moved to South Africa to get away from growing criticism in Britain of his heavy-handed, often brutal, attacks on German cities, especially Dresden, and remained there until 1953. Both Portal and Tedder were made barons after the war, and Portal was later elevated to viscount. Harris was made a baronet, although he initially refused the title in protest over his Bomber Command's being denied a campaign medal because of the February 1945 Dresden bombings.

Solly Zuckerman, the thorn in the side of the Americans, was also made a baron. His long career as a university professor was interrupted by his taking the post of chief scientific advisor to the British government in the 1960s. A continued interest in primates is evidenced by the titles of his two-volume autobiography, *From Apes to Warlords* and *Monkeys, Men and Missiles*.

Irving Krick, the Caltech meteorologist who became Hap Arnold's soothsayer of weather, remained in England after his successful—some would say masterful, others "damned lucky"—prediction of the weather for Big Week. As such, he was called upon to predict the weather, obviously of vital importance, for Operation Overlord. In the weeks ahead of time, Krick insisted that the weather would be fine on June 5, 1944, the day scheduled for the invasion. However, other meteorologists working for both the British and the Americans, predicted that a major Atlantic storm would blow through the English Channel that day. Fortunately, British meteorologist James Martin Stagg, who had once, coincidentally, studied under Krick, convinced him to go along with recommending a one-day postponement to General Eisenhower.

The storm appeared on June 5 as predicted, and blew through by June 6, and the rest is history. His having lost an argument saved Krick immense embarrassment, not to mention thousands of Allied lives. Krick was right, however, when he famously predicted sunny weather for Eisenhower's second inauguration as president in January 1957. After the war, Krick became a commercial long-term weather forecaster and made a great deal of money providing cloud seeding services to cause rain or, in the case of the 1960 Winter Olympics, snow.

As Eaker and Kuter were headed home to Washington, and Spaatz and Doolittle were packing their bags for the Pacific—and what they expected would be another bloody, hellish year of war—Richard D'Oyly Hughes was in Wiesbaden. Only one year earlier, this city in the Reich had been on the target list of the Eighth Air Force. Now there was no more Reich and the city was home to the headquarters of the 12th Army Group, the umbrella organization of the 1.3 million soldiers of four American field armies.

Dick Hughes had been on the continent since December 1944, when his years with strategic air operations had ended so abruptly and dramatically. As he moved across the continent with the headquarters of the Ninth Air Force—from Luxembourg into Germany—it continued to be collocated, for tactical coordination purposes, with that of the 12th Army Group. As such, Hughes found himself reunited with his old colleague from the Enemy Objectives Unit at 40 Berkeley Square, Charlie Kindleberger, who had made the transfer to the intelligence staff of the 12th in May 1944.

Around the first of May in 1944, as the German surrender seemed imminent, Hughes and Kindleberger decided to take a drive to see the once-secret underground factories in the Harz Mountains near Nordhausen, where the Germans had used slaves to manufacture their V-1 cruise missiles and V-2 ballistic missiles.

While they had been aware of Germany's having used slave labor in manufacturing as a desperate measure to keep their factories going in the final months of the war, they were unprepared for the horror of seeing the walking skeletons who were still living in the vicinity of their former camps, now under the care of the United States First Army.

The two former EOU hands, well versed in the nuances of econometric models, stared in incredulity at evidence of a practice that had never been discussed in any textbook in association with the economy of a modern industrialized nation.

The next day, while investigating a German plant that had generated hydrogen peroxide for rocket fuel, they were approached by a trio of well-dressed German gentlemen who explained that they had been managers at the facility.

As Hughes later described, they were "full of smiles and hospitable friendship, and attempted to shake our hands. This, after the sights of the concentration camp, to the great and obvious surprise of the Germans, we were not prepared to do, and Charlie Kindleberger, who was of German extraction himself, and spoke German fluently, quickly set them to rights about the position they were in."

Within a matter of days, World War II in Europe was over.

Dick Hughes never got to meet Albert Speer, the man who built and defended what the EOU and the USSTAF methodically tore down, but his friend, General Fred Anderson, did.

When the war ended, Speer retreated to Flensburg, near the Danish border to join Admiral Karl Doenitz, Hitler's designated successor. Doenitz was then still operating under the delusion that he could create a postwar German government that the victorious Allies would recognize. In a genteel setting that defied credulity against the backdrop of the global devastation of World War II, Speer was living in Schloss Glücksburg, a sixteenth-century castle that had been placed at his disposal by the duke of Schleswig-Holstein-Sonderburg-Glücksburg.

When Fred Anderson caught up to him there on May 16, he was in his comfortable sitting room, graciously entertaining guests—the members of the United States Strategic Bombing Survey.

These men had explained that American headquarters was accumulating data on the effects of the Allied bombings, and asked whether Speer would be willing to provide information.

"We discussed the mistakes and peculiarities of the bombings on both sides," the former armaments minister recalls. "The next morning my adjutant reported that many American officers, including a high-ranking general, had arrived at the entrance to the castle. Our guard of soldiers from a German armored force presented arms, and so—under the protection of German arms, as it were—General F. L. Anderson, commander of the bombers of the American Eighth Air Force, entered my apartment. He thanked me in the most courteous fashion for taking part in these discussions."

Within three days, others arrived, including Franklin Woolman D'Olier, handpicked by Harry Truman to head the Strategic Bombing Survey, and Henry C. Alexander of Morgan Guaranty Trust, his vice chairman. They were accompanied by Paul Nitze, George Ball, and the economist John Kenneth Galbraith—all of whom became influential, household-name policy makers and advisors to presidents in the decades following the war.

"During the next several days an almost comradely tone prevailed in our 'university of bombing,'" Speer relates in his memoirs. "We went systematically through the various aspects of the war in the air. From my own work I could appreciate the great importance of this division for the American military operations. . . . General Anderson paid me the most curious and flattering compliment of my career: 'Had I known what this man was achieving, I would have sent out the entire American Eighth Air Force merely to put him underground.' That air force had at its disposal more than two thousand heavy daylight bombers. I was lucky General Anderson found out too late."

On May 23, Speer's "university" was compelled to close its doors. Another, less congenial group of Allied officers arrived to place Speer under arrest. Tried at Nürnberg, he was convicted of war crimes and crimes against humanity—primarily because of the use of slave labor in German industry during the final years of the war. He was sentenced in October 1946 to twenty years and traded the comfortable castle for a cramped cell in Berlin's Spandau Prison.

Shortly after Fred Anderson had paid his call at Schloss Glücksburg, Dick Hughes received a phone call from Tooey Spaatz, who reminded

Hughes that he had long ago promised to release Hughes to return to civilian life as soon as Germany had been defeated.

The following day, Hughes was back at an Eighth Air Force base in England, where he was to catch a ride on a Flying Fortress that was headed back to the United States. To his surprise, he discovered that the aircraft was being piloted by General Frederick Lewis Anderson.

Anderson had been reassigned to the Pentagon, where he was to serve under Hap Arnold as the director in charge of relocating USAAF personnel, especially those of the Eighth Air Force, from the European Theater to the Pacific.

"I think that the most personally gratifying thing to me," Hughes writes in the conclusion to his wartime memoir, "was that Fred Anderson and I, who had sweated through together, and executed, the truly terrible decisions of 1943 and early 1944, should leave the European Theater in company."

Less than a week later, Dick Hughes was home in Clayton, Missouri, and two weeks after that he went to work at the Cupples Company in St. Louis as an executive assistant to the president. The Cupples Company, which would celebrate its centennial in 1951, was illustrative of the types of firms that were so much a part of the fabric of the United States economy in the two decades after World War II. A manufacturer of everyday home products, from American brand rubber fruit jar rings, to Kent double-edged razor blades, to the Good Housekeepers brand products, Cupples was typical of thousands of small businesses that flourished in those years but which have long since faded away as the consumer products industry has consolidated into larger and larger corporations.

Charlie Kindleberger, meanwhile, remained in government for a time and served as one of the leading architects of the Marshall Plan for the recovery of the European economy after World War II. One of the men who had been responsible for the deconstruction of the German economy was one of those who stepped in to save and restore that economy and the nations that it had occupied during World War II. As such, he helped to define the course of European history through the remainder of the twentieth century.

Kindleberger later settled in on the faculty of MIT and published a number of books on economics and economic history. His 1978 book *Manias, Panics, and Crashes*, about speculative stock market bubbles, is now considered prophetic because of its prediction of the "Dot-Com Bubble." It remains as required reading in many master's of business administration programs to this day.

While working on the Marshall Plan, Kindleberger was reunited with another one of the bright young men of the EOU, Walt Rostow, who also went on to serve on the faculty at MIT. Rostow, however, is best remembered for serving in the administrations of three American presidents. He was a speechwriter for President Dwight D. Eisenhower, the former commander at SHAEF, whose pre-Overlord London office was a few steps from 40 Berkeley Square.

Rostow joined John F. Kennedy when he was still a presidential candidate, and coined Kennedy's famous campaign phrase "New Frontier." When Kennedy was elected, Rostow became the deputy to McGeorge Bundy, the president's special assistant for national security affairs. He later served as Lyndon Johnson's national security affairs assistant.

Fred Anderson had returned to the United States to prepare for a phase of the war that became unnecessary almost before he had a chance to settle in at his Pentagon desk. Instead, he found himself presiding over a downsizing of the world's largest air force from 2.4 million people at its peak in 1944 to 305,827 in 1947.

Anderson himself became one of those heading for the door, and he, like Ira Eaker and thousands of others, chose 1947 as his retirement year.

Around that time, Anderson crossed paths with William Henry Draper Jr., a longtime investment banker with the New York firm of Dillon, Read & Company. Draper, who had held general's rank during World War II, had been part of the Economics Division of the Allied Control Council in Berlin immediately after the war. Here, as with Kindleberger and Rostow, who came later with the Marshall Plan, he was tasked with reconstruction of the same German economy that Anderson had worked to destroy.

In 1952, when Draper was named as the US special representative in Europe, and later became the American ambassador to NATO, he picked

Fred Anderson as his deputy. In turn, Draper and Anderson got to know Horace Rowan Gaither Jr., a San Francisco attorney and financier who had been a cofounder, along with Donald Douglas of Douglas Aircraft, of the RAND Corporation think tank. Coincidentally, during the war, Gaither had been assistant director of the MIT Radiation Laboratory, where they built the H2X (AN/APS-15) radar system for the Flying Fortresses that flew as pathfinders for Anderson's VIII Bomber Command.

In 1959, this trio moved to California's Santa Clara Valley, south of San Francisco, where the high-tech talent coming out of Stanford University was creating a new era of technological innovation. In 1959, they founded Draper, Gaither & Anderson (DGA), the first venture capital firm in the West, to invest in leading edge technology that could be seen as the H2X-type systems of the future. This was an exciting time in the rolling hills south of San Francisco, coincidentally just two years after two of the brightest young future household names in the area, Bill Hewlett and Dave Packard, went public with Hewlett-Packard, and at a time when top secret projects from missile guidance to spy satellites were going full bore in the Santa Clara Valley.

In turn, this was two decades before the valley became known as "Silicon Valley" and famous as the home of an archipelago of venture capital firms that were to underwrite another technological boom and another monumental change in the course of world history.

In 1992, David J. Mathies turned sixty-five and went back to the United Kingdom for the fiftieth anniversary of the "Friendly Invasion" of England by the troops of the United States armed forces. When it was learned that David was in the country, he was invited to give a talk at the Archibald Mathies NCO Academy at Upwood in Cambridgeshire.

Though Upwood, a US Air Force installation since 1981, would be abandoned, except for its hospital, by 2005, the words that David spoke there will live as long as the memory of Archie's heroism.

His words can also be taken to speak for that entire generation of young men, the later-named "Greatest Generation," who served bravely and selflessly in the United States armed forces during World War II. And of course, that generation included the analysts who worked at 40 Berkeley Square through the terrible and difficult days of Black Week and Big Week.

As Walt Rostow said in an address given in Washington one year before David Mathies went to Upwood, "I do not believe that the members of EOU, caught up in exciting headquarters business, ever forgot for long those for whom we were ultimately working. After all, they were of our generation. . . . Above all, there were the aircrews who flew up from the peaceful British countryside, assembled, and, in a matter of minutes, found themselves for much of the air war plunged into an inferno of antiaircraft fire and lethal air combat—some dying or going into captivity; others limping home with dead or wounded aboard; all undergoing traumatic strain carried gracefully or otherwise for the rest of their lives."

Rostow was aware of Archie Mathies and recognized that they shared the bond of being of that unique generation.

"In the aging of my memory, I always come back to England and the Eighth Air Force," David Mathies reflected in his talk that night in Upwood. "Always there echo and reecho in my ears, just as they probably echoed in Archie's ears, three words: 'duty, honor, country.' Duty. He felt that it was his job as a practicing Christian to try to save that pilot's life. It was certainly the honorable thing to do. Country. Oh yes, America, land of the free, and home of the brave. Archie certainly was brave on that fateful, final day of his life."

In closing, he recalled that when "Archie took off on that deep penetration mission to Leipzig, he had recently been promoted to staff sergeant, but before that day was over, he was a captain, the captain of his fate, the master of his soul."

SELECTED ACRONYMS

AAF Army Air Forces (short for USAAF)

AEAF Allied Expeditionary Air Force

AFCE Automatic Flight-Control Equipment

AFHQ Allied Forces Headquarters (the operational command of the MTO)

AFSC Air Force Service Command

AGO Apparatebau GmbH Oschersleben

AWPD Air War Plans Division (also the acronym for documents prepared by the division)

BBSU British Bombing Survey Unit

CBO Combined Bomber Offensive

CCOS Combined Chiefs of Staff (alternate form of CCS)

CCS Combined Chiefs of Staff (alternate form of CCOS)

COA Committee of Operations Analysts

COPC Combined Operations Planning Committee

COSSAC Chief of Staff, Supreme Allied Command (precursor to SHAEF)

EOU Enemy Objectives Unit (of the Economic Warfare Division)

ETO European Theater of Operations

ETOUSA European Theater of Operations, United States Army (organizational precursor to ETO)

EWD Economic Warfare Division

GASC Ground Air Support Command

GWF Gothaer Waggonfabrik

IP Initial Point (the map coordinates of the beginning point of a bomb run)

MAAF Mediterranean Allied Air Forces

MACAF Mediterranean Allied Coastal Air Force

MASAF Mediterranean Allied Strategic Air Force

MATAF Mediterranean Allied Tactical Air Force

MEAF Middle East Air Forces

MEW Ministry of Economic Warfare (United Kingdom)

MIAG Muhlenbau-Industrie AG

MTO Mediterranean Theater of Operations

MTOUSA Mediterranean Theater of Operations, United States Army
(organizational precursor to MTO)

NAAF Northwest African Air Forces

NACAF Northwest African Coastal Air Force

NASAF Northwest African Strategic Air Force

NATAF Northwest African Tactical Air Force

NATOUSA North African Theater of Operations, US Army
(later MTOUSA)

ORS Operational Research Section (of the Eighth Air Force)

OSS Office of Strategic Services

RAF Royal Air Force (United Kingdom)

RLM Reichsluftfahrtministerium (German Air Ministry)

SHAEF Supreme Headquarters, Allied Expeditionary Force

SKF Svenska Kullagerfabriken

USAAF US Army Air Forces

USSAFE United States Strategic Air Forces in Europe

USSTAF United States Strategic Air Forces

VKF Vereinigte Kugellagerfabriken

WPD War Plans Division

BIBLIOGRAPHY

Anderson, Andy. *One Pilot's Story: The Fabled 91st and Other 8th Air Force Memoirs.* Bloomington, Indiana: Author House, 2006.

Anderton, David. *History of the US Air Force.* New York: Crescent, 1981.

Andrade, John M. *US Military Aircraft Designations and Serials 1909 to 1979.* Earl Shilton, United Kingdom: Midland Counties Publications, 1997.

Arnold, Henry Harley (edited by John W. Huston). *American Airpower Comes of Age: General Henry H. "Hap" Arnold's World War II Diaries, Volume 1.* Collingdale, Pennsylvania: Diane Publishing, 2002.

Arnold, Henry Harley (edited by John W. Huston). *American Airpower Comes of Age: General Henry H. "Hap" Arnold's World War II Diaries, Volume 2.* Collingdale, Pennsylvania: Diane Publishing, 2002.

Arnold, Henry Harley. *Global Mission.* New York: Harper & Brothers, 1949.

Astor, Gerald. *The Mighty Eighth: The Air War in Europe as Told by the Men Who Fought It.* New York: Dell, 1998.

Ballew, Brian P. *The Enemy Objectives Unit in World War II: Selecting Targets for Aerial Bombardment that Support the Political Purpose of War.* Fort Leavenworth, Kansas: United States Air Force School of Advanced Military Studies, United States Army Command and General Staff College, 2011.

Bass, James L. *Fait Accompli: A Historical Account of the 457th Bomb Group (H).* Carthage, Tennessee: JLB Publications, 1995.

Bass, James L. *Fait Accompli II: A Historical Account of the 457th Bomb Group (H).* Carthage, Tennessee: JLB Publications, 1998.

Bass, James L. *Fait Accompli III: A Historical Account of the 457th Bomb Group (H).* Carthage, Tennessee: JLB Publications, 2000.

Biddle, Tami Davis. *Rhetoric and Reality in Air Warfare: The Evolution of British and American Ideas About Strategic Bombing, 1914–1945.* Princeton: Princeton University Press, 2002.

Birsic, Rudolph. *The History of the 445th Bombardment Group (H) (Unofficial).* Glendale, California: Birsic, 1948.

Boeing Company. *Pedigree of Champions: Boeing Since 1916*. Seattle: The Boeing Company, 1985.

Bowers, Peter M. *Boeing Aircraft Since 1916*. New York: Aero Publishers; Annapolis: Naval Institute Press, 1966; 1989.

Bowman, Martin W., and Theo Boiten. *Battles with the Luftwaffe: The Bomber Campaign Against Germany 1942–45*. New York: Harper Collins, 2001.

Bowman, Martin. *B-17 Flying Fortress Units of the Eighth Air Force (Part 1)* (Osprey Combat Aircraft 18). Oxford, United Kingdom: Osprey Publishing, 2000.

Bowman, Martin. *B-17 Flying Fortress Units of the Eighth Air Force (Part 2)*. Oxford, United Kingdom: Osprey Publishing, 2002.

Brauer, Jurgen, and Hubert P. Van Tuyll. *Castles, Battles, and Bombs: How Economics Explains Military History*. Chicago: University of Chicago Press, 2008.

Brett, Jeffrey E. *The 448th Bomb Group (H)—Liberators Over Germany in World War II*. Altgen, Pennsylvania: Schiffer Publishing, Limited, 2002.

Butler, J. R. M. *Grand Strategy, Volume 2, September 1939–June 1941*. London: Her Majesty's Stationary Office, 1957.

Byers, Roland O. *Black Puff Polly*. Moscow, Idaho: Pawpaw Press, 1991.

Byers, Roland O. *Flak Dodger*. Moscow, Idaho: Pawpaw Press, 1985.

Caidin, Martin. *Black Thursday*. New York: E.P. Dutton, 1960.

Caldwell, Donald, and Richard Muller. *The Luftwaffe over Germany: Defense of the Reich*. London: Greenhill Books, 2007.

Cannon, General John K. *The Contribution of Air Power to the Defeat of Germany*. Wiesbaden, Germany: Headquarters United States Air Forces in Europe, 1945.

Chalou, George C. (editor). *The Secrets War: The Office of Strategic Services in World War II*. Washington, DC: National Archives and Records Administration, 1991.

Childers, Thomas. *Wings of Morning: The Story of the Last American Bomber Shot Down Over Germany in World War II*. Cambridge, Massachusetts: Da Capo Press, 1996.

Churchill, Winston. *The Second World War. Vol. 1: The Gathering Storm*. Boston: Houghton Mifflin Company, 1948.

Churchill, Winston. *The Second World War. Vol. 2: Their Finest Hour*. Boston: Houghton Mifflin Company, 1949.

Churchill, Winston. *The Second World War. Vol. 3: The Grand Alliance*. Boston: Houghton Mifflin Company, 1950.

Churchill, Winston. *The Second World War. Vol. 4: The Hinge of Fate*. Boston: Houghton Mifflin Company, 1950.

Churchill, Winston. *The Second World War. Vol. 5: Closing the Ring*. Boston: Houghton Mifflin Company, 1951.

Churchill, Winston. *The Second World War. Vol. 6: Triumph and Tragedy*. Boston: Houghton Mifflin Company, 1953.

Clark, John A. *An Eighth Air Force Combat Diary: A First-Person, Contemporaneous Account of Combat Missions Flown with the 100th Bomb Group, England 1944 –1945*. Ann Arbor: Proctor Publications, LLC., 2001.

Cline, Ray S. *Washington Command Post: The Operations Division. United States Army in World War II, The War Department.* Washington, DC: Center of Military History, United States Army, 1990.

Closway, Gordon (editor). *Pictorial Record of the 401st Bomb Group.* San Angelo, Texas: Newsfoto Publishing Company, 1946.

Coffey, Thomas M. *Decision over Schweinfurt: The US 8th Air Force Battle for Daylight Bombing.* New York: David McKay Company, 1977.

Cox, John. *Storm Watchers: The Turbulent History of Weather Prediction from Franklin's Kite to El Niño.* Hoboken: Wiley, 2002.

Crane, Conrad C. *Bombs, Cities, and Civilians: American Airpower Strategy in World War II.* Lawrence: University Press of Kansas, 1993.

Craven, Wesley Frank (Princeton University), and James Lea Cate (University of Chicago), editors. *Army Air Forces in World War II Vol. I: Plans & Early Operations, January 1939 to August 1942.* Washington, DC: Office of Air Force History, 1947.

Craven, Wesley Frank (Princeton University), and James Lea Cate (University of Chicago), editors. *Army Air Forces in World War II Vol. II: Europe: TORCH to POINTBLANK, August 1942 to December 1943.* Washington, DC: Office of Air Force History, 1948.

Craven, Wesley Frank (Princeton University), and James Lea Cate (University of Chicago), editors. *Army Air Forces in World War II: Europe: Argument to VE Day, January 1944 to May 1945.* Washington, DC: Office of Air Force History, 1951.

Crosby, Harry H. *A Wing and a Prayer: The "Bloody 100th" Bomb Group of the U.S. Eighth Air Force in Action over Europe in World War II.* New York: Harper, 1994.

Currier, Lt. Col. Donald R., USAF (Ret). *Fifty Mission Crush.* Shippensburg, Pennsylvania: Burd Street Press, 1992.

Dallek, Robert. *Franklin D. Roosevelt and American Foreign Policy, 1932–1945.* New York: Oxford University Press, 1995.

Davis, Richard G. *Carl A. Spaatz and the Air War in Europe.* Washington, DC: Smithsonian Institution Press, 1992.

Doherty, Robert E. and Geoffrey D. Ward. *Snetterton Falcons II: In the Nest and On the Wing.* Dallas, Texas: Taylor Publishing Company, 1997.

Doherty, Robert E., and Geoffrey D. Ward. *Snetterton Falcons, the 96th Bomb Group in World War II.* Dallas, Texas: Taylor Publishing Company, 1989.

Dorr, Robert F. *B-24 Liberator Units of the Eighth Air Force (Osprey Combat Aircraft 15).* Oxford, United Kingdom: Osprey Publishing, 1999.

Dorr, Robert F. *B-24 Liberator Units of the Fifteenth Air Force (Osprey Combat Aircraft 21).* Oxford, United Kingdom: Osprey Publishing, 2000.

Douhet, Giulio. *Command of the Air.* New York: Arno Press, 1942.

Economic Warfare Division. *Handbook of Target Information.* London: Enemy Objectives Unit, 1943.

Ehrman, John. *Grand Strategy, Volume 5: August 1943–September 1944.* London: Her Majesty's Stationary Office, 1956.

Ehrman, John. *Grand Strategy, Volume 6: October 1944–August 1945.* London: Her Majesty's Stationary Office, 1956.

Emerson, William R. *Operation Pointblank: A Tale of Bombers and Fighters. The Harmon Memorial Lectures in Military History, Number 4.* Colorado Springs: United States Air Force Academy, 1962.

Fagg, John E. (New York University). Chapters regarding the strategic air war in the European and Mediterranean Theaters of Operations in *Army Air Forces in World War II: Europe: Argument to VE Day, January 1944 to May 1945.* (Edited by Wesley Frank Craven and James Lea Cate). Washington, DC: Office of Air Force History, 1948.

Fayers-Hallin, Linda and Vic, and Quentin Bland (384th BG Official Historian). *Keep the Show on the Road: The History of the 384th Bombardment Group (Heavy) 1942–1946.* The 384th Bombardment Group, no date.

Ferguson, Arthur (Duke University). Chapters regarding the strategic air war in the European and Mediterranean Theaters of Operations in *Army Air Forces in World War II: Europe: Argument to VE Day, January 1944 to May 1945.* (Edited by Wesley Frank Craven and James Lea Cate). Washington, DC: Office of Air Force History, 1948.

Ferguson, Arthur (Duke University). Chapters regarding the strategic air war in the European and Mediterranean Theaters of Operations in *Army Air Forces in World War II Vol. II: Europe: TORCH to POINTBLANK, August 1942 to December 1943.* (Edited by Wesley Frank Craven and James Lea Cate). Washington, DC: Office of Air Force History, 1948.

Frankland, Noble, and Charles Webster. *The Strategic Air Offensive Against Germany, 1939–1945, Volume II: Endeavour, Part 4.* London: Her Majesty's Stationary Office, 1961.

Frankland, Noble. *Bomber Offensive, The Devastation of Europe.* New York: Ballantine Books, 1970.

Futrell, Robert Frank. *Ideas, Concepts, Doctrine: Basic Thinking in the United States Air Force 1907–1960.* Collingdale, Pennsylvania: Diane Publishing, 1989.

Galland, Adolf. *The First and the Last: The Rise and Fall of the German Fighter Forces, 1938–1945.* New York: Henry Holt and Company, 1954.

Gann, Harvey E. *Escape I Must, World War II Prisoner of War in Germany.* Austin, Texas: Woodburner Press, 1995.

Gobrecht, Harry D. *Might in Flight: Daily Diary of the Eighth Air Force's Hell's Angels 303rd Bombardment Group (H).* San Clemente, California: 303rd Bombardment Group (H) Association, 1993.

Green, William. *Famous Bombers of the Second World War.* New York: Doubleday, 1957.

Green, William. *Famous Fighters of the Second World War.* New York: Doubleday, 1957.

Green, William. *Warplanes of the Second World War.* New York: Doubleday, 1964.

Griffith, Charles. *The Quest: Haywood Hansell and American Strategic Bombing in World War II.* Darby, Pennsylvania: Diane Publishing, 1999.

Gulley, Thomas F., Edmund Hicks Ph.D., William McClintock, Jerry Blackmer, and Christopher J. Karas. *The Hour Has Come: The 97th Bomb Group in World War II.* Dallas, Texas: Taylor Publishing Company, 1993.

Hansell, Haywood S. Jr. *The Air Plan That Defeated Hitler.* Atlanta: Higgins McArthur/ Longino and Porter, 1972.

Harper, Kristine. *Weather by the Numbers: The Genesis of Modern Meteorology.* New York: Harper, 2008.

Harris, Arthur Travers (edited by Sebastian Cox). *Dispatch on War Operations: 23 February, 1942, to 8 May, 1945.* London: Routledge, 1995.

Harris, Arthur Travers. *Bomber Offensive.* London: Pen & Sword Military Classics (first published 1947), 2005.

Harris, Peter, and Ken Harbour. *A Chronicle of the 351st Bomb Group (H) 1942–1945.* St. Petersburg, Florida: Byron Kennedy and Company, 1985.

Hartles, Andy. *Lightning Strikes: The Story of a B-17 Bomber (Fortunes of War).* Bristol, England: Cerberus Publishing Limited, 2005.

Harvey, G. Robert. *Memories from the Out House Mouse—The Personal Diaries of One B-17 Crew.* Bloomington, Indiana: Trafford Publishing, 2002.

Havelaar, Marion H. *The Ragged Irregulars: The 91st Bomb Group in World War II.* Altgen, Pennsylvania: Schiffer Military History, 1997.

Hawkins, Ian. *20th Century Crusaders: 392nd Bombardment Group (H), January 1943– September 1945: True Tales of the Air War Over Europe Told By Those Who Lived Them.* Paducah, Kentucky: Turner Publishing, 1998.

Hedley, John H. "The Evolution of Intelligence Analysis." In *Analyzing Intelligence: Origins, Obstacles, and Innovations* (edited by Roger Z. George and James B. Bruce). Washington ,DC: Georgetown University Press, 2008.

Hofemeister (Hrsg.). *100 Jahre Realschule Diepholz (100 Years of Secondary School Diepholz).* Diepholz: Schröderscher Buchverlag, 2000.

Howard, Michael. *Grand Strategy, Volume 4, August 1942–September 1943.* London: Her Majesty's Stationary Office, 1972.

Huntzinger, Edward J. *The 388th at War.* Cape Coral, Florida: Newsfoto Yearbooks, 1979.

Jackson, Julian. *France: The Dark Years 1940–1941.* New York: Oxford University Press, 2001.

Jansen, Harold E. *The History of the 446th Bombardment Group (H).* Rijkswijk: Elmar, 1989.

Johnston, Alan. "How an Italian pilot began the air war era." BBC News, May 9, 2011.

Katz, Barry M. *Foreign Intelligence: Research and Analysis in the Office of Strategic Services. 1942–1945.* Cambridge: Harvard University Press, 1989.

Kelsey, Benjamin. *The Dragon's Teeth: The Creation of United States Air Power for World War II.* Washington, DC: Smithsonian Institution Press, 1982.

Kindleberger, Charles Poor. *International Short-term Capital Movements.* New York: Columbia University Press, 1937.

Kindleberger, Charles Poor. *Manias, Panics, and Crashes: A History of Financial Crises.* New York: Palgrave Macmillan, 2005 (5th edition).

Kindleberger, Charles Poor. *The World in Depression: 1929–1939.* Berkeley: University of California Press, 1973.

Kreis, John F, Alexander S. Cochran Jr., Robert C. Ehrhart, Thomas A. Fabyanic, Robert F. Futrell, and Murray Williamson. *Piercing the Fog: Intelligence and Army Air Forces*

Operations in World War II. Washington, DC: Air Force Historical Studies Office, 1996.

Lambourne, Nicola. *War Damage in Western Europe*. Edinburgh: Edinburgh University Press, 2000.

Lee, Loyd E., and Robin D. S. Higham. *World War II in Europe, Africa, and the Americas*. Westport, Connecticut: Greenwood Publishing Group, 1997.

Lee, Wright. *Not As Briefed: 445th Bombardment Group (H) Eighth Air Force: Memoirs of a B-24 Navigator/Prisoner of War 1943–1945*. Spartanburg, SC: Honoribus Press, 1993.

LeMay, General Curtis E., and Bill Yenne. *Superfortress: The B-29 and American Air Power in World War II*. New York/Yardley, Pennsylvania: McGraw Hill 1988/Westholme 2006.

Levine, Alan J. *The Strategic Bombing of Germany, 1940–1945*. New York: Praeger Publishers, 1992.

Mackay, Ron, and Steve Adams. *The 44th Bomb Group in World War II: The Flying Eight-Balls Over Europe in the B-24*. Altgen, Pennsylvania: Schiffer Military History, 2007.

Mackay, Ron. *Ridgewell's Flying Fortresses: The 381st Bombardment Group (H) in World War II*. Altgen, Pennsylvania: Schiffer Publishing Limited, 2000.

MacPherson, Nelson. *American Intelligence in Wartime London: The Story of the OSS*. Portland: Frank Cass Publishers, 2003.

Mauch, Christof (Translated by Jeremiah Riemer). *The Shadow War Against Hitler: The Covert Operations of America's Wartime Secret Intelligence Service*. New York: Columbia University Press, 2003.

Maurer, Maurer. *Air Force Combat Units of World War II*. Maxwell AFB: Office of Air Force History, 1983.

McArthur, Charles W. *Operations Analysis in the US Army Eighth Air Force in World War II*. Providence: American Mathematical Society, 1990.

McFarland, Stephen L. *America's Pursuit of Precision Bombing, 1910–1945*. Washington, DC: Smithsonian Institution Press, 1995.

McFarland, Stephen L., and Richard P. Hallion. *America's Pursuit of Precision Bombing, 1910–1945*. Tuscaloosa, Alabama: University of Alabama Press, 2008.

McLaughlin, J. Kemp. *The Mighty Eighth in WWII: A Memoir*. Lexington: The University Press of Kentucky, 2000.

Menzel, George H. *Portrait of a Flying Lady: The Stories of Those She Flew with in Battle (401st Bomb Group)*. Paducah, Kentucky: Turner Publishing, 1994.

Miller, Donald L. *Masters of the Air: America's Bomber Boys Who Fought the Air War Against Nazi Germany*. New York: Simon & Schuster, 2007.

Mitchell, William L. *Winged Defense: The Development and Possibilities of Modern Air Power—Economic and Military*. New York: G. P. Putnam's Sons, 1925.

Morrison, Wilbur H. *The Incredible 305th: The "Can Do" Bombers of World War II*. New York: Jove, 1984.

Mrazek, Robert J. *To Kingdom Come: An Epic Saga of Survival in the Air War Over Germany*. New York: NAL Hardcover, 2011.

Neillands, Robin. *The Bomber War: The Allied Air Offensive Against Nazi Germany*. New York: The Overlook Press, Peter Mayer Publishers, 2001.

O'Neil, Myles. *Ploesti Raiders*. Chicago: Adams Press, 1993.

Osborne, David. *They Came from Over the Pond*. Madison, Wisconsin: 381st Bomb Group, 1999.

Parrent, Erik. *Defenders of Liberty: 2nd Bombardment Group/Wing, 1918–1993*. Paducah, Kentucky: Turner Publishing, 1996.

Penry, Jerry. *The Sunrise Serenade: A World War II Bomber Crew Story*. Milford, Nebraska: Bluemound Press, 2000.

Pitts, Jesse Richard. *Return to Base: Memoirs of A B17 Copilot, Kimbolton, England, 1943–1944*. Charlottesville, Virginia: Howell Press Inc., 2004.

Price, Alfred. *Battle over the Reich—The Strategic Air Offensive over Germany*. Hersham, Surrey: Classic Publications, 2005.

Quibble, Anthony. "The Eastern Front at the Turning Point: Review of a Logistics Estimate." *Studies in Intelligence* 6 (1962).

Robb, Derwyn D. *Shades of Kimbolton, a Narrative of the 379th Bombardment Group (H)*. San Angelo, Texas: Newsfoto Publishing Company, 1946.

Roosevelt, Kermit. *War Report of the OSS*. New York: Walker and Company, 1976.

Rostow, Walt W. "The Beginnings of Air Targeting." *Studies in Intelligence* 7, No.1 (1963).

Rostow, Walt W. "Waging Economic Warfare From London." *Studies in Intelligence* 36, No.5 (1992).

Rostow, Walt W. *Concept and Controversy: Sixty Years of Taking Ideas to Market*. Austin: University of Texas Press, 2003.

Rostow, Walt W. *Pre-Invasion Bombing Strategy: General Eisenhower's Decision of March 25, 1944*. Austin: University of Texas Press, 1981.

Rostow, Walt W. *War Diary, Volume 5, Office of Strategic Services, Research and Analysis Branch*. London: The Economic Outpost with Economic Warfare Division, 1945.

Royal Air Force. *RAF Bomber Command Campaign Diary* (http://raf.mod.uk/bombercommand/diary.html). High Wycombe: Royal Air Force, 2004.

Runyan, Timothy J., and Jan M. Copes. *To Die Gallantly: The Battle of the Atlantic*. Boulder, Colorado: Westview Press, 1994.

Ryan, Cornelius. *The Longest Day*. Greenwich, Connecticut: Fawcett, 1959.

School, Rick, and Jeff Rogers. *Valor at Polebrook: The Last Flight of Ten Horsepower*. Milwaukee: Ken Cook Company, 1998.

Seversky, Alexander de. *Victory Through Air Power*. New York: Simon & Schuster, 1942.

Shepherd, D. William. *Of Men And Wings, The First 100 Missions of the 449th Bomb Group*. Panama City, Florida: Norfield Publishing, 1996.

Shields, Doyle. *The History of the 447th Bombardment Group (H)*. Self-published, 1996.

Slater, Harry E. *Lingering Contrails of the Big Square A: A History of the 94th Bomb Group (H), 1942–1945*. Self-published, 1980.

Smith, Dale O. *Screaming Eagle: Memoirs of a B-17 Group Commander*. Chapel Hill: Algonquin Books, 1990.

Sokolski, Henry D. (editor). *Getting MAD: Nuclear Mutual Assured Destruction, Its Origins and Practice*. Carlisle, Pennsylvania: Strategic Studies Institute, U.S. Army War College, 2004.

Stansky, Peter. *The First Day of the Blitz: September 7, 1940*. New Haven: Yale University Press, 2007.

Stewart, Carroll. *Ted's Travelling Circus: 93rd Bombardment Group (H), United States Army Air Force, World War II*. Lincoln, Nebraska: Sun/World Communications, 1996.

Stout, Jay A. *Men Who Killed the Luftwaffe: The U.S. Army Air Forces Against Germany in World War II*. Mechanicsburg, Pennsylvania: Stackpole Books, 2010.

Strong, Russell A. *First Over Germany / a History of the 306th Bombardment Group*. WinstonSalem, NC: Hunter Printing, 1990.

Suchenwirth, Richard. *Historical Turning Points in the German Air Force War Effort (USAF Historical Study No. 189)*. Maxwell AFB: Office of Air Force History, 1968.

Tedder, Arthur W. *Air Power in War: The Lees Knowles Lecture, 1947*. London: Hodder and Stoughton, 1948; reprint edition, Westport: Greenwood Press, 1975.

The 305th Bombardment Group (H) Association. *The 305th Bombardment Group (H)*. Paducah, Kentucky: Turner Publishing, 1997.

The 385th Bomb Group Memorial Association. *A New History of the 385th Bomb Group (H)*. St. Petersburg, Florida: Southern Heritage Press, 1995.

Thixton, Marshall J. *Bombs Away by Pathfinders of the Eighth Air Force*. Trumbull, Connecticut: FNP Military Division, 1998.

Thom, Walter. *The Brotherhood of Courage: The History of the 305th Bombardment Group (H) in WWII*. 305th Bombardment Group (H) Association. New York: Walter Thom, 1986.

United States Strategic Bombing Survey, Equipment Division. *The German Anti-Friction Bearings Industry*. Washington, DC: United States Strategic Bombing Survey, Equipment Division, 1947.

United States Strategic Bombing Survey. *The Effects of Strategic Bombing on the German War Economy*. Washington, DC: Overall Economic Effects Division, United States Strategic Bombing Survey, 1945.

USAAF. *Army Air Forces Statistical Digest, World War II*. Washington, DC: Director, Statistical Services, USAAF, 1945.

Vaughn, Robert E. *Fame's Favored Few: The Men in the Lead Crew*. Paducah, Kentucky: Turner Publishing, 1999.

Vickers, Robert E. *The Liberators from Wendling: The Combat Story of the 392nd Bombardment Group (H) of the Eighth Air Force During World War Two*. Manhattan, Kansas: Sunflower University Press, 1977.

Wagner, Ray. *American Combat Planes*, Third Enlarged Edition. New York: Doubleday. 1982.

Walker, James W. *The Liberandos: A World War II History of the 376th Bomb Group (H) and Its Founding Units*. Waco, Texas: 376th Heavy Bombardment Group Veterans Association, 1994.

Watson, Mark Skinner. *Chief of Staff: Prewar Plans and Preparations*. Washington, DC: Historical Division, Department of the Army, 1950.

Webster, George. *Savage Sky: Life and Death on a Bomber over Germany in 1944 (Stackpole Military History Series)*. Mechanicsburg, Pennsylvania: Stackpole Books, 2007.

Webster, Sir Charles, and Noble Frankland. *The Strategic Air Offensive Against Germany*. London: Her Majesty's Stationary Office, 1961.

Welch, John F. *Dead Engine Kids*. Rapid City, South Dakota: Silver Wings Aviation, Inc., 1993.

Werrell, Kenneth. *Who Fears? The 301st In War and Peace, 1942–1979*. Dallas, Texas: Taylor Publishing Company, 1991.

Wilson, Paul, and Ron MacKay. *The Sky Scorpions: The Story of the 389th Bomb Group in World War II*. Altgen, Pennsylvania: Schiffer Publishing Limited, 2006.

Wolk, Herman S. *Strategic Bombing: The American Experience*. Manhattan, Kansas: MA/AH Publishing, 1981.

Yedlin, Benedict, with Alexander Jeffers. *Brother Men Who Fly: A World War II Gunner's Personal Quest*. Princeton, New Jersey: Liberator Crew Productions, 2002.

Yenne, Bill, and Robert Redding. *Boeing: Planemaker to the World*. New York: Crown/Random House, 1983/1989.

Yenne, Bill. *Convair: Into the Sunset*. Greenwich/San Diego: Greenwich/General Dynamics, 1995.

Yenne, Bill. *The History of the US Air Force*. New York: Simon & Schuster, 1984, 1992.

Yenne, Bill. *Lockheed*. New York: Random House, 1987.

Yenne, Bill. *McDonnell Douglas: A Tale of Two Giants*. New York: Random House, 1985.

Yenne, Bill. *Rockwell: The Heritage of North American*. New York: Random House/Crescent, 1989.

Yenne, Bill. *Secret Weapons of World War II*. New York: Penguin Putnam, 2003.

Yenne, Bill. *The Story of the Boeing Company*. San Francisco/Minneapolis: AGS BookWorks/Zenith Press, 2005, 2010.

Zuckerman, Solly. *From Apes to Warlords: The Autobiography (1904–1946) of Solly Zuckerman*. London: Hamilton, 1978.

Zuckerman, Solly. *Monkeys, Men and Missiles: An Autobiography, 1946–1988*. New York: Norton, 1989.

INDEX

ABOUT THE AUTHOR

Bill Yenne is the author of more than three dozen nonfiction books, especially on aviation and military history. These have included histories of the Strategic Air Command, the US Air Force, and his recently updated *The Story of the Boeing Company*. He has contributed to encyclopedias of both world wars. Mr. Yenne's recent dual biography of Dick Bong and Tommy McGuire, published by Berkley and entitled *Aces High: The Heroic Story of the Two Top-Scoring American Aces of World War II*, was described by pilot and best-selling author Dan Roam as "The greatest flying story of all time." General Wesley Clark called Mr. Yenne's recent biography of Alexander the Great the "best yet." The *New Yorker* wrote of *Sitting Bull*, Mr. Yenne's biography of the great Lakota leader, that it "excels as a study in leadership." Mr. Yenne lives in San Francisco, and on the Web at www.BillYenne.com.